THE WRITER'S DIGEST
HANDBOOK
OF
NOVEL WRITING

EDITED BY
TOM CLARK
WILLIAM BROHAUGH
BRUCE WOODS
BILL STRICKLAND

Writer's
Digest
Books

CINCINNATI, OHIO

The Writer's Digest Handbook of Novel Writing. Copyright © 1992 by
Writer's Digest Books. Printed and bound in the United States of America. All
rights reserved. No part of this book may be reproduced in any form or by any
electronic or mechanical means including information storage and retrieval
systems without permission in writing from the publisher, except by a reviewer,
who may quote brief passages in a review. Published by Writer's Digest Books,
an imprint of F&W Publications, Inc., 1507 Dana Avenue, Cincinnati, Ohio
45207 (1-800-289-0963). First edition.

This hardcover edition of *The Writer's Digest Handbook of Novel Writing* features
a "self-jacket" that eliminates the need for a separate dust jacket. It provides
sturdy protection for your book while it saves paper, trees and energy.

96 95 94 93 92   5 4 3 2 1

Library of Congress Cataloging in Publication Data

The Writer's Digest handbook of novel writing / edited by Tom Clark
  . . . [et al.].
        p.   cm.
  Includes index.
  ISBN 0-89879-507-9 (hardcover)
    1. Fiction—Technique. 2. Authorship—Marketing. I. Clark, Tom,
1958-   . II. Writer's Digest (Cincinnati, Ohio)
PN3365.W75   1992
808.3—dc20   91-38678
                                                        CIP

Designed by Sandy Conopeotis

The following page constitutes an extension of this copyright page.

Permissions

Table of Contents

About the Authors

John Gregory Betancourt is the author of nine science fiction and fantasy novels, including *Johnny Zed, Rememory, The Blind Archer* and a number of young adult novels. He has published some twenty short stories in such magazines as *Amazing Stories, Fantasy Book* and *The Dragon*. He is science fiction editor for Byron Press Visual Publications.

Jack M. Bickham is the author of more than sixty-five novels, including the Brad Smith suspense series for Tor Books.

Lawrence Block is the author of such novels as *A Dance at the Slaughterhouse, A Ticket to the Boneyard* and *Out on the Cutting Edge*. His short stories have appeared in *Playboy, Ellery Queen's Mystery Magazine* and others.

Hal Blythe and **Charlie Sweet** teach creative writing at Eastern Kentucky University. Frequent contributors to *Writer's Digest*, they have published more than a hundred stories. They are currently working on a novel—the right way, of course.

Dorothy Bryant has published nine novels, including *The Kin of Ata are Waiting, Ella Price's Journal, Miss Giardino* and *Confessions of Madame Psyche*, for which she won the Before Columbus Foundation's American Book Award in 1988. Her publishing house, Ata Books, was honored with the Publishing Award of the Bay Area Book Reviewers Association in 1988. Her play *Dear Master* was produced in 1991 with the help of a Skaggs Foundation award.

Orson Scott Card is the author of the Alvin Maker series, *Ender's Game, Speaker for the Dead*, and *Xenocide*. His nonfiction includes *Characters & Viewpoint* and *How to Write Science Fiction & Fantasy*. He lives in Greensboro, North Carolina, with his wife and three children.

Louis Catron is professor of theater at the College of William and Mary (Williamsburg, Virginia), where he teaches playwriting, play direction and acting. He's the author of published plays plus *Writing, Producing, and Selling Your Play, The Director's Vision* and *Playwriting*. He is a frequent contributor to magazines such as *Dramatics* and *Writer's Digest*.

Tom Clancy is the author of *The Cardinal of the Kremlin, The Hunt for Red October* and other bestsellers.

Jack Dann is the author or editor of more than thirty books, including the novels *Junction, Starhiker* and *The Man Who Melted*. His short stories have appeared in *Omni, Playboy, Penthouse*, and other magazines and anthologies.

He has been a finalist for the Nebula Award ten times and a World Fantasy Award Finalist twice. He has also been a finalist for the British Science Fiction Award.

Loren D. Estleman writes both mystery and western novels, including *Whiskey River* (Bantam), *Sweet Women Lie* (Houghton Mifflin) and *Sudden Country* (Doubleday).

Russell Galen, an agent and vice president with Scott Meredith Literary Agency in New York City, covers the book industry in his New York Overheard report, which appears every other month in The Markets section of *Writer's Digest* magazine.

David Groff is a senior editor at a large New York publishing house.

Helen Haukeness has contributed to *North American Review*, *Overtures*, and many other magazines, as well as being syndicated by *Fiction Network*. She is a freelance editor for Scribner's.

Mary Kittredge won the 1987 Mystery Writers of America's Robert L. Fish Award for her short story "Father to the Man." Her novels include *Murder in Mendocino* and *Dead and Gone*.

Dean R. Koontz is a bestselling author of suspense novels, including *Hideaway*, *Cold Fire*, *The Bad Place* and *Midnight* (all Putnam).

Nancy Kress is the author of five novels and one collection of short stories, all science fiction or fantasy. She won the 1985 Nebula award for her short story "Out of All Them Bright Stars." She writes the monthly Fiction column for *Writer's Digest* magazine.

David Madden, writer-in-residence at Louisana State University, is the author of seven novels, two collections of stories, and more than twenty works of nonfiction, including *Revising Fiction*, *Bijou*, *The Suicide's Wife* and *The New Orleans of Possibilities*.

Raymond Obstfeld teaches literature and creative writing at Orange Coast College, Costa Mesa, California. He is the author of more than thirty novels, a book of poetry, and several plays. Four of his screenplays are currently under option. His mystery novel, *Dead Heat*, was nominated for an Edgar Award. *Doing Good*, his nonfiction book on ethics, was coauthored with Dirk Jamison. He has written a young adult novel, *Wise Acres*.

Gary Provost is the author of eighteen books, including *Make Your Words Work* and *Perfect Husband*.

Joel Rosenberg's science fiction novels include *Hero, Ties of Blood and Silver, Emile and the Dutchman* (all ROC/Penguin) and others. There are more than one million copies of Rosenberg's novels in print.

Stanley Schmidt is the author of four novels (the most recent being *Tweedlioop*) and numerous short stories and articles. As editor of *Analog Science Fiction/Science Fact* since 1978, he has been nominated eleven times for the Hugo Award as Best Professional Editor. He coedited and wrote several chapters of *Writing Science Fiction and Fantasy*, published in 1991 by St. Martin's Press.

Darrell Schweitzer is the editor of *Weird Tales*. He has worked as editorial assistant of *Isaac Asimov's Science Fiction Magazine* (1977-82), and assistant editor of *Amazing Stories* (1982-86). He has also written novels, including *Shattered Goddess* and *The White Isle*, and has had more than one hundred stories published.

George H. Scithers, publisher of *Weird Tales*, is the recipient of four Hugo Awards. His short stories have appeared in *Analog* and *Worlds of If*. He is former editor for *Isaac Asimov's Science Fiction Magazine* and *Amazing Stories*.

Michael Seidman is mystery editor of Walker and Co., and is the author of *From Printout to Published*.

Art Spikol writes the monthly Nonfiction column for *Writer's Digest*. His novels include *The Physalia Incident*.

W.C. Stroby is book editor of *The Asbury Park Press* and is a frequent contributor of Profile in *Writer's Digest* magazine.

Dwight V. Swain, Professor Emeritus of the University of Oklahoma's Professional Writing Program, is the author of *Creating Characters: How to Build Story People*.

Ronald B. Tobias is a professor in the Department of Media and Theatre Arts at Montana State University. His fiction includes *Kings and Desperate Men and Other Stories* and *The Bodywasher*. He is the author of *Theme & Strategy*.

Maron L. Waxman is the Executive Director of Book Development of the Book-of-the-Month Club. She has been an executive editor at Scribner's and Macmillan. She teaches at the Publishing Institute of City University and has also taught at New York University's Publishing Center.

Editors' Introduction

I t was over a plate of cold noodles at our favorite Szechwan restaurant that the editorial director of Writer's Digest Books suggested the book you're now holding. "Let's put together the best articles we've published on writing novels," he told me and the other editors of *Writer's Digest* magazine. (He used to be editor of *Writer's Digest*, so we still let him say "we.")

By the time my Kung Pao beef arrived, we'd convinced ourselves of the book's viability. Now came the real fun: picking the candidates for inclusion. Though I've been at WD since the February 1984 issue—and have one of the world's worst memories—long-forgotten favorites sprang readily to mind. We made notes quickly, trying not to confuse pencils for chopsticks. It was a good meal all around.

In the months that followed, the editors of *Writer's Digest* spent hours paging through bound volumes of the magazine. We buried ourselves in the library, exploring the books published under the Writer's Digest Books imprint. We considered, debated, reconsidered, rejected and selected (frequently in that same restaurant) as we searched for just the right mix of advice and encouragement and pragmatism.

You'll recognize many of the authors who have shared their wisdom with *Writer's Digest*'s readers. You've read the novels of Dean R. Koontz, Tom Clancy, Loren D. Estleman, Lawrence Block, Orson Scott Card and many of the others. Still others of the writers collected here won't be as familiar to you, but you'll want to get to know what these agents and editors have to say.

You'll want to get to know them because now it's up to you. Up to you to take the advice out of these pages and put it to work at your keyboard. Up to you to start—and then finish—your novel. Up to you to chart your path to the bestseller list.

And while you're doing that, we'll be editing new pieces that may eventually turn up in *The Writer's Digest Handbook of Novel Writing, Volume 2*.

And, well, I've got this idea for a novel . . .

Thomas Clark
Senior Editor
Writer's Digest

"I Have an Idea . . ."

by George H. Scithers and Darrell Schweitzer

You'll know you've arrived as an author when a friend or neighbor takes you aside and makes you an offer you'll find surprisingly easy to refuse: he'll provide ideas, you'll write them into stories, and he'll only take half of the proceeds. . . .

But by then, you'll *know* the difference between an idea and a story, which will be precisely *why* you'll be a professional writer: You'll have learned just how cheap ideas are. And ideas *are* cheap; everyone has them. As Obis's Law puts it, "Somebody else probably has the same idea — so (a) get started and (b) plan to do it better." We hope this article will help you accomplish (b). We cannot do this, however, just by presenting the bare idea.

An idea is no more than a spark that sets the story process into motion, even in such a literature of ideas as science fiction. Except in a few, very specialized cases, where a short-short story is actually a form of commentary or parody (often designed to give some cliché its comeuppance), the idea itself is not what makes a story distinctive. Consider the difference between a sensational tabloid headline, WOMAN SLEEPS WITH HER HUSBAND'S CORPSE FOR FORTY YEARS and William Faulkner's treatment of the same idea in "A Rose for Emily." And Robert Bloch's *Psycho* has a basic idea different only in detail: A boy argues with his mother's corpse for ten years. Yet, the story Bloch told is altogether different from Faulkner's — and the tabloids.

An idea is essential — but an idea is not enough. As science fiction editors, we see altogether too many "stories" that do no more than present ideas. Mystery magazine editors have the same experience: ingenious methods of lessening the planet's population which completely fail to *tell a story*. What made Homer's *Iliad* great is not the basic idea — soldiers squabble in the lulls between battles (even then, some twenty-five hundred years ago, the idea wasn't new) — but how he developed the consequences of those squabbles, and especially how he dramatized it all: "I sing of the anger of Achilles. . . ."

If you find you've written an idea presentation instead of a story, write a sequel, then throw away the original. Do *not* recapitulate the content of the first version in the sequel; just assume that our idea-premise is a real part of the lives of your cast of characters. Then show your readers what that idea means to the characters: How do they respond? Do they grow and mature? Do they adapt and learn? Do they try to cope, yet fail?

Beware of surprises; very few ideas are so shocking and wonderful and original that their mere revelation (or even: Revelation!!) will work as a surprise ending. If the reader's response is a *what happens next?*, then write *that*, and dispense with the buildup. (Yes, we know that Homer didn't throw away the *Iliad* after he wrote the *Odyssey*. But then, you aren't as good as Homer . . . yet.)

Mind Games

Let's see what can be done with a simple idea: *Boy meets girl. One of them joins a group mind.*

In science-fictional terms, a "group mind" can be precisely that: a collection of people (or more generally, beings) who telepathically share one another's consciousness to the extent they form one overall "person" spread over many bodies. This confers a kind of immortality, since the death of one body leaves the overall entity almost intact. But the act of someone joining that group mind would seem to be the same as dying, since the formerly independent individual has ceased to exist—which leads to all kinds of horrific situations, along with questions about identity, individual rights, free will, and the like. What if one member of the group mind kills another: is it murder—or amputation?

In another setting—historical, say—the same basic idea produces a tale of the Children's Crusade, around A.D. 1212: Either the boy or the girl gets totally swept up into the hysteria of the Crusade and, abandoning all previous commitments and relationships, goes off to what the other character recognizes as certain destruction. But at the same time, the non-Crusading character must decide if his/her concern is selfish: Is he/she trying to save the Crusader, or merely satisfying his/her own emotional needs? The story can be one of faith and duty *vs.* self-delusion and self-gratification.

In a contemporary setting, the story shifts to someone who joins a bizarre cult—perhaps even the Nazi party. It is still a story of loss and longing, of seeking identity and a place in the world, but both the setting and the characters are markedly different.

Yet all these—science-fictional, historical, and contemporary versions—are based on the same idea. And, while the subject matter seems to be inherently serious and conducive to heart-wrenching tragedy, it can also be done as comedy—slapstick, absurdist, existential, black, or whatever. So many stories can spring out of a single idea that editors can assign the same idea to a dozen or so writers and publish the resulting stories as an anthology. Arthur C. Clarke's 1969 anthology, *Three for Tomorrow*, is an example, with stories by Robert Silverberg, Roger Zelazny and James Blish.

Getting Situated

Distinguish between an idea and a situation. Strictly speaking, "Boy meets girl; one of them joins a group mind," is both an idea *and* a situation. The pure idea is that there is a group mind (or Children's Crusade, or Nazi party, or whatever), just *sitting* there, so to speak. The situation—emotional attachment, put under strain by one character joining the whatever—is what drives your cast to react to that strain.

Editors see far too many manuscripts in which the idea or the idea-and-situation combination are just presented, with no additional development. These manuscripts tend to be quite short. Suppose, in about five pages, the author shows us the lofty hall of the Order of Cosmic Oneness, where the viewpoint character is being presented with the robe of membership. He goes through certain rituals. Maybe he signs papers. Maybe he drinks ritual wine (which is drugged to open his telepathic receptors) while chatting with other members about how wonderful membership in the Order can be. Then hundreds of other members file in, and the initiation ceremony takes place, and suddenly he realizes that this is a group mind, and these are not hundreds of individuals but *one*, of which he is now a tiny part.

The End. It's a fascinating idea, but the author has merely worked up to it, then stopped. This is the very sort of story that needs to have a sequel written—and the original story abandoned.

Sometimes the author goes a few paragraphs further, and there is an emotional tug at the end: The character's last independent thought, before he is wholly submerged in the Order of Cosmic Oneness, is the realization that he will never be able to see (or at least care for) his true love again.

A little better, but not much. We've moved from raw idea to idea and situation, but still this is where the story must *start*, not finish.

You must develop your characters, deciding how each would respond to the situation as it develops, and then *show* your readers those characters in action. If the girl joins, and the boy is Conan the Barbarian, one kind of story will evolve; if he is Sherlock Holmes, quite another will result. But again, the really interesting action is that each shows what happens *next*.

He has joined the Order, or maybe the Crusade, which is disaster looking for fodder; she misses him . . . all of that is past history when your story opens: what is she going to *do* about the situation, what will go wrong when she tries, what will she do next, and so on through complication, stress, rising tension, continuing to a resolution, happy or tragic. She may begin, for example, by trying to persuade him to renounce the cult and leave it; then she finally resolves the problem by becoming the cult's high priestess and dissolving the whole organization. She may, through her struggles to regain him, come to realize that he is hopelessly flawed and that her true love is a man who has lost *his* girl to that same organization.

Unless you are writing a deliberately shallow action-adventure story, the overall plot and the development of your characters must come to mean something: As Mark Twain put it, "a tale shall accomplish something and arrive somewhere." Don't preach an obvious moral—but build your plot around one to some degree or other. If your story touches on such basic and important matters as life and death and personal identity, it's entirely appropriate for your characters to learn and change and grow as a result. All this should make you tell a *story*, quite different from every other story based on the same idea and situation.

The Naked Truth

Many editors tell you that what they want more than anything else are "new ideas." Yes, they do—but not naked and alone on the page. They want *stories* that incorporate new ideas, or that approach familiar ideas in new ways. If you can move from an *idea* to the *story* that grows out of that idea, you're well on your way to becoming a professional writer.

Five Questions Every First Novelist Must Answer

by W.C. Stroby

C hances are the idea has simmered in your subconscious for months, maybe years. You've filled half a dozen spiral notebooks with scrawled notes recopied from cocktail napkins and envelopes. A few characters crouch on your shoulders, whispering dialogue in your ear, daring you to bring them into existence.

You're ready to write your first novel.

Or are you?

Starting a novel and finishing it are two different things. Whatever type of novel you plan to write, it's going to involve a significant outlay of time, energy and emotion. So unless you're content to fill up reams and reams of paper with a narrative that goes nowhere, you should know what you're getting into *before* you start. Once you climb on that tiger's back, you might find it hard to jump off without mauling your creative ego.

Here are five questions about yourself and your material that you absolutely, positively must know before you sit down to write.

Am I Ready For This?

Ambition is fine, but know when you're getting in over your head. A beginning mountain climber doesn't set out to scale Everest his first time out, and the budding novelist shouldn't take on a task that would daunt even a hardened veteran. Melville wasn't ready to write *Moby Dick* until he was five novels into his career. A good idea undertaken at a time when you don't have the skill or resources to bring it off can be a painful and ultimately frustrating experience, even if you finish the book. Be ambitious, but be realistic in your own goals.

"You have to know your own level of craft," says F. Paul Wilson, author of the horror/fantasy novels *The Keep*, *Black Wind* and *Re-Born*. "The guy who wrote *Healer* and *Wheels Within Wheels* [Wilson's first two novels] couldn't have written *Black Wind* with any justice to the theme and the characters and the sweep of the thing. There's a talent part of writing and then there's the craft, and they're two different things. The talent comes in while conceptualizing a story; the craft is what lets you put it on paper in a coherent form. You've got to have the tools. If you don't have the necessary skills, you can have some great ideas for stories, but it's going to be awfully hard to tell them."

"A lot of people have the ambition to write novels," says Stephen Coonts, author of the bestselling *Flight of the Intruder* and *The Minotaur*. "But what the average reader doesn't understand is the sweat, blood and tears that go into doing it."

Many first-time novelists don't consider how much time they're likely to spend feeling their way around a new medium, just learning how to make it work for them.

"A novel is not just something about which you can say, 'Okay, I'll write four pages a day and in one hundred days I'll have four hundred pages,' " Coonts says. "It doesn't work that way. You may write for a week at four pages a day and then have to throw it all away because you see it didn't work. So you have to go back and do it again, and so the one hundred days becomes two hundred or three hundred or four hundred."

Coonts says the only way to get anything done is to set up a regular writing schedule—and stick to it.

"When I wrote *Flight of the Intruder*, I worked every night, four hours a night, sometimes five," he says. "I worked every Saturday, Sunday and holiday—at least ten hours on those days. And I was holding down a forty-hour-a-week job the rest of the time, trying to make a living. While everybody else was skiing and whooping it up and going to parties, I was sitting there and tapping away."

A good target schedule for first-timers, suggests Coonts, is two to four hours a day, at least five days a week.

"For a book of any size, from start to finish, plan on spending at least two thousand hours on it," he says. "That's on a very regular basis, not two hours every Sunday morning before you go to church. People tell me they only write on weekends; they've had a novel in progress for five years. They'll never get it done."

Ex-Secret Service agent Gerald Petievich, author of *To Live and Die in LA*, *Shakedown* and *Earth Angels*, began writing his first novel while a special agent in the Service's Los Angeles bureau. During that time, he got up every morning at 3:30 so he could get in four solid hours of writing before leaving for the office.

"I more or less gave up everything else in my life," Petievich says. "I went to bed early every night, I had no social life; on the job I refused promotions just so I could stay in one place and write. That's the kind of commitment you have to make for fiction. But when you take on that kind of obsession—which is what writing is, what art is—nothing else can stop you if you choose to do it."

Few first-time novelists have the luxury of endless hours to work on a book at their leisure, unencumbered by other responsibilities. Unless you're independently wealthy, you'll probably be holding down another job when you make that first stab at novel writing—even if that job is caring for a family, which can be even more demanding.

Resist the temptation to blow off your regular job once you feel the calling of a novel, says Petievich. "That's a big mistake. Don't say: 'Well, I'll just quit my job and go write a book.' Books don't pay very well, and the financial pressure that comes makes people write faster and faster. And the faster you write, the worse it is."

What Is My Story About?

As complex as your novel might turn out to be, it's essential you be able to state clearly what your basic story is and where it's going.

"One sentence," says Gerald Petievich. "Two at the most. If you can't tell yourself what your story is in one or two sentences, you're already running into trouble.

"Even in *Moby Dick*, it comes down to *Captain Ahab chases a whale and doesn't get it.* Now that's simplistic, but it's the way you have to look at it. Melville could have been writing a police story — it could have been anything — but he did have in mind the story of an obsession, an obsession where a man does not reach his goal. All the other things that are added into it, all the religious symbolism and so on, is only to help tell *that* story."

First novelists often stumble in translating a promising idea into a workable, functioning story with a beginning, a middle and an end.

"A story is not a setting," warns Stephen Coonts. "For example, *war in the jungle* — that's not a story. A story is an adventure, a conflict that happens to people that's either resolved in the story or cannot be resolved for reasons that become clear in the story. Ideas are a dime a dozen. I've got a dozen of them right now. I can get one usually by reading the morning newspaper. But that doesn't mean it's going to be a good story."

A clearly defined story — who, where, what and when — is the most important groundwork for your novel. But, says Coonts, understanding your story doesn't mean you have to know in advance every twist and turn it's going to take along the way.

Plotwise, "I know exactly where I'm going," he says. "The only question is how to get there. Your destination may be Pike's Peak, but there are an infinite number of ways to get to Pike's Peak."

Crime novelist Robert Campbell (*Juice, Sweet La-La Land*) says he often starts a novel with only a vague idea of how it's going to end.

"You know certain things going into it," he says. "For instance, you know that your villain is going to get his comeuppance, but that doesn't mean you know he's going to pull a gun at some point and a certain character is going to come out of left field and shoot him. But as I'm writing, as I'm feeling my way toward it, I pretty much intuitively or instinctively know how I want it to turn out. If I go into it with an ending mapped out and it changes midway, I usually go with it. I know that's my subconscious at work, and my subconscious has probably done more work on it than my conscious mind has."

Outlining the entire novel beforehand may be useful. Once you know where your story's headed and have chosen a starting point, mapping out the rest is just a question of whatever works best for you.

"You don't really need a page-for-page outline, or even necessarily a chapter outline," Petievich says. "But you have to know the events that are going to occur, where the book's going. Writers who say they make it up as they go along are fooling themselves."

"I just start on chapter one, page one," says Coonts. "It's the basic story that's critical, that's what carries you along. If you have to do an outline, then do it. Do whatever you feel you have to do. If you don't need to do it, then don't waste the time."

If you know your story works before you begin writing, that confidence helps steer you through the rockier spots of plotting later in the book. But as you move toward your ending, be ready to adapt to changes along the way.

"If your creative talent is working correctly, it will pull (the plot) along in the way it should go," Petievich says. "Our subconscious mind really rules in a creative endeavor. So if it starts to change, don't try and force it back into some sort of dogma that you've established."

If you do that, you've undermined one of the fundamental joys of writing, says Jude Deveraux, author of more than twenty novels, including the bestselling *A Knight in Shining Armor* and *Mountain Laurel*.

"There are no new stories," she says. "It all depends on how you handle them. In romances, the characters are going to fall in love with each other; you know that when you see the syrupy cover. It's how you get there that's the fun."

Do I Know Who My Characters Are?

To convince readers that what you're writing about can — or has — happened, you're going to need characters who not only move the plot along, but also are real enough to get readers believing.

"Your characters are going to make or break your story," says Stephen Coonts. "In a perfect world, readers are going to fall in love with your main characters and they're going to be moved in one way or another by the ending."

Bringing your characters to life means getting them down on paper. List them before you start writing and know something about each of them beyond just their plot functions.

"You have to know something about the characters, but not everything," says Gerald Petievich. "You should know their age; their social class, their sex and their nationality. That's enough. Remember that the story comes first. The characters are created for the purpose of telling the story, not vice versa. The characters can change, the story remains."

"Writers shouldn't fall in love with characters so much that they lose sight of what they're trying to accomplish," says Coonts. "The idea is to write a whole story, a whole book. A writer has to be able to look at that story and see whether or not a character works — whether or not a character needs further definition."

This doesn't necessarily mean knowing the location of every mole on their bodies or what the characters had for breakfast. The trick is to bring them alive within the context of the story.

"Physical descriptions for your main characters don't matter, they're passe," says Petievich. "Minor characters can be described at great length, and that helps to create mood and define the characters when you don't really have time to deal with them. But for the main characters, I don't think you should do like Dashiell Hammett and describe Sam Spade in great detail so that you can see his face. Because what if you're the reader and you don't like his face?"

"Most romances, I think, deal too much with the physical looks of people," says Jude Deveraux. "How beautiful she is, how gorgeous and handsome he is. I'm not interested in that, so I don't put much of that in. But I am very interested in their personalities. So rather than describing them at length, I try to come up with actions to show what they're like."

Do I Know the Genre?

No one writes in a vacuum. No matter what genre you're tackling—and this includes "mainstream" books—you must know who and what has gone before you. You need to know what you're up against and you can learn from everything you read, good or bad. But most of all, you can't afford to not be familiar with the genre you're writing in, because your intended reader almost certainly will be.

"You need to know the structure," says Jude Deveraux. "You need to know what you can and cannot do. A lot of new writers come to me and say: 'I'm going to give the reader two romances in one book.' My response is always: 'You couldn't come up with enough plot for one, right, so you're going to stick a second one in?' Well, that's a taboo. People who read romances only care about the hero or heroine. Some writers mix murder mysteries in with their romances, and you can do that but you have to know how much. And you can only learn that from reading lots of books."

If the genre you've chosen isn't one you particularly like, it might be wise to reconsider.

"You have to like it," says F. Paul Wilson. "If you're writing something that you don't really like to read, you're going to fall down miserably. If you've tried a couple of romance novels and you hear that Cyberpunk is hot and you figure you're going to knock off a Cyberpunk novel, you're wasting your time. If you don't know science fiction, if you don't know computerese and stuff, you're not going to be able to bring it off.

"Every genre has its own ambiance and you have to know that," Wilson says. "You've got to know what other people have done. If you talk to science fiction magazine editors who read the slush pile, they'll tell you every fourth story has an Adam-and-Eve ending. Those writers are people who don't know the genre, who don't know that this ending has been done to death already.

If you're not familiar with the genre, you won't know it's one of the hoariest clichés going."

At the same time, warns Deveraux, don't subvert your own writing style to something you think may be more "marketable."

"You should really stay true to your own style," she says. "When I first started writing, everybody said to me, 'your style just isn't right because you don't use the really flowery language that romances have.' My romances—compared to what's out there—are very strange, very odd, very different. And I think that's one of the reasons they're selling. Within romance novels, Danielle Steel is in a genre all her own. Nobody writes like she does. Stephen King's books are quite different from most horror novels. So it's a genre within a genre. You stay within the genre but you do something different with it."

There's room for experimentation within any kind of fiction, provided you give the readers their money's worth in terms of story and characters. But as Stephen Coonts advises, "Try and find a subject that nobody else has touched."

Read a good dozen novels in the genre you've chosen. Chances are you'll have a better idea of what you should—and shouldn't—be doing.

Am I Excited By the Story I'm Going To Tell?

The answer to this question makes the difference between a completed, publishable novel and several months worth of manuscript left to rot in a bureau drawer. Write a story that excites you, challenges you, that keeps you awake at night every time you start to think about it. If you can't get fired up over it, who will?

"Writing a novel involves a lot of work and a long time without any positive reinforcement," says F. Paul Wilson. "It better not be a story you're lukewarm about. You really have to think *This is great*."

"Some books I've written come to me because I've seen something in the paper that outrages me," says Robert Campbell. "A lot of them come out of a philosophical position that has cooked in my mind for many years, until I found the story to tell it. Either way, it has to be something that, in a sense, *demands* my attention."

Jude Deveraux remembers when a former agent talked her into writing an "epic family saga" of a sort popular at the time, though she wasn't happy with the idea. That novel, *Casagrande*, is the only book of hers no longer in print.

"The best advice is to write what you're really passionate about," she says. "My first books are not the best written things, but there's a lot of passion in them and it got me through."

Of course, no matter what your idea is, there will come a time when you wonder if you can pull it off. Once you're into a book, a grandiose idea boils down into a lot of time-consuming—and sometimes tedious—labor. The going can get very dark indeed.

"It's never going to wind up as great as you think it'll be when you start," says Wilson. "The more excited you are with a book to start out with, probably the harder that realization will hit you. When you start a book, it has all these possibilities, all this great potential. But the book you hope it will be, I don't think ever really materializes. You find out you're limited by your talent."

No matter how experienced a writer you eventually become, that moment of doubt and uncertainty is still almost sure to rear its head at some point.

"I get that all the time," says Wilson. "You get off to a strong start and maybe you have a strong finish planned, but to hold up the belly of the book is the toughest part. From an objective outside viewpoint, the book may be going great. But to you it won't be, because there are going to be parts where you're just slogging through, and every page—every paragraph—is a strain to get it to come out and to get it to work."

What it all adds up to, says Campbell, is preparing yourself for a certain amount of disappointment, but learning how to move beyond it as well.

"The great courage of the creative artist—whether it's a composer, a writer, a painter or whatever—is that he or she is willing to sit down and write that first line of dialogue, make that first stroke on the canvas," he says, "even though the artist realizes that by that act he is beginning to destroy the vision he has in his mind. Because the vision you've got for a book is monumental, it flows like water, it's beautiful, it's this, it's that. But to write it, you have to struggle into the real world."

"The chief thing is desire," says Wilson. "You've really got to want to do it, you've really got to want to tell that story. And you have to be able to set goals for yourself to get it done.

"It does get easier," he says. "The longer you do it, the easier it gets to do. You learn how to get your ideas down on paper; you learn how to think in those terms. Look at Robert Heinlein's Rules of Writing. The first one is: You Must Write. The second one is: You Must Finish What You Write.

"It's just a matter of sitting down and doing it."

Stranger Than Truth

by Art Spikol

In July of 1985, on a beach in Bermuda, I noticed a sign warning of a dangerous stinging jellyfish, Physalia physalis, the Portugeuse man-of-war.

That sign must have been the catalyst I needed, because the moment I saw it I decided to start writing fiction. I'd write a mystery ("Aim low," I told myself, "this is just to get the gears oiled"). But first, to get myself into the proper mood, I picked up an Inspector Maigret novel (the only mystery in the old bookcase in the hotel where I was staying), read it and determined that I could, ahem, write more compelling stuff than Georges Simenon with my eyes closed. Since then I have learned that I was out of touch with the genre, and I now realize that Maigret, while entertaining in a 1940s sort of way, is not exactly *au courant*—he's sort of a French gumshoe who solves mysteries by finding the obvious, and the book I read had that kind of plodding effect about it. Perhaps, in that sense, my choice was somehow preordained; if I'd read something that was state-of-the-art detective, or even a better Maigret, I might not have had the same degree of confidence.

This happened when I was in my late forties, and the last time I'd written fiction (or read a mystery, for that matter) was when I was in my teens. But I'd often thought about doing it, wondering if it was possible to just *do* it—to simply sit down at the keyboard and apply my nonfiction-writing skills to fiction, letting nature take its course.

The Mystery, Explained

Well, now that I've trapped you with this irresistible lead, I owe you an explanation. Why am I talking about fiction in a column dedicated to the opposite? Answer: the column is, always has been, as much about writers as writing. And occasionally I digress. This month I digress as a nonfiction writer who decided to write fiction, a category in which I am sure many of you fit. The rest of you I'll see next month.

The Portuguese man-of-war, I decided, would play a major role in my book. I didn't know just how. I didn't have to know too much at all, since I intended to write just four or five chapters. Within that arena I would determine if I had the staying power, the interest, the enthusiasm, the talent for fiction—and if I did, I would put the chapters on a diskette and file them somewhere and then go on to write something entirely different: the Great American Novel. You see, I didn't really *want* to write a mystery at all. I picked the genre, as I said, just to oil the gears.

13

So I wrote four chapters, and I was a little way into the fifth when I got a phone call from an ex-colleague of mine, an editor from whom I hadn't heard for years. She said she was in New York, was a literary agent, and did I have any books in the works?

"Just a mystery," I told her, and to make a short story long, she read what I had and said she thought it would sell. Was I thrilled? You bet. Suddenly I wanted to finish the book after all, and eventually we got a couple of offers, went with Viking, and the book will be out in March. When I got the news that it had sold, I started crying. And this is strange behavior indeed for a middle-aged man in a pool hall. Viking kept my working title, *The Physalia Incident*, and the jacket bears the imprimatur "A Viking Novel of Mystery and Suspense." I take it that this is the statement Viking puts on certain of its books to distinguish them from works of genuine literary merit, but what the hell, I'm happy. It's a good read, an unusual mystery with a terrific central character ("modeled," Spikol admits sheepishly "somewhat after me"), and because I'm one of those people who gets better as he goes along, I'm already looking forward to the next book.

Making the Leap

Since I've gone through the process, I'd like to tell you a little about the transition from nonfiction to fiction, and some of the things I learned along the way.

In many respects, fiction is like nonfiction, and the mere fact of being in complete charge of the story does not make it easy. If the story is based on facts and requires digging and understanding, the research is demanding whether it's fiction or nonfiction. *The Physalia Incident*, while fiction, is a scientific mystery that involves marine biology and toxicology, computers, medicine, several real locations, and real, checkable facts. In short, it required research and travel and interviewing. What I thought would be a piece of cake turned out to be work, because in fiction, and *especially* in a mystery (since the readers tend to watch very closely), things must hang together.

Had I known this, I probably would not have started a mystery in the first place, because the history of the book extended over the course of two and a half years, one year of which was playful, a sort of seeing what would happen (and assuming that it was all for the fun of it anyway, so not caring intensely); another year of which was damn hard work writing the remaining thirty-five chapters to meet a deadline; and a half year of which was spent fine tuning: assimilating input from my editor at Viking, rewriting, getting the copyedited manuscript back, agreeing, disagreeing, justifying, and so on. I could have written *War and Peace*.

What makes fiction good is not much different from what makes nonfiction good. I have always known that in nonfiction a burden is on the author to make things sound real, that a central character in an article, if he or she is to come alive, needs just as much description and characterization as does one in a short story. Quotations in fiction have to sound plausible, but quotations from real life have to sound no less plausible—even though readers may know they're genuine and accept them as such. It has less to do with credibility than with the nature of the writing itself and its ability to be taken seriously.

The interview process is the interview process whether you're retrieving data for a true story or a made-up one. There is one notable exception: there's less fear of the interviewer when it's fiction. In nonfiction, for the most part, the interviewees expect to be quoted directly, to see their names interwoven with their comments; in fiction, they understand that they are being used for background. The latter is, of course, less dangerous and in some ways more fun, since being associated with a work of fiction may mean that someday you will be associated, even if indirectly, with a popular bestseller or a movie or a TV series.

In fiction, the writer controls everything. Along the way I came to identify fairly strongly, as you might have gathered, with my main character, a guy named Alex Black who is the editor of the science section of a weekly news magazine. In fact, it was at that point that I decided to write the book in the first person instead of the third person, which was how I started out. Alex (we are on a first-name basis) is a lot like me, only less secure. I *made* Alex less secure—gave him, in fact, a few of the earmarks of a midlife crisis—because I figured he had to have more problems than I do. (Any hero worth reading about would have to have more problems than I do.) I gave him a lady friend, a boss, co-workers, a nemesis or two, a femme fatale. I made him younger, which automatically meant he had more problems. But when I sat him down in a bar or on a motorcycle or put him in bed with a woman, Spikol was there.

But I also learned that **with the freedom to create characters goes the responsibility to keep those characters from sounding too much like real people.** This can be a problem: say you have set your fiction in a small town, and one of your characters is a big brain surgeon in that town. And let us say that you live in a small town, or that you have interviewed many people in a small town in order to get the perspective you need. Now, that means a certain number of people know you are writing about a town modeled after their town, or at least they surmise as much—and that could conceivably cause you trouble if the leading brain surgeon of your fictional town turns out to be anything like a surgeon in the real town, or, perhaps, even if people secretly suspect that the real surgeon was the model for the fictional one. This never used to be much of a problem, but these are litigious years, and people are more easily wounded now that they know how much it's worth.

If you expect to write a book in your spare time, you can forget it. There is no such thing as spare time. You have to define the time, whittle it out and decide when it's going to be. And you need discipline to keep that time sacrosanct. In my case, I certainly couldn't drop everything and work on the novel.

So I gave myself an assignment: I would spend two hours a day on *The Physalia Incident*, and at the end of a year, based on my calculations, I would have a book. Those two hours were from 8 to 10 A.M., and if I missed any time during the week I made up for it on the weekend.

The writer decides what happens. The nice thing about fiction, and the big difference between it and nonfiction, of course, is a sense of freedom unlike anything I've ever felt in nonfiction, but it's paralyzing in a way. In nonfiction, the problem is different: you have to take something that happened and dramatize it, weave in the quotations and the facts, bring the characters to life. You know where the road ends and you have a handful of buildings to erect along the way, and you know what those buildings should look like. In fiction, there's only the horizon, and you can build whatever you want on the land that precedes it. But you have to make sure your buildings will stand on their own, and hold the right stuff.

And it doesn't take much wind to blow them down. Let characters act "out of character" and your readers will know it. Solve a problem by including a convenient but inappropriate plot twist and your readers will feel cheated. It may not ruin your book, but it may diminish the sense of reality you want it to have. In my entire writing career, I never used an outline—until now. Sure, I veered from it, changed my mind about some things, etc., but it was there when I needed it. And I needed it.

So there is freedom, and a lot of it, but in fiction you have to earn it sentence by sentence, page by page. As for me, I came away from my first stab at it with a little more respect. And an appetite.

How Fictional Can Fiction Afford to Be?

by George H. Scithers and Darrell Schweitzer

Every story you write must be true, at least to some extent. There are, of course, many levels of truth: The story must be true to the human spirit, to the basic realities of life. If it doesn't contain real feelings of love, loneliness, mirth, glory, disappointment, horror, or whatever, it is a *lie* in the worst sense, and wholly unconvincing, no matter how realistic its setting or subject matter.

But on another level, fiction is lies. There is the Great Lie, the simple fact that the story is a *story* and not reportage. Even most historical dramas contain *some* imaginary characters. And fantastic fiction of all sorts contains another lie: events that the writers know are impossible, or that are at least impossible in the here and now.

Fiction writers, therefore, are liars—and they have to be good ones. Here's how to improve your lying skills:

Remember the old saying: He who lies least lies best. Readers have already accepted the ultimate lie that is at the core of fiction. They will, of course, accept additional lies. But heap falsehood upon falsehood, untruth upon untruth, and the entire story starts to sound fishy.

Closely related to that:

Give your lies credibility by getting the *truths* right. Get so many facts—historical, scientific, or just commonsensical—right that your departures will pass unnoticed. Or, if sophisticated readers notice them, you will have gained their confidence by showing them that you *do* know what you are doing, and they will be willing to allow you some license.

On the simplest level, the reason for doing this is to build a convincing picture of the setting—a whole world if necessary—in which the story or novel takes place. A novel set in Rome, circa A.D. 100, must present that Rome as a real, lived-in place, through which the cast moves in a natural way.

Note that we didn't call that date 100 A.D.; *A.D.* comes first. Note too that the people of that time didn't use the A.D. dating at all (it wasn't invented until around A.D. 700 or so). They might say it was the Year of the City—A.U.C.—853, although more likely they'd just call it the third year of the reign of the emperor Trajan. So what? So the people in the story don't make unlikely references to something that probably wouldn't concern them—the birthdate of the leader of an obscure Eastern cult—and so your picture of a convincing, lived-in Roman setting builds up, piece by piece.

No detail is so small that it doesn't matter. If it truly doesn't, it is *irrelevant*, which is another thing entirely. If it belongs in the story, your job is to get your information right.

The attitude that no one will notice, that it's not worth the trouble, is one of the things that keep unpublished writers unpublished. If, in your Roman novel, you don't know the difference between an atrium and peristyle (and you haven't bothered to find out), it is true that many people will not notice. But some of them *will*, and you have lost them at that point. They no longer trust you to tell a convincing story, and immediately assume that all the facts that are *not* in their area of expertise are wrong, too. And when you put an empress in a toga, you lose some more, and when the swords are made of rustproof steel, you lose yet more—and this is even before you locate Mount Vesuvius along the Po River and announce that Nero was the godson (The *what*? Never mind, *nobody will notice*) of Cleopatra.

Any writer should respect facts simply because there is a joy in knowledge, and in sharing it. Further, reality has a certain grittiness that's easy to recognize and difficult to fake. This is why the best war novels are usually written by men who have actually experienced combat. There is no substitute for having seen it and been there.

Present your outright lies firmly—and early—and then get on with the story. And the bigger the lie, the earlier—and the more boldly—you should establish it. Make your huge departure from reality at the beginning, state it as such immediately, and trust the reader to suspend his disbelief. This is a convention of all fiction, a tacit agreement between the reader and the writer: *We will pretend _____ , and tell a good story about it.*

Thus, you can state at the outset that in your story, the South won the Civil War. (There is a whole subgenre of science fiction devoted to this form of alternate history.) The reader will allow you that much, but *only* if you make your imaginary reality convincing: you had better know which side General Hooker fought on, whether Maryland was Union or Confederate or neither, and whether the pistols of 1861-1865 were one-shot or revolvers.

And consider *Star Wars*, when the *Millennium Falcon* flees a desert planet. The pilot activates the faster-than-light drive: the *Falcon* escapes. Now, by all *we* know of physics, moving faster than light is about the most impossible thing going. But for the plot of *Star Wars*—and most other deep-space science fiction stories—to work at all, we must assume that there *is* a way to go faster than the speed of light. In the *Star Wars* universe, everyone *knows* that it's possible to go that fast—and it is therefore possible to cross the vast, interstellar distances in far less than a human lifetime—and so the concern in that particular scene is whether or not *this* rickety specimen of faster-than-light drive is going to work when it is needed in the worst way.

The classic blooper in the western story is the hero's gun that just happens to be an eight-shooter at the crucial showdown. Silly, right? Instead, equip him with this unusual weapon at the outset. Even if you want those last two shots to be a surprise, you must mention the eight-round weapon early. Then divert the reader's attention. This is fair; omitting necessary data is not. At the end, after the surprise has occurred, you want the reader to think, "Of course!" rather than "You lied to me."

Investigate your lies to see if you can base them in truth. This is another call to do your research. In the matter of the eight-shot handgun, a little research — either in the library or in conversation with a friendly gun collector — will reveal that in a modern story you don't have to invent an imaginary weapon after all. The hero can either pick up a .22 revolver with eight chambers in the cylinder, or else he can use a .45 automatic with one round in the chamber and seven more in the standard magazine. In either case, this requires having a round under the weapon's firing pin — an inherently dangerous condition, but one that furthers the characterization of the hero — is he knowledgeable and willing to take the risk, or stupid enough to shoot himself in the foot? Which gun — the .22 or the .45 — will depend on the purpose of the gunfire. In either case, you can be specific about just which make and model of weapon is in the hero's hand. Ian Fleming and Leslie Charteris were very good at using specific, realistic details to make believable some of James Bond's or Simon Templar's more improbable exploits.

Be consistent within your lies. Don't draw attention to the lies by making one claim early on, then later making another that disputes or contradicts the first. In the *Star Wars* universe, for example, it has been established that to cross the interstellar gulfs, one must use faster-than-light drive. Further, it is established that the small spacecraft — the X-wing fighters used by the good guys, and the Tie-fighters of the bad guys — do *not* have faster-than-light capacity. Yet somehow Luke Skywalker is able to pilot an X-wing fighter between solar systems. Anywhere in the universe (except perhaps inside a globular star cluster, where the accumulated radiation would fry any planets there might be) solar systems must be several light-years apart. That is how far apart the stars are. A light-year is roughly 5.8 trillion miles. Luke would probably have spent more than a human lifetime on that trip. It is an allowable lie that faster-than-light is possible in the *Star Wars* universe, but it remains a *fact* that solar systems are too far apart to be reached any other way, unless the voyage is to take decades or even centuries.

Slip both *facts* and *fiction* into the story delicately. The *story* is most important. Avoid pedantry. Some writers can't resist stopping the story to lecture, either directly or through dialogue (characters talking to one another about what they already know, for the benefit of the reader; this is called "idiot lecture" in editorialese), to explain the history of the world up to the point of the story ("The Sirians had first arrived on Earth early in the twenty-first century. At first their presence was welcomed. But then their baleful influence became apparent. Open warfare began in the mid 2060s. Mankind lost, and was driven underground. Three generations later, the cult of the Savior of Earth arose. Joseph Q. Hero was the grandson of the legendary Prophet, and much looked-up-to by his contemporaries. . . .") The would-be historical novelist may easily succumb to the urge to show off everything he has learned about the first century, whether it has anything to do with the story or not. Remember that a novel is not a master's thesis. It need not be studded with scholarly references. You aren't so much trying to convince the reader of your vast erudition as trying to create a believable facade so you can get on with the story.

Thus, you as writer and researcher have a duty to *make* yourself familiar with what material you need. Then, having taught yourself a great deal about the subject, you must learn what to *leave out*. Your hero has a history—*you* know how he came to have experience with eight-shot pistols, how old he is, where he was raised, what he plans to do when this adventure is over. But most of this is irrelevant to the story at hand, and so should be left out; it only serves as a self-consistent background that is larger than the story itself. You must know *more* than you actually put down, so you have the freedom to pick and choose among the details for the ones you think you actually need.

Then—get *on* with it! H.G. Wells said that eighty years ago. George Lucas and Steven Spielberg make millions by doing exactly that: getting on with the story while the illusion holds. Since they have the facilities of a superb special-effects group and—more important—the immediacy of film, they can get away with things a writer on the printed page cannot. Nevertheless, the same principle applies: Make it worth the reader's while to stay with the action, rather than dropping out to say, *Hey, wait a minute!* either in the middle of a page or on the way out of the theater.

The object is to tell a story, not to show off your arcane learning. But at the same time, you mustn't give readers who *do* know better the impression that you don't.

Remember your limitations as a liar. Heed writer David Gerrold's Rule: "Half of being smart is knowing what you're dumb at." Do not volunteer information you are uncertain about. If you are not sure, and can't find out what you need to know, avoid that subject. At the same time, make certain you *are* sure about enough for there to be a basis for a story.

You don't have to know everything about everything—only give the impression that you do. Fit your plot and cast to what you know, and deftly avoid what you do not know. In your Roman novel, if you can find vast amounts of information about court life in Rome itself, but nothing at all about village life among Spanish peasants of the same period, maybe your hero shouldn't take off for that particular province.

Similarly, don't feel compelled to tell the truth when it doesn't really matter. In our story set in ancient Rome, you might, by careful omission, avoid getting involved in whether the cast is speaking Latin or Greek (Educated Romans of the first century spoke both. The army used Latin. By the very late Empire, Greek had declined in the West, even as Latin did in the East.) If the details are irrelevant to your story, you may safely ignore them.

Don't be taken in by other writers' lies, or by what "everybody knows." Go to the original sources, if you can, when researching. For your Roman novel, get your information from Tacitus, Suetonius and Cassius Dio, then go to the sober, scholarly works on Roman daily life, religion, military technology, and the like. *Do not* rely on hearsay—what your friend remembers having read once—or on other people's novels, or, worse yet, on reruns of *Quo Vadis?* For one thing, you may well trip over someone else's sloppy research. For another, you may be perpetuating a cliché that has long since deserved a gory and *final* demise in the arena.

Most especially, avoid the conventions of one medium when writing for another. Meteors and starships do not go "whoosh!" in the vacuum of space. Nor does Dodge City (which is in Kansas) look at all like the desert terrain where most westerns are filmed. If you are writing a screenplay, you may have to consider the unique properties of the film medium—silent starships are boring on the big screen—and the problem of budget—Kansas farmland is expensive, compared to Arizona desert. But if you are writing for a printed page, there's no excuse for not sticking to reality.

Give your inventions the trappings of realism, so that your lies aren't readily indentifiable as such. This means giving them detail, and then describing the detail so matter-of-factly that the reader will "believe" the inventions to be true. Characters with depth and quirks are more believable than one-dimensional characters. A fictional city with a sleaze district and well-described suburbs and unusual names will be more credible than a vaguely described Anytown.

For this reason, avoid stereotypes. Not only are they unoriginal, but they also call attention to themselves as fictional concoctions—and poor ones, at that.

This is especially important, of course, with characters. If they aren't believable, no amount of inspired imagination or diligent research will save your story. Your cast, like other elements of fiction, is a mixture of autobiography, reportage and lies. Your cast, far more than any other elements, must be convincing.

The Depths of Truth

There are, of course, truths that go far deeper than mere facts. A character must act true, speak true. That's why your research must include listening to people, both for what they say and how they say it. You may not be able to directly "research" the life and attitudes of a starship captain, but it might help to know an airline pilot, or the captain of your local tugboat. *Then* you can see how fictional captains—like James T. Kirk or Horatio Hornblower—are or are not like your real-life sample of the profession.

Be wary of basing all your research on a single source. Your local tugboat captain probably *doesn't* share many of the characteristics of, say, a Russian admiral. Instead, use many sources, including, if you can find it, the memoirs of a Russian admiral, in addition to other firsthand accounts of navy life, from many navies and many centuries. From all these, you may be able to find some general principles that apply to all cases.

It's a good idea to read books produced by other cultures, or written in other eras, everything from the *Histories* of Herodotus to World War II memoirs written by Japanese soldiers and sailors. Much will seem utterly strange, but much will seem *familiar*. These familiar elements are more universal. From such research you can pick up specific facts previously unknown to you (the strange parts) and see how ordinary people adjust to them (the familiar). This will help you give your setting that lived-in feeling.

And the more lived-in your setting feels, the more receptive readers—and editors—will be to the lies you stage there.

The Right Way to Write About What You Know

by Hal Blythe and Charlie Sweet

L ast spring in our creative writing class, a student spent an entire semester trying to write a single two-thousand-word story. Her basic idea was good. A divorced teaching assistant in the humanities falls in love with a well-organized ROTC professor, somebody who represents all that she dislikes in life. Although Penny labored through four rewrites, she never produced a draft that satisfied either her or us. Eventually, unable to get a fictional handle on her story, she abandoned it.

What went wrong? After all, she had begun with a good idea.

Talking with Penny at the end of the semester, we belatedly discovered a few facts:

- Penny's marriage had broken up the previous year.
- Penny was a graduate assistant in the History Department.
- Penny had fallen in love with a lieutenant in Military Science.
- Penny was still unable to reconcile her free-spirited, antiviolent life-style with that of the officer.

Maybe Penny should have enrolled in Autobiography 200 instead of Creative Writing.

You Know What's Coming

Has there ever been a creative writing course, book, magazine, professor, or little old English teacher who hasn't introduced the godfather of all creative clichés — trumpets please — WRITE ABOUT WHAT YOU KNOW? Come on, confess. Since you decided to become a writer, you have seen it scribbled on subway walls, printed on matchbooks, and chiseled on stone tablets so often you repeat it ritualistically in your sleep.

Well, writing about what you know is a good commandment, but even Moses had to go back up the mountain for a little revision. If you don't use *some* personal experience in your writing, your story is apt not to sound true to life, to touch those common chords of human experience. Without those moments drawn from real life, your fiction will tend toward the artificial, the hollow. On the other hand, just as a prime cut of steak must be cooked, raw experience must be treated a bit, or it won't achieve the flavor that transforms it into art.

Penny's story suffered from some of the usual problems created by "undercooked" personal experience.

23

Lack of Objectivity/Distance. Penny was too close to the situation she was trying to portray. While her protagonist was agonizing over whether to become the bride of an officer and a gentleman, Penny was trapped in the same struggle. How could the writer direct her character's choice when she hadn't resolved the dilemma herself? Writing of this sort may be good psychological therapy, but when practiced by the novice it usually doesn't result in publishable fiction. In addition, Penny's lack of general perspective contributed to more specific problems in constructing her story.

Lack of Artistic Unity. Despite the existence of the slice-of-life technique, most publications prefer stories that offer a beginning, a middle and a conclusion. Penny, in a real sense, had no idea when her "story" actually began and wouldn't know its ending for quite some time. Good writing has a sense of wholeness, unity. Every word, description, and piece of dialogue contributes to what Poe called "that certain unique and singular effect." Embroiled in the experience itself, Penny put into her story every one of the problems that swirled around her: her lack of money, her desire to complete her Master's, her ties to family and area (marriage would mean, among other things, a move overseas), a reluctance to enter a new relationship so soon after another had failed, her new feminist perspective, her deep-seated antimilitary sentiments, etc. Any one of these concerns could have been the focus for an excellent story, but she, living these conflicts, tried to include them all — in two thousand words. Had Penny been writing a novel, perhaps she could have created a major river into which these tributaries flowed, but in her short story she had only a hodgepodge of individual streams meandering in many directions. Stories very often tighten and compress reality into a simpler, more unified version.

Lack of Causality. In fiction, a discernible link exists between Event A and Event B, between B and C, and so on. E.M. Forster stressed the notion of causality between two distinct events by using the example of the story wherein the king died and the queen died *out of grief*. Penny knew that her queen was attracted to her king, but she, unable to unravel the complex of her emotional and intellectual state to determine why, could not logically connect Event A to Event B in her story. In short, fiction demands a more clear-cut cause-and-effect relationship than real life. Life is often stranger than fiction because of this demand. In real life, trawlers do by chance assist lone fishermen in distress, but such an action would have destroyed the fictional impact of Santiago's rugged individualism at the end of *The Old Man and the Sea*. One reason we pick up fiction is that it offers us an order we do not find in our everyday life.

Lack of Background Awareness. Throughout the story, Penny's main character had what seemed an inordinate fear of her Military Science prof pulling up stakes in the middle of the academic year and leaving. In real life Penny knew a detail she never introduced into her story, but unconsciously assumed her reader would know. One day, when we were playing in a local softball league, a friend of ours from our college's ROTC department announced to the team that he would be leaving because his stint at the university was up. When he explained to us that every three years he was reassigned to a new position in a different location, the motivation for Penny's protagonist's fears became clear. The moral? When you live in the middle of the forest, the individual trees are so much a part of your reality that you don't stop to point out each one to visitors.

The Shape of Things to Write

In short, Penny let her life control her story. Fiction is not autobiography. The Greek root for poet (*poiētēs*) and the term *wright* (as in playwright or wheelwright) refers to a maker, a shaper of things. A writer molds the raw material of life into a new entity rather than simply transcribing the life experience. The writer is a painter, not a photographer whose only responsibility is to aim and shoot. The writer must control the material, not vice versa.

In simple terms, a writer selects bits and pieces from different portions of life and restructures them in different and unique combinations. Thomas Wolfe, for example, came out of the Carolina mountains with reams of personal reminiscences, but it took Maxwell Perkins to edit these experiences into fiction. Ross Macdonald's relationship with his father appears in the background of most everything he has written, but names, locations and plots vary. Obviously, every writer must draw on personal experience to some degree, and occasionally real life provides the writer with an experience that can be set down almost *in toto* in fiction; but this is rare. In more than a hundred published stories, we have never written one that in beginning, middle and end reproduced a real-life experience (of course, that may be more a comment on the inherent dullness of our lives).

Rather than trying to lift the whole experience from real life and call it fiction, we suggest employing *segmented reality*. Through this technique, the writer fuses, for instance, a character from childhood, a present-day conflict, and a setting taken from last summer's vacation. The writer shapes these varied experiences into a new reality and thus avoids the a-four-mentioned horsemen) of the novice's apocalypse. In addition, this use of segmented reality allows — indeed forces — the writer to fill in the gaps of personal experience.

What Hamlet told his friend, "There are more things in heaven and earth Horatio, / Than are dreamt of in your philosophy," is especially true for us as mystery writers, as it is for those of you who wish to write historical romances, thrillers or science fiction. If, before writing, we waited around our small college town until we ran into international jewel thieves, fugitive war criminals, mafia capos and the like, we'd never touch pen to paper.

Therefore, in creating "The Turning Point" (which appeared in *Mike Shayne Mystery Magazine*), we used segmented reality to help us avoid Penny's pitfalls. Although the story's genesis was something that had really happened to one of us — an unscrupulous professor stole part of one of our doctoral dissertations — the resulting tale we concocted was miles distant. First, as the event had happened ten years ago, we believed we had achieved the necessary aesthetic distance to treat the incident objectively. And a dispassionate review of the real event told us it was nothing more than a stale pastry served up daily in faculty lounges around the country. Furthermore, whereas Penny's real-life situation had been replete with possibilities, ours was a bit too small in itself; nonetheless, it had the advantage of not being a complete story. So, second, to give our story a sense of artistic unity, something the incident inherently lacked, we created a fictional beginning and ending to surround our real-life middle. Having no idea what motivated our real-life villain, we were forced to create a cause (the publish-or-perish problem so prevalent at universities larger than ours). While in real life we had done nothing about the purloined passages, we wondered what would have happened if we had, and if we had, how the professor would have protected himself. Bingo.

From the small grain of real-life sand, we had manufactured a fictional pearl. Since the beginning and ending had never happened, we had to invent the third element lacking in purely autobiographic writing, causality. Though we had discovered the real-life plagiarism in a journal, we decided it would be much more dramatic for our story if the theft was discovered during a confrontation between the two antagonists, the original writer and the professor. Imagining this scene allowed us to furnish the office in our story with anything we wanted. Unhindered by a real-life setting, we could draw our verisimilitude from other personal experiences. We combined the office we share with the study of Charlie's father, who being an amateur historian, has such medieval martial artifacts as swords, shields and, in particular, an arbalest. Other segments of reality filled in the background pieces. The hardnosed police officer who investigates the crime, for instance, was drawn from a local officer with whom we coach girls' softball.

"The Turning Point," then, is not simply a documentary account of an incident that really happened, but a distanced, unified, casual and realistic piece of fiction.

Tip-Off

Here are a few tips for turning personal experiences into salable fiction.

Never lift an entire experience from real life and call it fiction. First there's the problem of intellectual dishonesty, and second you will find the situation presents more dangers than advantages, as we have shown.

Make sure you have achieved enough distance from the real-life incident to treat it objectively. Sometimes this needed distance is spatial, sometimes temporal. Remember how Wordsworth defined his type of poetry: "the spontaneous overflow of powerful emotions" but that are "recollected in tranquility." Even Ralph Ellison, whose *Invisible Man* is heavily autobiographical, waited until adulthood after he had left his native Oklahoma to set down the painful memories of childhood.

Make reality into fiction by changing names. This is done not only, as Joe Friday used to say, "to protect the innocent," but also partially to protect yourself legally. When it comes time to construct your story, your sister can become Aunt Jane, that Holiday Inn in Clearwater a Caribbean haunt of the very rich, and your next-door neighbor's grocery a shoe store. Yet, the most important reason to change names is to further distance yourself from the story. Both of us, for instance, have a handicapped child. We have written several stories involving this situation, but in each case we changed the child's name, sometimes his handicap, and once his sex. Even though we are still emotionally caught up in our sons' lives, these changes give us the kind of objectivity as if we were dealing with someone else's child.

Experiment with point of view. One of the surest ways to separate fiction from reality and maintain control over the fictionalized incident is to change the method of narration. The natural way of revealing a powerful emotional experience is to begin "I was walking down Elm Street when . . . ," but if you shift the perspective to "Mary was walking down Elm Street," you force yourself to do all that fiction demands. In "The Turning Point," for instance, we thought we achieved the ultimate distance by telling the story from the point of view of the purloining professor.

Record poignant experiences. Wordsworth was lucky in that his sister kept a precise record of the things he said and did. When the muse struck, it was often more a matter of reading her journal than receiving a bolt from the blue. Henry James captured his powerful moments in a series of voluminous notebooks, and when it came time for the next story, he read over his jottings, drawing bits and pieces from various volumes. Jack London had a unique way of recording his experiences: he noted them on a small piece of paper, which he stuck to his clothing to be collected at the end of the day.

Supplement personal experience with research. While Scott Fitzgerald and Zelda lived every day to the fullest and hence found sufficient fodder for fiction, the mass of writers, looking for something to happen, live lives of quiet exasperation. In the late seventies for example, to brighten our otherwise pedestrian existence, we ventured forth to the local disco. What a great spot, we thought, for a murder. But even though Charlie's wife taught dancing, we didn't feel secure in the world of flashing lights, quadrophonic sound, and classy women in Halston skirts (in the interests of research we may have gone more than once). Even so, between the Latin Hustle and the Bus Stop, we read magazine articles, watched TV, and even suffered through a bout with *Saturday Night Fever*. One phenomenon struck us: people in the dark of the disco did not act the way they did in daylight. We used this evidence of dual personality, supplemented by Jung, as the basis for our killer of "In the Key of Murder," which we sold to *MSMM*. And because our killer psychotically believed herself the illegitimate daughter of Humphrey Bogart (the Bogie revival was in full swing), we aided and abetted our movie-buff knowledge with a short biography.

Apply the "what if . . . ?" principle. No matter how complete, how vivid a real-life situation seems, be willing to ask yourself these questions: What if it hadn't happened exactly as it did? What if Event X had preceded it? What if Event Z had followed it? Sticking to pure autobiography gives you the possibility of but one story—using an incident and altering it here and there gives you potentially many stories. One day Hal was interrupted at home by a particularly obnoxious door-to-door salesman. A common experience and a good irritant. But what if Hal had been a burglar interrupted *in medias ransack*? The answer became "Sign of the Times," which we sold to *Spiderweb*. Remember Kent State? We do. One of us at the time was a Reservist, the other a grad student. History records what happened that day, but that didn't stop us from asking, "What if one of the National Guardsmen involved had a personal ulterior motive for firing on a specific protester?" The results appeared as "The Five Sides of Murder" in *MSMM*.

Apply the I.C.E. Test to your finished story. Does your fictionalized incident have a definite Introduction, at least one Complication, and a satisfying Ending? And, does it have Incidents containing logical Cause and Effect? If your story doesn't pass both parts of the I.C.E. Test cold, it may be that you're still too close to the real-life basis.

In summary, the next time you undergo a powerful emotional experience, don't automatically sit down and start to write. Do jot down the highlights in a journal and give yourself a chance to digest it, to let it ferment. Then, when you think you have had time to get a handle on it, bottle it, cork it, and try to sell it.

By the way, we recently ran into Penny. She's married, finishing up her degree, and ready to move overseas at the end of the semester. She has found the conclusion to one of her stories. Let's hope the other can have as happy an ending.

To Make a Short Story Long . . .

by Orson Scott Card

In the 1936 Munich Olympics, the Germans were very clever. They didn't let the equestrians from other nations see the course the horses would have to race. At one point in the course, after the normal obstacles that all the horses easily coped with, was a fence. And beyond the fence was a strip of water dozens of yards across, far too wide for any horse to jump.

When the non-German equestrians reached that obstacle, they all tried to jump, of course, and floundered. But the German rider, knowing all about it, had his horse daintily step over the fence and walk gently through the water with perfect form.

It was cheating. But it's the kind of thing many of us face when we try to switch from writing short stories to writing novels. We're used to coping with three thousand or even ten thousand words. But suddenly there yawns before us a huge expanse of words—a hundred thousand or more. And when we try to leap over it as we would with a story, we end up with a soaking, as often as not.

In 1977, six months after I got my first check for a short story sale, I took stock of my earnings. I had sold a total of four stories in that time, for which I had been paid a total of $980. This was still $20 less than my monthly salary at my magazine editing job.

It didn't look like I would be able to freelance very soon, not on short story sales alone. If I wanted to be a fulltime writer, I was going to have to write a novel.

So I sat down at the typewriter and began writing. I was confident. After all, what was a novel, if not a short story that had more things happen before the end? So, page by page, my first novel flowed from my typewriter. It was a science fiction epic that spanned a thousand years and dealt with the lives of twenty characters.

And it lasted only one hundred twenty pages.

I began to suspect there was more to writing a novel than just "having more things happen."

Longer Is Shorter

More of us who write fiction begin with short stories. There are several practical reasons for this: short stories look easier to write. If you write a bad one that never sells, you have lost only twenty pages' work, not three hundred. And—perhaps the most common reason of all—short stories are what your college creative writing teacher wanted to see, and now you're in the habit.

How do you make the leap from short stories to novels? That intimidating stack of blank pages you have to fill is enough to frighten off most would-be novelists. But if you're one of the rare ones who is determined to go ahead, there are some things you can do to help yourself over the hurdle.

How do I know the arcana of switching to the novel form? I learned from experience. I wrote some bad novels. And each one's flaws taught me how to write the next one better. Take that first novel—that one-hundred-twenty-page, thousand-year epic. I knew something was terribly wrong with it. So I took it to a friend, a fine editor who had been criticizing my short stories for me. He read it; he returned it to me silently.

"Well?" I asked.

"Um," he said. "Sure is long."

Long? A hundred and twenty pages? "The problem is it's too short."

"No," he insisted. "The problem is it's too long. It's absolutely boring. From page three on, I could hardly get through it."

The novel began like any of my short stories. I jumped into the main character's problem with both feet, and tried to make him personally interesting. It worked fine.

But on page three, I started really getting into the plot. I introduced two more characters and moved my protagonist into a life-and-death struggle. By page five, he had resolved that problem and was off on another adventure. By page ten, he had saved the world. By page thirty, he had saved another world.

I wasn't writing a novel at all. I was writing a plot outline. I was so keenly aware of how much story line I had to cover that I had raced ahead and not paused to give the reader time to absorb anything.

Short stories are designed to deliver their impact in as few pages as possible. A tremendous amount is left out, and a good short story writer learns to include only the most essential information—only what he needs to create mood, get the facts across, and prepare the reader for the climax.

But novels have more space, more time. When readers sit down with a book, they are committing several hours of their lives to reading it. They will stay with you for much more peripheral material; they expect, in return, that you will provide them with a fuller experience than they could possibly get from a short story.

In my first draft of my first novel, I had written second-rate *history*—a bare retelling of events. When I set out to write the second draft, I knew I had to write *biography*—a detailed exposition of what my characters thought and said and did, and what in their past made them act that way.

My second draft was more than three hundred pages long, and included only half the plot of the first draft. But it was a much better book. That is, it could be read by a person who actually stayed awake without liberal doses of NoDoz.

My friend read it again, and came back much happier. "It still isn't very good, but at least it's *shorter* this time."

Cards' Law of Novel-Writing: Longer Is Shorter.

Don't Get Buried in Plot

One of the things that fooled me on that first draft was the idea that if a novel is ten times the length of a short story, it must have ten times the plot. But that is rarely the case.

Think of John Fowles's novel *Daniel Martin* — 629 pages of always excellent, often brilliant prose. Yet the plot, the actual, essential plot, could have been expressed in a forty-page novelette. I suspect it would be a mediocre story at best, but it could easily be done, because not that much happens on the direct plot line. Reduced to its absurd minimum, *Daniel Martin* is the story of a financially successful screenwriter who returns to England at the request of a dying friend with whom he feuded years ago. The friend's wife was the woman the screenwriter really loved and wanted to marry back in their days at Oxford; the dying friend reveals that he knew his wife had an affair with the screenwriter, and wants the two of them to get together after his death. Having delivered his message, the friend kills himself, and the screenwriter and the woman he once loved do indeed fall in love again, much to their own surprise.

Sounds like a melodramatic little story doesn't it? And it might have turned out that way — except that stories and novels are not just devices for recounting plot.

When I first plotted that first novel of mine, I was thinking of a short story as a sort of thread through time, a few events long; I thought of a novel as simply a longer thread to fill up the pages. My metaphor was all wrong, however. Writing is not just one-dimensional.

So when you plot your novel, don't try to come up with ten times the number of events you usually put in a story. You will usually want more events than in a story, of course, but you should still leave yourself plenty of leisure to explore from character to character, from thought to thought, from detail to detail. A novel need not cover a thousand years or forty-eight characters or the Renaissance in Italy; you have the freedom to use the novel form to write about a single life or a single year or a single incident. Despite the deceptively simple plot of *Daniel Martin*, or perhaps because of it, Fowles was able to take his readers by surprise, bringing us to love the seemingly jaded and shallow narrator as he reluctantly shows us his true self a layer at a time.

Gulps and Swallows

My first novel went through several more drafts, and I thought I had finally found a system for coping with its length. I was a short story writer, wasn't I? So why not cut up the plot into five or six novelettes? They would all lead to a climax at the end, and yet I would be on familiar ground, writing thirty or forty pages in each section, just like a story.

Well, it worked — and it didn't. I sold the novel, and people even bought copies of it and read it, and some liked it. But the critics didn't, and much as it pains me to say it, they were fundamentally right. Because that little trick of cutting the novel up into short stories simply doesn't work.

A novel isn't a half-dozen short stories with the same characters. The seams invariably show. Why? Because a novel must have integrity. The novel, no matter how dense and wide-ranging it might be, must have a single cumulative effect to please the reader. Every minor climax must point toward the book's final climax, must promise still better things to come.

But in my first novel (all right, I'll name it: *Hot Sleep*), instead of a series of minor climaxes leading toward the final climax of the book, I had six completely unrelated climaxes. In the first short story, my protagonist, as a child, faces a terrible dilemma that shapes his whole future. But when I start the second story, years have passed and those earlier events are not very important anymore—it's hard to see any real effect they might have on the events of the rest of the novel. And at the end of the second story, all but one of the major characters lose their memories in a disaster in space, and to all intents and purposes the third part of the book is another entirely new beginning. All the readers' emotional investment is gone, and they must begin all over again. No wonder some readers got impatient!

In a way, however, my instinct was correct. You can't write a novel all at once, any more than you can swallow a whale in one gulp. You do have to break it up into smaller chunks. But those smaller chunks aren't good old familiar short stories. Novels aren't built out of short stories.

They're built out of scenes.

Lights! Camera! Action! Cut!

Think of the way a movie works. A new setting is almost always introduced with an establishing shot, showing the audience what characters are present and where they are. Almost every time the film skips from one place to another without actually following the character there, the audience is given some time to get its bearings.

Then, as the film progresses, the camera cuts from one point of view to another, or follows as the characters travel from one place to another. The camera is able to focus on a particular thing that a character is looking at—or that the character is unaware of. But all through a single action, the camera keeps our attention tightly focused on the important matters. Then, when that scene ends, there is another establishing shot; another line of action begins.

As you see the story unwind on the screen, you aren't really aware that between each old and new setting are actually *many* scenes, small bits of action leading to a single, small climax or revelation. After all, neither novelists nor filmmakers show *everything* that happens. Tremendous amounts of detail are skipped over, left out—hinted at, perhaps, but never shown. All the action is compressed into the events that *are* shown. While a filmmaker must compress everything into two hours or so, a novelist has a great deal more freedom. Within reasonable limits, you can include all the pertinent information, and the reader will be right there with you.

Like a filmmaker, however, you must present that information carefully. You can't just list the events and motives and speeches of the characters — that's history. Bad history, in fact. Instead, you present the information dramatically, through characters who have understandable desires and who are carrying out understandable actions, and with a structure that helps the readers notice and understand and feel what you want them to.

And the structure you use comprises hundreds of different scenes of varying lengths and varying degrees of importance — each one a single continuing action.

A single continuing action may be, for instance, a sword fight that begins with an insult at a party and continues all over the palace until one man finally gasps with a sword in his chest and the hero, panting, watches his enemy die.

A single continuing action may be a man standing at the window of an apartment in a tall building, looking out over a city, watching a helicopter land, regretting his decision not to be aboard it.

A single continuing action may be a journey across the United States, summarized by telling, in two paragraphs, the routine of a single day of travel; that summary is extended to cover all the days of travel.

Each such scene is a unit, designed to have its own effect on the reader. When the scene ends, the reader knows something more — and feels something more.

How is that different from writing a short story? Ideally, a short story is an indivisible unit — every sentence in it points toward the single climax that fulfills the entire work. One moment in the story controls all the rest. But in a novel, that single climax is replaced by many smaller climaxes, by many side trips or pauses to explore. If you keep shaping everything to point to that one climax, your readers will get sick of it after a hundred pages or so. It will feel monotonous. To keep the readers entertained (that is, to keep them reading) you must give them many small moments of fulfillment along the way, brief rewards that promise something bigger later.

How does this work in a particular novel? Let's go through chapter twenty-seven of Stephen King's *The Stand* (as it was originally published). After each scene number, the number of paragraphs in the scene appears in parentheses, followed by a synopsis of the scene:

1. (4) Characters Larry and Rita have noticed that the electricity is beginning to go off, and the smell of the decaying bodies is terrible; Larry is afraid New York will soon be unlivable.

2. (2) Flashback: they found the body of a man they had been aware of, murdered. It affected Rita deeply.

3. (20) Dialogue: Larry and Rita eat breakfast, and Larry makes the decision to leave.

4. (8) Rita suddenly rushes to the bathroom, vomits. She is fast becoming unable to cope with the disaster.

5. (3) Flashback: Rita is not as strong as Larry had thought at first.

6. (1) Larry wonders if he can take care of her.

7. (13) Dialogue: she decides to go with him, even as he comes to resent her more because of her weakness.

At this point, King takes a larger break. There is a line space, and suddenly we are with Larry and Rita as they walk along the streets of New York. In those first seven scenes, there is a definite sense of building toward a single climax, the moment in scene 1, where Larry catches himself hating her. King writes:

> Then he felt the familiar surge of self-contempt and wondered what the hell could be the matter with him.
>
> "I'm sorry," he said. "I'm an insensitive bastard."

It is a pivotal moment for Larry; it is the reason why he takes responsibility for her even though he hates the thought of taking her along. It explains his motive. It also sets us up for tension in later scenes, and finally, in a small way it leads us to the climax of the novel.

Yet, each of the small scenes leading to that climax had a closure of its own. Scene 1 closes with Larry's dark dream of a black thing that wants him. Scene 2 closes with the observation that seeing the dead man had made a powerful change in Rita. Scene 3 ends with a startling change — after a peaceful conversation, Rita suddenly has an expression on her face that scares Larry. And so on.

Every scene advances the reader toward the minor climax in the seventh scene. Each scene conveys the necessary information and then closes in a way that increases the tension, the reader's expectation of a climax. And the scenes vary — first bare exposition in the author's voice, then a flashback in Larry's mind, then dialogue between Larry and Rita, then physical action as Rita rushes to the bathroom to vomit, then flashback, then reflection, and then dialogue again.

It is as if King had cut from camera to camera, showing us the continuing action from different points of view, revealing bits of information that together built to a whole — the superscene that ends with the line space. And the chapter is composed of five superscenes of varying length that, together, tell a complete episode. The chapter as a whole cements Larry and Rita together in our minds, despite the tension between them. We end up understanding and liking both. They have managed to get out of New York alive, but we know their adventures are just beginning.

Cliffhangers

These are the gulps you can use to down a whole novel. You never sit down to write three hundred or five hundred or one thousand pages. You sit down to write a series of scenes that create a superscene with its own minor climax;

you then add superscenes together to create the climax that completes the chapter.

Yet, while each closure, each minor climax, each chapter climax is fulfilling to the reader, none of them is *completely* fulfilling. Inherent in every climax is the promise of more tension and greater fulfillment later. In its crudest form, this is the cliffhanger technique—putting the protagonist into an awkward dilemma and then leaving him hanging there while the reader waits to buy the next day's installment. Such obvious tricks irritate most readers; but the technique, in more subtle form, is essential to creating a novel as a whole. After all, what is a novel if not the writer's attempt to involve the readers emotionally in a dilemma and keep them involved until its resolution? In your short stories, you could hold off until your single climax because the reader would stay with you for such a brief time; but in a novel, the reader's patience is not infinite.

Of course, I seriously doubt that Stephen King sat down and planned out each of those seven scenes. I wonder if he even outlined chapter by chapter. The selection of what scenes to present is art; it is felt, not intellectualized. For me, most of those decisions are unconscious. It feels right to include this scene; it feels right to interrupt the action here for a flashback that reveals important information; it feels right to describe this particular setting in loving detail.

You *can* consciously plan, however, to keep yourself aware of the possibilities open to you, so that you use all your tools. You can concentrate on the scenes and superscenes at hand, instead of letting the climax of the novel, hundreds of pages away, distract you from what you are creating now.

And, while you aren't writing short stories anymore, you *have* cut that whale of a novel into pieces small enough that you, like the reader, can forget about the hundreds of pages ahead and concentrate on only the few pages needed to reach the climax of this particular scene.

As a friend of mine once said, "I'd a lot rather fight two tons of tiny lizards than a two-ton fire-breathing dragon."

The Second Will Be Better Than the First

Even if you keep in mind all the things I have pointed out, you will probably find new mistakes or problems I haven't mentioned. After all, there were some things I did *right* in my first novels that you might do wrong. And undoubtedly there were some things I'm *still* doing wrong that I haven't caught yet—and therefore can't warn you about.

I was lucky. Years after that first novel was published, Susan Allison at Ace Books gave me a chance to do it again. *Hot Sleep* was taken out of print, and I replaced it with *The Worthing Chronicle*. I had not realized how much I had learned in the intervening years. I told the same story, but not a scene from the first book was usable in the second.

ᴇach novel you write will make the next one easier. I'm not talking about mere confidence, either, though finishing one novel will certainly make the next one seem less intimidating. Whether or not you notice what you're learning, you *are* learning. When I was an eight year old first throwing a ball at a basketball hoop, I missed time and time again. But gradually I began to be able to hit the backboard every time, and eventually I got good enough to have the ball come somewhere near the basket on every shot. Though I'm still a miserable basketball player, I did unconsciously learn and improve. In writing novels, of course, each shot takes a long time, and you aren't able to see so easily whether you missed. But your brain is still plugging along, learning to become comfortable with the form.

Too comfortable, sometimes. I studied Spanish for eight years and was pretty good in it—but then I lived in Brazil for two years and spoke Portuguese the whole time. Those languages are so similar that by the end of those two years, I literally could not speak Spanish at all—Portuguese had taken over.

Something similar has happened with my fiction. I am now a "novelist," and I find it increasingly hard to use that similar but still different "language" of short stories. I keep forgetting that I don't have hundreds of pages to work with. I have *started* short stories, but any that were any good kept going until they were hundreds of pages long. In other words, when I have a story to tell, my "native" language is the novel.

Anybody have any advice on how a novelist can learn to write short stories?

The Ten Essentials of Popular Fiction

by David Groff

I t's Friday afternoon and on the table behind my desk is a stack of manuscripts to read this weekend. The trade publisher I work for makes a good portion of its profits from the commercial or "popular" novel, so many of those manuscripts are novels intended to make a lot of money. This weekend, if I'm very lucky, I'll find a novel by some author that will turn out to be a blockbuster.

Here are the weekend's offerings:

• *Hollywood Hype*, a novel about a young Chicago woman who gets off the bus in Burbank and within two tumultuous years is the head of a major movie studio—until a long-hidden secret threatens to topple her.

• *Waco*, the story of a Texas wildcatter who makes a fortune taking over wells abandoned by the big oil companies, but who seems to meet his match in a young woman rancher and her crazy brother who are determined to rescue their land from his drills.

• *Cuba*, in which an ex-merchant marine uncovers a drug-smuggling ring based in Miami, which may or may not be run by a renegade FBI agent.

• *Princeton*, a novel of two generations of Ivy League alumni and the financial scandal that puts their fortunes and reputations at risk.

All of these are fundamentally good ideas for novels. And as you may notice from my descriptions of them—the kinds of descriptions that appear in manuscript cover letters and publishers' jacket copy—they are written to reach a wide audience. They aim not for posterity or Pulitzers but for profit. They are commercial novels.

Which one of these (and in a weekend's reading there is at best only one) is worth being considered seriously for publication? When we ask that question, we're really asking what makes a successful commercial novel.

Why are some books classified instantly as commercial while others are assigned to the literature shelves of a bookstore? Is a novel about a young woman growing up poor and Jewish on the Riviera a novel with a commercial destiny? What about the story of a Dutch prisoner of war who starts his own spy network and dies at the end to save a beautiful woman from the Nazis? As in the case of obscenity, we may know commercial fiction when we see it, even if we have trouble defining it.

But here are some typical characteristics of a successful commercial novel in any genre:

- It is about a subject that already fascinates its readers, such as love on the Riviera or espionage in London.
- It employs—to a varying degree—a formula that allows it both to fulfill and play with the readers' expectations.
- It speaks to its readers in a language they understand—it is not "experimental" or *avant garde* in its style. It provides a recognizable narrative that moves forward clearly in time.
- It has a hero or heroine (or both) who ends up surviving, changed and usually happier.
- It is less significant for its meaning than for its game content; it is plotted.
- It speaks neither up nor down to its audience, but across.
- It presents its readers with interesting facts about the world.
- However lusty or violent it may be, it is conservative, both stylistically and morally.
- It is meant primarily to entertain.
- It falls largely or completely into a particular genre and—at its best— toys with the reader's expectations of that genre.

I'm sure you can point out six or ten successful novels that violate a few of these tenets and still end up on the *New York Times* bestseller list. A novel like *The Good Mother*, by Sue Miller, for instance, or Mona Simpson's *Anywhere But Here*, were not intended to be commercial novels; good reviews and good promotion hefted them onto the lower rungs of the list. But when writers set out to create lucrative fiction, these rules generally apply. Let's explore some of them individually.

Author and Audience

Perhaps more than in any other kind of writing, the relationship between the author and his or her audience is primary in commercial fiction. An author should ask exactly who that reader is. Is it a woman who will be reading the novel on the bus on the way to her word-processing job? Is it a man who reads to fall asleep at night? Will the reader—man or woman—be reading the novel fast or slow? Will that reader keep the book after finishing it, or throw it away? Is that reader on vacation or—like my father's secretary—sneaking looks at the novel when she should be typing?

The first question, whether your reader is a man or woman, is somewhat misleading. Detective novels are not sex-specific, nor are so-called women's novels read only by women. Some 40 percent of the readers of Jackie Collins's *Hollywood Husbands* probably were men; boys like glamour just as much as girls do, and women adore Mickey Spillane.

Nevertheless, a writer should keep in mind some ideal reader—identifying that reader not only by sex, but also by personality. What about that reader who devours your novel on the bus to work? Her name is Mary Ann Cowan. Give her an entire life: Make her thirty-five years old and newly married, with a sluggish husband she loves and a job that leaves her restless and distracted; give her a brand-new ranch house in Clinton, Iowa; give her a religion, parents, types of men and women she considers ideal, and a particular sexual fantasy.

Now for your hypothetical male reader. Let's say he always wanted to be James Bond (I always wanted to be James Bond). His name is Paul Winters. He's thirty-seven, overweight, making a lot of money, with a wife and three children who tie him down. College-educated, he spends two weeks of every month on the road, selling computer furniture (Mary Ann Cowan sits on a padded chair he sold her company). Every night in his Missouri motel rooms he turns off the TV about midnight and reads for half an hour. He likes action; he likes computers; he likes blondes.

If these descriptions sound at all stereotyped, please forgive me—and then make them real for yourself. I'm not trying to create a stereotypical reader for commercial fiction. Publishers of commercial fiction, especially paperback publishers, sometimes try to do that via market surveys. They may discover that the average romance-novel reader is a thirty-one-year-old woman living in Dayton, Ohio, fifteen pounds overweight, with two and a half children—but such surveys tell most writers very little that's helpful in the writing process. Instead of some sort of mental market-probe, try to create a genuine reader who looks over your shoulder. Ask your reader some questions like this:

- What places fascinate you?
- How do you connect your morality with what you read?
- How much action do you like, compared with the amount of exposition?
- Do you find this particular description of Madame Beaufort making your spine tingle with excitement?
- Would you like to sleep with Pete Fountain, famous TV anchorman? Or is he selfish and arrogant? Do you trust him at this point in the plot?
- Would you recognize this character on the street, or is he too generic?
- Is the plot something you truly believe could happen?

Putting these questions to Paul Winters and Mary Ann Cowan will help you achieve that rare quality among writers: objectivity. If you can be convinced that your reader is seeing what you are seeing, feeling what you are feeling, you'll be on your way to creating some compelling commercial fiction. After all, your primary task is not to *express yourself* but to *communicate* to your readers and create in them the same strong sense of character and story that you feel yourself.

Talking Across to Your Reader

Let's go back and take a look at that fiction manuscript called *Waco*. The author, who has a doctorate in geology, knows exactly how you drill oil wells and how you beg, borrow and mostly steal the money to do it. But listen to this dialogue:

"Well, I'm a gonna git that well drilled even if I have to git you all murdered to do it," Digger said.

Shem Lamston stared at him, centuries of hatred visible in his spring-chicken face. "Over my dead body," he snarled. "That land is made for cows, pardner, and you're a gonna have to scrape me and a hundred head of steer offa that ground afore you dig your way to hell!"

Outside, the Texas sun glared through the windows like an ugly woman.

Ouch. The author has no ear. People don't talk like that, even in Texas. But beyond that, our Ph.D. is making a major error. He is underestimating his reader. You can tell by his dialect, by his inadequate, farcical description, by the inelegant and careless sentences, even the characters' names. He's decided he's a gonna make some money writing a schlock novel to be read by stupid people, and you can hear that on every single page.

One fatal flaw in many manuscripts I read is condescension. Writers too often talk down to their readers; they seem to have no respect for the buyers of their novels. They oversimplify their plots; they use plot devices so silly, ancient and transparent that Mary Ann Cowan would throw the novel across the bus in disgust; they create characters in such broad strokes that no reader would recognize them as human beings; they write sentences so plain that they are clearly intended for readers who didn't make it past Head Start.

Such tactics demonstrate contempt for the craft of popular fiction and for the very readers a writer is trying to communicate with. Anyone who can spend even $5.95 for a paperback novel has a measure of sophistication and sense. Readers (and editors) can figure out when an author is talking down to them. They compare the novel to real life and real people, and if the novel falls short, they won't finish it.

Talk across to your reader; use your intelligence and gauge your reader's reactions as if he or she were a friend who shares your education and your interests. *Remember that no matter what kind of novel you are writing, you must write the best possible novel you can.* Paul Winters and Mary Ann Cowan will appreciate it.

Princeton, one of the novels I took home for the weekend, turns out to be intricate and exciting. The author clearly knows New Jersey's intellectual and financial oasis intimately; his novel is the story of five university graduates, three women and two men, who fall in and out of preppylove over the course of their fifteenth college reunion. But *Princeton* is only incidentally a love story; two of the characters are investment bankers, and the plot revolves around some fairly complex insider trading. It's really a business novel, and as such it challenges the intelligence of its readers while breaking some of the rules of the class-reunion-love-story genre. The prose is taut but occasionally lyrical in its descriptions of the elegant campus and often-elegant characters, and downright pungent in its evocation of the mores of a privileged young generation and its constricted society.

The author has taken pains to be precise and lucid, so that the average reader can follow all the romantic, social and financial machinations by reading carefully. Both Paul Winters and Mary Ann Cowan would find things to like in the novel. And because it treats its readers as sophisticated and educable equals, *Princeton* could potentially succeed on a large scale, appealing to both men and women and to all those who can shell out twenty dollars for a hardcover novel or who will wait breathlessly for the eventual paperback edition. The novelist has written the best possible book he could write, and it shows; he makes his readers the best possible readers they can be.

Morality and Other Commercial Mores

While this may surprise you, commercial fiction is always morally conservative. It doesn't matter how many Dirks bed how many Ambers, or how many KGB agents kill off innocent Berliners on the way to find CIA operative Tim Sheahan. A literary novel may, like a piece of contemporary music, be atonal — and leave the reader feeling discord; but in a commercial novel the narrative ends on the tonic note, with balance restored and order reigning. The good doctor marries the actress even though she has had to sleep with half of the Screen Actors Guild. The renegade Miami cop manages to blow up the drug smugglers' trawler before it docks in Tampa. In every case, the values and balance of the civilization are reaffirmed, at least temporarily.

This is particularly true of so-called "women's novels." The heroine may sleep around, but she does it out of necessity, to survive or get ahead in a cruel world, or to gain what is rightfully hers. But, much like Shakespearean comedy, the novels end with marriage, or at least true love, unimpeded by the outside world. Even shoot-em-up espionage novels do not exist in moral darkness. They may be tragedies — except that the hero usually survives, scarred — but they too end on the tonic, with at least a temporary restoration of order, with the world saved. However dirty it may get, the good guy never loses his white hat. And the amoral means are always justified by the moral ends.

Commercial novels, then, are by nature optimistic. They show characters not only surviving but also triumphing, and through their manipulation of formula they provide a lastingly conservative moral lesson: You, too, can make it. That is, at least in part, why such novels are popular. They *are* society.

What does this imply for the writer intending to compose a popular novel? It doesn't mean you should keep in the forefront of your mind the idea that you are a keeper of society's code. That is your ultimate and inevitable goal, but if your novel is successful, it's a goal you'll accomplish without even intending to. What's more important — and more difficult — is to create a world, and to populate that world, in a way that will entertain your reader.

And that means interesting characters. Consider *Hollywood Hype*. Our heroine was born in Chicago, worked as a typist, blackmailed her boss into sending her to the California office, and promptly sleeps her way to the middle. As assistant head of production at an independent studio, she bullies a director into choosing the stars she wants and making a movie *her* way. It works, but she makes a lot of enemies. Then, for her next effort, she smears a starlet and takes over her movie role. And so on, until she vanquishes her enemies, gets rich, gets married and gets good.

But besides being about as likable as Imelda Marcos, our heroine has another problem. She is boring and predictable. Nothing motivates her beyond meanness and money. She has no past, no particular reasons for acting as she does. She is a machine that propels the plot, and the plot she propels is also compulsively predictable.

I'm tired of reading about feisty young actresses, hardboiled detectives, frosty matriarchs and steely-eyed spies. Genre fiction doesn't require genre characters. Novelists are duty-bound to write about people who are complex, vivid, ever-changing. A writer should work like an actor, creating motivations, building that character from the inside out. Why does our Hollywood producer/starlet so ruthlessly claw her way up the success ladder? More than money motivated Imelda Marcos.

Too often I feel as if the novel I'm reading is floating in some indeterminable space-bubble environment that's a product less of lived experience than of the *Star*, the *Enquirer*, *Entertainment Tonight*—and, especially, other novels in the same genre. This is another problem with *Hollywood Hype*. The author lives in Chicago, and her opening scene, when our heroine boards a bus to Los Angeles, is more vivid than anything that occurs in Hollywood. Clearly this author has visited her local Greyhound terminal. It is less clear that she's ever crossed the Mississippi.

I suspect that the *Hollywood Hype* author was aware of this problem. She has without a doubt read every pop novel about the silver screen, and she's made an effort to create a milieu for her leading character. But the details feel secondhand. When we read about the skylight directly over her heart-shaped bed, that skylight and that bed could just as easily exist in a particularly palatial Michigan Avenue penthouse. There's no precise sense of society or social detail to bring the novel alive. Likewise, the studio machinations we hear so much about could, it appears, occur just as easily among Amway distributors in Glencoe. I am not convinced.

To create a sense of place, and to populate that place believably—that's the greatest task any commercial fiction writer has to face. Most fail at it. They simply don't know enough about the world they're trying to create.

Fact and Fiction

Why should anyone put down the newspaper to read your novel about drug runs from Grenada to Miami? Quite possibly the front page tells them all they need to know. And why should anyone turn off *Entertainment Tonight* to open the first page of *Hollywood Hype?* Why does anybody read fiction, anyway?

Pundits call this the age of information. It does seem as if we have an insatiable hunger to *know* things, to find out facts. People are both entertained and informed when they read about the social order of a particular Ivy League university, the way scrub is cleared in preparation for an oil rig, or where exactly on their boats drug runners store their coke. They want to be entertained, but they also want to *know*.

And how can you tell them if you don't know yourself? If you are writing about horse racing and you spend every afternoon at the track, that's great. But if you are putting together a spy novel set in Berlin and you're relying on one *National Geographic* article, you're lost. And readers will know if you don't know.

The best way to write a novel is to have lived it first. Become a movie executive; go to Princeton; smuggle drugs. But if you're in Chicago, and you have decided that Chicago lacks the glamour you desire, be sure to learn absolutely everything in your fictional world. Do your research. Read everything you can, fact and fiction. Talk to people who have lived your novel, if you can. As if you were writing a novel about the Indians who first settled the Cincinnati area, you must first recreate that remote world accurately for yourself. Then, with deftness, detail and urgency, transmit that precise vision to your reader.

Beyond Genre

What I like about the novels *Princeton* and *Cuba* is that they evoke for me a milieu I might not know at all, and yet — after I've finished the manuscript — I feel I could travel it without a map. *Cuba* not only tells me where the cocaine gets hidden (in trash bags taped to the hull of the boat), but also makes me smell the brine and feel the same adrenaline surge that the characters do. It's well-paced, thoughtful, and ultimately not a genre novel at all; it is the story of a weary, jaded ex-merchant marine who discovers not only cocaine — but also God.

Cuba, it turns out, breaks the rules. It's not just a thriller but a novel that combines well-paced action with reluctant religious redemption. While it will appeal to those who love action, it will reach those who read for the protagonist's spiritual quest. The author has used the elements of genre to touch the largest possible audience and to transcend genre itself.

There are a lot of ways to break the rules — and breaking the rules can often bring you more success than following them. You may decide your novel necessitates a less-than-happy ending and is strong enough to bear up under the pressure. You may simply have your CIA agent by a woman or be gay, or place your movie-studio novel not in Hollywood but in Toronto.

To cross from one genre to another and still be popular is a real challenge, but it can be worth it. It may garner more attention than hewing the genre-line. But it requires that you write even better than the norm, structure your story superbly, and shape and channel your reader's expectations. But if you manage it well, you may find yourself the author of a novel that doesn't just sell but endures—on the store bookshelf and in your readers' minds. Maybe Mary Ann Cowan will miss her bus stop to finish it, or maybe Paul Winters will stay up all night with it, long after the TV plays "The Star-Spangled Banner."

I certainly will stay up all night with it. While *Waco* and *Hollywood Hype* will make their sad way into the rejection pile, *Cuba* and *Princeton* will get a second set of readers come Monday morning. If those other editors like the manuscripts as well as I did, both just might end up as novels published by my company, with all the accompanying hoopla.

This is quite a spectacular harvest for one weekend's reading.

Never write a commercial novel just for money or fame. Become a financier instead, or the kind of character others will want to write about. If you write for cash only, and not because you *have* to write, then your reader will sense the residue of your unhappy toil. Whether you're in it for glamour or in it for cash, to truly succeed you must make sure you're also in it for love.

What Kind of Story Are You Telling?

by Orson Scott Card

When you invent a character, you depend on your sense of what is important and true to make your decisions. This will continue throughout your telling of the tale—but once you start setting down words, you also have to make many decisions based on what is right for the whole story. Now it's time for this newly created character to get to work.

It is a mistake to think that "good characterization" is the same thing in every work of fiction. Different kinds of stories require different kinds of characters.

But what are the different kinds of stories? Forget about publishing genres for a moment—there isn't one kind of characterization for academic/literary stories, another kind for science fiction, and still others for westerns, mysteries, thrillers, and historicals. Instead we'll look at four basic factors that are present in every story, with varying degrees of emphasis. It is the balance among these factors that determines what sort of characterization a story *must* have, *should* have or *can* have.

The four factors are *milieu*, *idea*, *character*, and *event:*

The milieu is the world surrounding the characters—the landscape, the interior spaces, the surrounding cultures the characters emerge from and react to; everything from weather to traffic laws.

The *idea* is the information that readers are meant to discover or learn during the process of the story.

Character is the nature of one or more of the people in the story—what they do and why they do it. It usually leads to or arises from a conclusion about human nature in general.

The *events* of the story are everything that happens and why.

These factors usually overlap. Character A is part of the milieu surrounding character B. The idea in the story may include information about the nature of a character; the idea we are meant to discover can be some aspect of the milieu, some previously misunderstood or overlooked event, or the nature of a character. The events of the story are usually performed by characters or emerge from the milieu, and the discovery of an idea can also be an event in the tale.

Each factor is present in all stories, to one degree or another. Every factor has an implicit structure; if that factor dominates a story, its structure determines the overall shape of the story.

Milieu

It has become a figure of speech to say that a story "takes place." But it is quite true: The characters must have a place in which to perform the acts that make up the story—the setting, the milieu of the tale. The milieu includes all the *physical locations* that are used—one city or many cities, one building or many buildings, a street, a bus, a farm, a clearing in the woods—with all the sights, smells and sounds that come with the territory. The milieu also includes the *culture*—the customs, laws, social roles, and public expectations that limit and illuminate all that a character thinks and feels and says and does.

In some stories the milieu is very sketchy; in others, it is created in loving detail. Indeed, there are some stories in which the milieu is the primary focus of attention. Think of *Gulliver's Travels* or *A Connecticut Yankee in King Arthur's Court*: The point of these stories is not to explore the soul of a character or resolve a tense and thrilling plot, but rather to explore a world that is different from our own, comparing it to our own customs and expectations.

The structure of the pure milieu story is simple: Get a character to the setting that the story is about, and then devise reasons for her to move through the world of the story, showing the reader all the interesting physical and social details of the milieu. When you've shown everything you want the reader to see, bring the character home.

In most pure milieu stories, the main character is a person from the writer's and readers' own time and place, so that the character will experience the world with the reader's attitudes and perceptions.

In a pure milieu story, the *less* you characterize the main character, the better. Her job is to stand in the place of all the readers. If you make the character too much of an individual, you draw the readers' attention to her and away from the milieu; instead, you want to keep the readers' attention on the milieu. So the main character's reactions to everything that happens must be as "normal" as possible (what the reader would expect *anybody* to do in those circumstances). The character might have a wry humor or a particular slant to her observations, but the more you call attention to the character, the less the story tends to be about the milieu.

Few stories, however, are "pure" milieu stories. Travelogues, utopian fiction, satires, and natural science tend to be the only genres in which the pure milieu story can be found. More often, stories emphasize milieu but develop other story factors as well. Although the setting might be the primary focus, there is also a strong story line. The reader then absorbs the milieu indirectly. In these stories, the major characters don't have to come from the readers' own time; usually, in fact, they'll be permanent residents of the story's milieu. The characters' own attitudes and expectations are part of the cultural ambience, and their very strangeness and unfamiliarity is part of the readers' experience of the milieu.

Such stories will seem to have the structure of another kind of tale—but the author will reveal that the milieu is a main concern by the close attention paid to the surroundings. The characters will be chosen, not just for their intrinsic interest, but also because they typify certain kinds or classes of people within the culture. The characters are meant to fascinate us, not because we understand them or share their desires, but because of their strangeness, and what they can teach us about an alien culture.

This kind of story is fairly common in science fiction and fantasy, where the milieu, the world of the story, is often the main attraction. Frank Herbert (*Dune*), and J.R.R. Tolkien (*The Lord of the Rings*) are most noted for works in which the story line is not tightly structured and the characters tend to be types rather than individuals, yet the milieu is carefully, lovingly drawn. In such milieu stories the author feels free to digress from the main story line with long passages of explanation, description, or depiction of the culture. The reader who isn't interested in the milieu will quickly become bored and set the story aside; but the reader who is fascinated by the world of the story will read on, rapt, through pages of songs and poetry and rituals and ordinary daily life.

How much characterization does a milieu story need? Not very much. Most characters need only be stereotypes within the culture of the milieu, acting out exactly the role their society expects of them, with perhaps a few eccentricities that help move the story along. It is no accident that when Tolkien assembled the Fellowship of the Ring in his *The Lord of the Rings* trilogy, there was only one dwarf and one elf—had there been more, it would have been nearly impossible to tell them apart, just as few readers can remember the difference between the two generic hobbits Merry and Pippin. Because *The Lord of the Rings* was not a pure milieu story, there are some heroic major characters who are more than local stereotypes, and some that approach full characterization—but characterization simply isn't a major factor in the appeal of the book.

Besides science fiction and fantasy, milieu stories often crop up in academic/literary fiction ("This story absolutely *is* contemporary suburban life") and historical fiction (though most historicals nowadays focus on the romance rather than the setting), while milieu plays an important role in many thrillers. Milieu is the entire definition of the western.

Are you writing a milieu story? Is it mostly the setting that you work on in loving detail? That doesn't mean that you can ignore character, especially if you're trying to tell a compelling story within the milieu; but it does mean that a lot of fully drawn characters aren't really necessary to your story, and might even be distracting.

Idea

The idea story has a simple structure. A problem or question is posed at the beginning of the story, and at the end of the tale the answer is revealed. Murder mysteries use this structure: Someone is found murdered, and the rest of the story is devoted to discovering who did it, why, and how. Caper stories also follow the idea story structure: A problem is posed at the beginning (a bank to rob, a rich and dangerous mark to con), the main character or characters devise a plan, and we read on to find out if their plan is in fact the "answer" to the problem. Invariably something goes wrong and the characters have to improvise, but the story is over when the problem is solved.

How much characterization is needed? In puzzle or locked-room mysteries, there is no need for characterization at all; most authors use only a few eccentricities to "sweeten" the characters, particularly the detective.

In classic English mysteries, like those of Agatha Christie, characterization rarely goes beyond the requirement that a fairly large group of people must have enough of a motive for murder that each can legitimately be suspected of having committed the crime.

The American detective novel tends to demand a little more characterization. The detective himself is usually more than a tight little bundle of eccentricities; instead, he responds to the people around him, not as pieces to be fitted into the puzzle, but as sad or dangerous or good or pathetic human beings. Such tales, like those of Raymond Chandler or Ross Macdonald, require the detective to be a keen observer of other people, whose individual natures often twist and turn the story line. However, such characters—including the detective—are rarely *changed*; the story only *reveals* who they are. In these novels, the characters' true natures are among the questions that the detective—and the reader—tries to answer during the course of the story.

Caper stories, on the other hand, generally don't require that their characters be much more than charming or amusing, and only rarely is there any attempt to show a character being transformed by the events in the tale.

In fact, it is the very lack of change in the characters in mystery, detective and caper stories that allows writers to use the same characters over and over again, to the delight of their readers. A few writers have fairly recently tried to change that, developing and changing their detective characters from book to book. But that very process of change can end up severely limiting the future possibilities of the character.

When the title character of Gregory McDonald's *Fletch* series became very rich, it made it very difficult to put him in situations where he actually *needed* to solve a mystery; McDonald finally resorted to writing the prequels *Fletch Won* and *Fletch, Too*, which took place *before* Fletch got rich, and has announced his intention to stop writing Fletch novels.

Robert D. Parker took his character Spenser even further, showing him with ongoing and developing relationships, with friendships and transformations that begin in one book and are not forgotten in the next. The result, however, has been a tendency in recent years to reach for increasingly far-fetched plots or to repeat story lines from the past. It's *hard* to do full, rich characterization in an idea story.

Don't get me wrong, though—I don't think it's a mistake to attempt full characterization in idea stories; Fletch and Spenser are two of my favorite mystery characters precisely because of the richer-than-normal characterization and the possibility of permanent change. You simply need to recognize that if you choose to do full characterization in an idea story, complete with character transformation, there is a price.

There are idea stories in other genres, of course. Many a science fiction story follows the idea structure perfectly: Characters are faced with a problem—a malfunctioning spaceship is one of the favorites—and, as with a caper, the story consists of finding a plan to solve the problem and carrying it out, with improvisations as needed. Characterization is not needed, except to make the characters entertaining—eccentricity is usually enough.

Allegory is a form in which the idea is everything. The author has composed the story according to a plan; the reader's job is to decode the plan. Characters in allegory are rarely more than figures standing for ideas. While allegory is rarely written today, many writers of academic/literary fiction use symbolism in much the same way—characters exist primarily to stand for an idea, and readers must decode the symbolic structure in order to receive the story.

Does all this mean that idea stories require "bad" characterization? Not at all. It means that appropriate characterization for an idea story is not necessarily the same thing as appropriate characterization for another kind of story. Characters stand for ideas, or exist primarily to discover them; a character who fulfills her role perfectly may be no more than a stereotype or a bundle of eccentricities, and yet she'll be characterized perfectly for that story.

Character

The character story is about a person trying to change his role in life. It begins at the point when the main character finds his present situation intolerable and sets out to change; it ends when the character either finds a new role, willingly returns to the old one, or despairs of improving his lot.

What is a character's "role"? It is his network of relationships with other people and with society at large. My role in life is father to my children—with a different relationship with each; husband to my wife; son and brother to the family I grew up with. I have a complex relationship with each of the literary communities I write for, with the full assortment of fans and critics; I also have a constantly shifting role within my religious community, for which I also write. Like every other human being, I have some interests and longings that aren't satisfied within the present pattern of my life, but in most cases I forsee ways of fulfilling those desires within the reasonably near future. All of these relationships, together, are my "role in life." I'm reasonably content with my life; it would be difficult to write a character story about me, because stories about happy people are boring.

The character story emerges when some part of a character's role in life becomes unbearable. A character is dominated by a vicious, whimsical parent or spouse; an employee has become discontented with his job, with growing distaste for the people he works with; a mother is weary of her nurturing role and longing for respect from adults; a career criminal is consumed by fear and longing to get away; a lover whose partner has been unfaithful can't bear to live with the betrayal. The impossible situation may have been going on for some time, but the story does not begin until the situation comes to a head—until the character reaches the point where the cost of staying becomes too high a price to pay.

Sometimes the protagonist of a character story cuts loose from the old role very easily, and the story consists of a search for a new one. Sometimes the new role is easy to envision, but breaking away from the old bonds is very hard to do. "Cutting loose" doesn't always mean physically leaving—the most complex and difficult character stories are the ones about people who try to change a relationship without abandoning the person.

Needless to say, the character story is the one that requires the fullest characterization. No shortcuts are possible. Readers must understand the character in the original, impossible role so that they comprehend and, usually, sympathize with the decision to change. Then the character's changes must be justified so that the reader never doubts that the change is possible; you can't just have a worn-out hooker suddenly go to college without showing us that the hunger for education and the intellectual ability to pursue it have always been part of her character.

Remember, though, that not all the people in a character story must be fully characterized. The protagonist—the character whose change is the subject of the story—must be fully characterized; so, too, must be each person whose relationship with the protagonist is part of his need for change or his new and satisfactory role. But other people in the story will be characterized less fully, just as in many milieu, idea, and event stories. Characterization is not a virtue, it is a technique; you use it when it will enhance your story, and when it won't, you don't.

Event

Every story is an event story in the sense that from time to time something happens that has causes and results. But the story in which the events are the central concern follows a particular pattern: The world is somehow out of order—call it imbalance, injustice, breakdown, evil, decay, disease—and the story is about the effort to restore the old order or establish a new one.

The event story structure is simple: It begins when the main characters become involved in the effort to heal the world's disorder, and ends when they either accomplish their goal or utterly fail to do so.

The world's disorder can take many forms. It can be a crime unpunished or unavenged: *The Count of Monte Cristo* is a prime example, as is *Oedipus Rex*. The disorder can be a usurper—Macbeth, for instance—who has stolen a place that doesn't belong to him, or a person who has lost his true position in the world, like Prince Edward in *The Prince and the Pauper*. The disorder can be an evil force, bent on destruction, like Sauron in *The Lord of the Rings* or Lord Foul in *The Chronicles of Thomas Covenant the Unbeliever*—that is also the way Nazis, Communists, and terrorists are often used in thrillers. The disorder can be an illicit love that cannot be allowed to endure and yet cannot be denied, as in *Wuthering Heights* and the traditional stories of Lancelot and Guinevere or Tristan and Isolde. The disorder can be a betrayal of trust, as in the medieval romance *Havelok the Dane* — or the romance of Watergate that was enacted in America's newspapers and television news during the early 1970s.

I think that the event story — the structure at the heart of the romantic tradition for more than two thousand years — might well be the reason for the existence of Story itself. It arises out of the human need to make sense of the things happening around us; the event story starts with the assumption that some sort of order should exist in the world, and our very belief in order in fiction helps us to create order in reality.

How important is characterization in the event story? Most of the time, it's up to the author. It's possible to tell a powerful event story in which the characters are nothing more than what they do and why they do it — we can come out of such tales feeling as if we know the character because we have lived through so much with her, even though we've learned almost nothing about the other aspects of her character. (Although Lancelot, for instance, is a major actor in the Arthurian legends, he has seldom been depicted as a complex individual beyond the simple facts of his relationship to Arthur and to Guinevere.) Yet it is also possible to characterize several people in the story without at all interfering with the forward movement of the tale. In fact, the process of inventing characters often introduces more story possibilities, so that event and character both grow.

Your Contract With Readers

Whenever you tell a story, you make an implicit contract with the readers. Within the first few paragraphs or pages, you tell the readers implicitly what kind of story this is going to be; the readers then know what to expect, and hold the thread of that structure throughout the tale.

If you begin with a murder, for instance, and focus on those characters who have reason to find out how, why, and by whom the murder was committed, the readers can reasonably expect that the story will continue until those questions are answered — the readers expect an idea story.

If, on the other hand, you begin with the murder victim's wife, concentrating on how widowhood has caused a sudden, unbearable disruption in the patterns of her life, the readers can fairly expect that the story will use the character structure, following the widow until she finds an acceptable new role for herself.

Choosing one structure does not preclude using another. For instance, in the first version of the story — the murder mystery — you can also follow the widow's attempts to find a new role for herself. Readers will gladly follow that story line as a subplot, and will be delighted if you resolve it along with the mystery. However, the readers would feel cheated if you began the novel as a mystery, but ended it when the widow falls in love and remarries — without ever solving the mystery at all! You can do that once, perhaps, for effect — but readers will feel, rightly, that you misled them.

On the other hand, if you establish at the beginning of the story that it is about the widow herself and her search for a new role in life, you can also weave the mystery into the story line as a subplot; if you do, readers will expect you to resolve the mystery, but they won't regard that as the climax of the story. They would rightly be outraged if you ended the book with the explanation of the mystery — and left the widow still in a state of flux.

The rule of thumb is this: Readers will expect a story to end when the first major source of structural tension is resolved. If the story begins as an idea story, the readers expect it to end when the idea is discovered, the plan unfolded. If the story begins as a milieu story, readers will gladly follow any number of story lines of every type, letting them be resolved here and there as needed, continuing to read in order to discover more of the milieu. A story that begins with a character in an intolerable situation will not feel finished until the character is fully content or finally resigned. A story that begins with an unbalanced world will not end until the world is balanced, justified, reordered, healed — or utterly destroyed beyond hope of restoration.

It's as if you begin the story by pushing a boulder off the top of a hill. No matter what else happens before the end of the story, the readers will not be satisfied until the boulder comes to rest somewhere.

That is your first contract with the readers. You will end what you began. Digressions will be tolerated, to a point; but digressions will almost never be accepted as a substitute for fulfilling the original contract.

You also make a second contract all the way through a story: Anything you spend much time on will amount to something in the story. I remember seeing one of Bob Hope's and Bing Crosby's road movies when I was a child — *The Road to Rio*, I think. In it, the director constantly interrupts the main story to show Jerry Colonna, their mustachioed comic sidekick, leading a troop of mounted soldiers to rescue our heroes. In the end, however, the story is completely resolved without Colonna's cavalry ever arriving. The director cuts one last time to Colonna, who pulls his horse to a stop, looks at the camera, and says something like, "It didn't amount to anything, but it *was* thrilling, wasn't it?" It was very funny — but the humor rested entirely on the fact that when a story spends time on a character, an event, a question, or a setting, the audience expects that the main thread of the story will somehow be affected by it.

Examine your story, either in your head, in outline, or in draft form. What is it that most interests you? Where are you spending the most time and effort? Are you constantly researching or inventing more details about the setting? Is it the detailed unraveling of the mystery that fascinates you? Do you constantly find yourself exploring a character? Or is it the actual events that you care about most? Your story will work best when you use the structure demanded by the factor that you care most about.

If you love the mystery, structure the tale as an idea story—begin with the question and devote the bulk of your story time to answering it. If you care most about the milieu, let the readers know it from the start by beginning with a character's arrival in the new world (how long does it take Alice to get down the rabbit hole or through the looking glass into Wonderland?) or by concentrating on the details of the place and culture; then spend the bulk of your time discovering the wonders and curiosities of the milieu. If you care most about a character, begin with his or her dilemma and spend the bulk of your time on the effort toward change. If you care most about the events, begin at the point where the characters become involved with the world's sickness, and spend the bulk of your time in the story on their efforts to restore balance.

The techniques and structures of the other story factors are always available to you for subplots or complications, but keep them in a relatively subordinate position. In *The Lord of the Rings*, there are several event stories going on within the overall milieu story—Aragorn, the out-of-place king, coming to take his rightful throne; Denethor, the steward who reached for power beyond his ability to control, threatening the safety of the kingdom and the life of his son until Gandalf finally succeeds in stopping him; Frodo, Samwise, and Gollum, the three hobbit ringbearers, in their twisted, braided paths to the cracks of doom where, by casting in the ring, they will be able to put an end to the evil, destructive power of Sauron.

Yet when all these story lines are resolved, the reader is not disappointed to find that the story goes on. Tolkien begins a completely new story line, the Scouring of the Shire, which is related to the other stories but is barely hinted at until the hobbits actually come home.

Even then the tale is not done—Tolkien still must show us Frodo sailing west, along with the elves who can no longer live in Middle Earth, at least not in their former glory. Was this the resolution of a question raised at the beginning of the book? No. Nor was it the resolution of a character dilemma—Frodo was quite content when the story began. And Frodo's and the elves' presence in Middle Earth was not, when the story began, a disequilibrium that needed to be resolved.

So why are we still reading? Because *The Lord of the Rings* is a milieu story. The author establishes from the beginning that he is going to spend large amounts of time simply exploring the world of Middle Earth. We are going to have detailed accounts of birthday parties, village life, customs and habits of the people; we will visit with Tom Bombadil, who has almost nothing to do with the story, but has everything to do with the underlying mythos of Middle Earth; we linger with the Ents, we pass through the Mines of Moria, we visit the Riders of Rohan, travel with the legendary dead; and while Tolkien weaves all these places and peoples into a story that is generally interesting, sometimes creating characters we care about, there is no story line or character that becomes our sole reason for reading. It is the world itself that Tolkien cared most about, and so the audience for the story is going to be those readers who also come to love the world of Middle Earth. So it is no accident that the story does not end until we see, clearly, that Middle Earth has ceased to exist as it was—we are entering a new age, and the milieu we were exploring is now closed.

All four story factors are present in *The Lord of the Rings*, but it is the milieu structure that predominates, as it should. It would be absurd to criticize *The Lord of the Rings* for not having plot unity and integrity, because it is not an event story. Likewise, it would be absurd to criticize the book for its stereotyped one-to-a-race characters or for the many characters about whom we learn little more than what they do in the story and why they do it, because this is not a character story. In fact, we should probably praise Tolkien for having done such a good job of working creditable story lines and the occasional identifiable character into a story that was, after all, about Something Else.

I'm dwelling on these structural matters at some length because for us writers to characterize *well*, we must characterize *appropriately*.

Character stories really came into their own at the beginning of the twentieth century, and both the novelty and the extraordinary brilliance of some of the writers who worked with this story structure have led many critics and teachers to believe that only this kind of story can be "good." This may be a true judgment for many individuals—that is, the only kind of story they enjoy is the character story—but it is not true in the abstract, for the other kinds of stories have long traditions, with many examples of brilliance along the way.

However, character stories have been so dominant that they have forced storytellers in the other traditions to pay more attention to characterization. Even though a story may follow the idea, milieu, or event structure, many readers expect a deeper level of characterization. The story is not *about* a transformation of character, but the readers still expect to get to know the characters; and even when they don't expect it, they are willing to allow the author to devote a certain amount of attention to character without regarding it as a digression. This is the fashion of our time, and you can't disregard it.

But it's a mistake to think that deep, detailed characterization is an absolute virtue in storytelling. You must look at your own reason for telling a story. If it's the puzzle—the idea—that attracts you, then that will probably be the factor in your story that you handle best; your natural audience will consist of readers who also care most about the idea. A certain amount of attention to characterization may help broaden your audience and increase your readers' pleasure in the story, but if you go into characterization as an unpleasant chore, something you must do in order to be a "good writer," chances are your characterization will be mechanical and ineffective, and instead of broadening your audience, it will interfere with your story. If you don't care about or believe in a character's deepest drives and troubled past, neither will your readers.

So if you choose not to devote much time to characterization in a particular story, this won't necessarily mean you "failed" or "wrote badly." It may mean that you understand yourself and your story.

And because you chose to tell one story in which characterization played a lesser role doesn't mean you "can't characterize." A good understanding of characterization includes knowing when it's appropriate to concentrate on character—and when it isn't.

Hot to Plot! A Plotting "System" That Works

by Mary Kittredge

What happens next in your novel or short story? Asking yourself—and supplying the answers—is plotting. Sometimes it's easy: The story arrives in your mind, whole and perfect as an egg; your job is just hatching it.

Other times, though, it's not easy at all: You know the beginning but not the end of your tale, or maybe you're stuck in the middle. Now you must construct a plot. How?

You *could* wait for inspiration (which is almost as useful as waiting for a watched pot to boil). *Or* you can do what I've been doing since I got smart, which not by coincidence is also when I started selling my stories and novels: You can use a system.

You might fear that a system is mechanical, uninspired, not artistic—but I promise: once you get the hang of this plotting system, you'll think *it* is artistic, too—and besides, it works.

Plotting Your Plot

Start with a story idea. If you don't have one, go copy the phone book. You can stop copying as soon as you get an idea, which will be in about . . . yep, about three minutes.

Now, what's your idea? For the purposes of explaining the system, let's say you want to write a mystery. About an attic that drips blood. Lovely. We'll build a story plot around that idea. *Why?*, you ask. Because an idea is just . . . an idea. Everyone's got 'em; that's why you can't sell 'em. A plot, on the other hand, leads directly to a story—one you can write, finish, polish, and maybe even sell. Let's start building our plot by thinking up a main character suitable to the idea we want to write about. A main character needs three attributes:

• *A need or want*: to find the secret of the lost gold mine, to escape the evil dragonmaster, to win the heart of his or her one true love—whatever. Characters who want something are interesting, and the higher you set the stakes, the more interesting their stories will be.

• *A strong point*: courage, love, generosity—some personality trait that confers on him or her the potential for triumph.

• *A fatal flaw*: fear, greed, laziness, gullibility—some trait that, unless overcome, may lead to the character's downfall.

Now, we'll put our character in a fairly stable situation and then *introduce the story problem*. The story problem is what the character must solve, to get what he or she wants. For instance, if the cops think I killed my rich uncle for his money, I have a problem. I must solve it—establish my innocence—to get what I want—that is, cleared of suspicion.

Our character will try to solve the problem, but his or her efforts will only *worsen the problem*. Still, our hero or heroine won't give up; instead, through actions and insights that grow from the *strong point*, he or she will learn about the *fatal flaw*. With this knowledge, the character will make a *final, enormous story-climaxing effort*—overcoming the fatal flaw, using the strong point, and triumphing over the story problem.

In short, we're deliberately putting these attributes—what's wanted, a strong point, and a fatal flaw—into our main character because we're going to *use* them in developing the plot.

Back to Our Story

Who is this character whose attic drips blood? Let's make her an ordinary housewife, with a couple of exceptions: a few weeks ago her husband vanished, and the cops think she might have killed him (remember, we said a *fairly* stable situation). For her strong point, let's give her an intense love for nature. Her weakness: fear of authority.

Story problem: any murder suspect with blood dripping from his or her attic definitely has a story problem. Cops hear about this, they'll be on her like butter on bread—an idea that scares here even more than the blood does.

So she tries to solve the problem. She calls a friend to help her inspect the attic, since clearly whatever is dripping is coming from up there, and likely from a horrid source. But—and she doesn't know how this happens—her call is overheard, and the police arrive to investigate. (See above: the character's efforts make the problem worse, because they grew out of fear, our character's fatal flaw.)

Here we are at the crunch. The police go upstairs—and guess whose body is in the attic? The husband's. (No, they didn't need a warrant; they just asked her if they could go up there, and of course she said yes. Fear, again.)

This is where you MAKE THINGS LOOK JUST AS TRULY AWFUL AS YOU CAN, otherwise known as creating the story's Black Moment: The cops, of course, think our heroine put the body in the attic. And since hiders of dead bodies are often responsible for having made those bodies dead in the first place, the cops think they've got their man, or in this case their woman.

In short, she's about to be arrested for murder. Her mission, which she has little choice but to accept, is to prove she didn't do it. And this is where the strong point comes in: *Your* mission is to use that strong point. You must develop an event that a) grows out of the character's strong point, and b) shows the character her own fatal flaw.

We've established love of nature as this character's strong point. Use it . . . let's say she feeds the birds. It's winter, and just outside her living room window is a bird feeder, which she can see from her favorite chair.

Now, start the action: The cops accuse her. She sinks into the chair. She can see the birds at the feeder. But—one of the policemen goes out to look around the house, frightening the birds away. Our heroine thinks, somewhat distractedly: *If the birds get frightened away from the feeder—even by something that isn't really a threat—they don't eat. If they don't eat, they die, not because it's cold or because there isn't food, but because they are afraid. Their fear kills them.*

From there, it's only a short mental hop to: *my fear will kill me—unless I overcome it*. That's what she realizes about her own fatal flaw: She *must* stop being afraid—and she does. She summons all her strength and *decides* not to be like the birds, not to be mindlessly fearful, not "To Die in Winter" (this story's title, by the way).

Once she casts off her fear, she can *think*. Once she thinks, she can ask herself the obvious: How did the police know the attic was dripping blood? Obvious answer: her "friend" told them—the "friend" our heroine called for help. Obvious conclusion: the "friend" is the real murderer, and called the cops so our heroine would get the blame. But, how to prove it, or at least establish her own innocence?

Back to the strong point—love of nature. Nature isn't just animals. It's also weather and earth, air and water, plants, the sky and stars. And—the sun.

So far, our heroine has successfully recognized her fatal flaw, determined to overcome it, and begun doing so. Now she must make the second part of her effort: having eliminated the negative, she must accentuate the positive. She must use her strong point to get herself out of this jam.

Let me add here that she need not know, herself, what her strong point is; in fact, it's more realistic if she doesn't. Once she sees her fatal flaw, she need only make her best effort to solve the story problem. But you must consciously know and use this plot element in order to plot the story. (That's true of all plot elements, in fact: You must identify them as mechanically as if they were car parts, handle them as coolly and competently as a member of a pit crew at the Indy 500. If you do, your story will win the race. If you don't, you'll get this sucker rolling along at three hundred mph and then the engine will explode. *That's* why writers must be good plot mechanics.)

Our heroine's about to get hauled to jail for a murder she didn't commit. She *was* scared witless; now she's calm, determined to face the future without fear. She's thought things through clearly, recognized the crucial question, and answered it: her "friend" must be the real killer. Thus she's ready to make her final effort, which is moving the cops' suspicion from herself to the true culprit.

In the attic near where the body was discovered, the police saw bunches of herbs and flowers drying (love of nature, again). Now our heroine calmly explains what those herbs and flowers are, how they grow, and what their uses may be. Next she recites the temperature in different parts of the attic, and tells what spot on the outside wall sunshine hits at this time of day, and where it shines on the attic floor.

She demonstrates, in short, her strong point: she knows a lot about nature and its effects, both indoors and out. And she shows she knows that all winter the attic is cold, except for the spot where her husband's body was found.

So she asks the police to think, too. "Do you really believe I'd have picked there to put him? Anywhere else and he'd have frozen solid. I could have saved him until spring, oh, quite easily. And when the ground thawed, I could have put him into it. No one ever would have known."

In other words, putting a body in the attic's only warm spot would have been stupid. And whatever else this shy, simple woman may be, she isn't stupid. So the cops know that someone else put the body there on purpose, to get our heroine arrested.

She finishes the job by remarking mildly that her "friend" gained financially from her husband's death, will gain more if our heroine's locked away, and adds that the "friend" happens also to have a key to this house.

And since the cops aren't stupid, either, that's the end of the story. Of course, when you write it you'll early on establish the love of nature, hint at the possibility of the friend's financial gain and mention that the friend has a key. But at this point you have a working machine, plot parts all present and in running order.

I didn't know how our story would end when I began writing this article (and I chose to plot a short story because it's brief enough for demonstration purposes; these techniques will help you plot a work of any length). I *used* the system, mechanically, but the story *grew*, naturally, and mostly from two key questions:

• *What's the character's fatal flaw?* This is crucial; half the plot comes from it. For example, if the fatal flaw is prejudice, the character must first recognize prejudice, and then overcome it, perhaps by accepting help from someone previously thought inferior. If the flaw is bitterness over a past event, that event must be viewed in a new light—perhaps through another character's memories—and the present and future seen more hopefully and determinedly, too.

• *How can I show my character recognizing his or her fatal flaw?* That's half of what the character's strong point is for. In our story above, for instance, the woman's knowledge of her own fear grows from her love of nature. She feeds the birds, so she sees them at the feeder, so she notices their fear, so she recognizes her own. The event that demonstrates her own flaw to her is *developed from her strong point*.

Shifting Gears

By changing the balance of the plot elements I've described here, you can write all sorts of stories, including those that—unlike the one we developed here—don't have happy endings. To see how the balance of the elements might change, think about why the story above had a "happy ending." After all, it was clear early on that we weren't going to let this lady lose. We knew things had to come out right for her. But—how did we know? And how did we make it happen?

We knew it and did it by remembering that fiction is not real life. Fiction is life *by design*. And fictional design, like other kinds of design, comes from *design elements*—from the plot elements we have been discussing. In choosing the particular elements we did in our mystery, we decided to build a kind of plot called "Good Character Wins."

In a "Good Character Wins" plot, the strong point is stronger than the fatal flaw. Our strong point was love of nature; our fatal flaw was fear. Love was stronger than fear, love won out, and we got a happy ending. But what if we'd drawn our character differently, given her a flaw stronger than her strong point? What if her flaw were vanity, for instance, and her love of nature not strong enough to overcome it?

She still didn't kill her husband, remember; she's still falsely accused. But the events of this story would have to be much different: instead of staring out at those birds, she might be looking into a mirror, combing her hair and fixing her makeup. Now the event dramatizing her "big effort" must grow out of that: maybe she makes a play for the cop who suspects her, thinking she'll win him over because she's gorgeous.

And of course she's wrong. This plot is "Good Character Loses (A)." In it, the character makes a fatal error that grows from the fatal flaw. There's also a bleaker form, "Good Character Loses (B)," in which through no fault of his or her own the character is overwhelmed by evil outside forces. If you try it, I suggest you write like an angel, make it darkly funny, or both, because "Good Character Loses (B)" is depressing and readers won't finish reading it unless you give them something to make feeling so bad worth their while.

Then, too, not all characters are good characters, and sometimes rats do win. How to set up a bad main character's plot so the story can end happily? One way is by balancing the character's big fatal flaw with a small but powerful strong point—a saving grace. For instance: he's a liar, a con man, a crumb, but he loves women. Really loves 'em. He always treats them right, as long as he's around. And even though he leaves them in the lurch, each remembers him fondly. Of course, someday this guy will leave the wrong lady. Then her daddy the mobster is going to get mad. How does our guy escape? Via his saving grace. True love means understanding, and our guy understands women. None of his macho strengths can help him now, but the ones he learned by paying attention to women will help him—because they're real and because he earned them honestly. I'll let you finish this plot, which is called "Bad Character Wins (A)."

There's also "Bad Character Wins (B)," in which the bad guy wins by sheer force of rattiness. Like "Good Character Loses (B)," this plot's depressing— or funny, if you're really good. To get away with it, you've got to do it right— absolutely right—or readers will hate it and hate you for inflicting depression—or worse, flopped humor—on them.

For that matter, "Bad Character Loses"—the final kind of plot we'll be discussing here—is also pretty depressing. That's because it centers around a toad, who in the end gets the slimy comeuppance he or she deserves. Remember that in a "Bad Character Loses" plot, the strong point must have *some* chance to overcome the fatal flaw; otherwise, there's no suspense.

Happy Endings

To recap:
- Get an idea.
- Create a main character suitable to the idea.
- Decide what this character wants.
- Determine the characters fatal flaw and strong point.
- Let the character's efforts to solve the problem only make matters worse, until things look as bleak as possible.
- Create an event that grows from the character's strong point, and forces him or her to recognize the fatal flaw.
- Finally, let the character determine to overcome the flaw, and the story problem, and let him or her make a last, enormous effort—one that also grows, necessarily, from the strong point. If the strong point is stronger than the flaw, the character succeeds. If the flaw is stronger than the strong point: the character fails.

Sure, you still need crisp dialogue, vivid description, true-to-life characters, and more—because good writing, too, is a necessary element of interesting, salable fiction. But plot's the engine that revs your story up to racing speed. Plot keeps readers reading and editors buying; it's the solid technical element on which all your other skills must hang.

I didn't invent the *elements* of a plot; storytellers have known them since humans began telling tales to entertain and amaze one another. They were taught to me by masters of plotting like science fiction writers Jack Williamson, Barry B. Longyear, and many others. And I'm not trying to suggest that by slavishly following this plotting *system*, you can write successful stories as mechanically as you'd crank sausages out of a machine; your own creativity is a vital part of your fiction, and one you must add as your own creative spark dictates. But constructing a plot *systematically*, using classic, time-honored plot elements *and* your own creativity—well, that's one writing skill you simply can't afford to be without.

A "hot-shot plot" is one whose parts are present and working *because you put them there*. So—put them there. Do it again . . . and again, until plotting comes to you as naturally as breathing. Before you know it, you'll be building more than plots. You'll be writing the *stories* that go with them.

Creating Characters That Readers Care About

by Orson Scott Card

I n Stephen King's *The Dead Zone*, a traffic accident puts the main character in a coma for many years; he loses his career, the woman he loves, and precious years of his life. When he finally recovers from the coma, he remains in constant pain. The magnitude of his suffering makes readers care about him deeply and see him as a hugely important character—great enough, in fact, to sustain the weight of a novel.

Although minor characters can stick in readers' minds simply by being colorful or eccentric, the characters who actually move the action forward, whose choices determine the events of the story, must be made both important and sympathetic in readers' eyes. If readers are not made to feel that the characters are important—if they don't truly care what happens to the major characters—why will they care enough to keep reading?

There are three tools you can use to lend stature to your major characters, and we'll see just how vital it is to be a successful story that your readers feel sympathy for the people your story is about.

The Sharp Edge of Pain

Pain is a sword with two edges. The character who suffers pain and the character who inflicts it are both made more memorable and more important.

Of course, not all pain is alike. A cut finger doesn't particularly magnify a character. But, as I mentioned, the main character in *The Dead Zone* suffers terribly. Notice that his pain is both physical and emotional. The loss of a loved one can weigh as heavily in the mind of the audience as the loss of a limb. However, *physical* pain is much easier to use because it doesn't have to be prepared for. If a character is tortured, readers will wince in sympathetic agony even if they have never seen the character before. Emotional loss does not come so easily. In *The Dead Zone*, King devoted several pages to creating a warm, valuable relationship between the main character and the woman he loves. His terrible traffic accident occurs at a vital moment in their relationship. Now when he discovers that she married someone else during his coma, readers know how much he loved her, and so the pain of losing her actually outweighs the physical pain he suffered.

Pain loses effectiveness with repetition. The first time a character is hit in the head, the pain raises his importance; the third or fourth time, the character becomes comic, and his pain is a joke.

You increase the power of pain not so much by describing the injury in greater detail as by showing more of its cause and its effect. Blood and gore only make the audience gag. But watching the character try to cope with his pain can heighten the audience's identification with and sympathy for the character.

Even more powerful is the character's degree of choice. Suppose Pete has broken his leg on a hike, and Nora must set it for him. That scene will be painful, and will certainly magnify both characters as they cause and suffer pain. But Pete's pain will be far more powerful if he is alone and has to set the leg himself. As he ties a rope to his ankle, passes it around a tree trunk, braces his good leg and pulls on the end of the rope, the agony he inflicts on himself will make the scene unforgettable, even if we never see his face, even if his agony is never described at all.

And when one character willingly inflicts pain on another, the torturer becomes as important, in our fear and loathing, as the victim becomes in our sympathy.

Jeopardy

Jeopardy is anticipated pain. As anyone who has been to a dentist knows, the anticipation of pain is often more potent than its actuality. When a character is threatened with something bad, the audience automatically focuses its attention on him. The more helpless the character and the more terrible the danger, the more importance the audience will attach to the character.

That is why children in danger are such powerful characters — so powerful, in fact, that some films become unbearable to watch. The film *Poltergeist* was strong stuff for that reason. Some horror-movie buffs pooh-poohed the film because "nothing really happened"; nobody got killed. But a dozen creative slashings of teenage kids in a splatter movie don't equal the power of a single scene in which children are being dragged to terrible deaths while their mother struggles vainly to try to reach them in time.

In the TV movie *The Dollmaker*, the threshold was crossed for me. Perhaps before I had children I could have borne it; but I have children now, and when the mother runs, screaming, to try to snatch her little girl before her legs are run over by a moving train, the tension builds beyond what I can bear. When the wheels finally reach the girl before her mother does, the girl's pain, combined with the climactic release of the exquisite jeopardy, is more than I can stand.

Now, I can watch a slasher stalk his teenage prey without batting an eye — what American moviegoer and insomniac cable-watcher can't? And I've seen *Alien* and *Indiana Jones and the Temple of Doom*; I'm not a complete sucker for whatever suspense they throw at me. Why did this moment of jeopardy in *The Dollmaker* affect me so strongly?

The writer had set up this jeopardy to be as powerful as it could be. The little girl and the mother had already suffered so much emotional pain in the film that the audience cared deeply about them both. And the girl was off by herself because of a painful emotional confrontation. So the audience's stake in these characters was already strong.

As the jeopardy develops, the girl is absolutely helpless—she has no idea the train is about to move. The mother is powerless to rescue her—how can she stop a train? And the power of the train is like the fist of God, irresistible, uncompromising.

As a result, during the seconds—it feels like half an hour—when the mother is struggling to get into the train yard, racing to try to reach her daughter, the jeopardy made the characters more important to me than any characters in my experience of reading and seeing stories. I could not bear to watch that scene again. I don't have to. I can relive every moment of it in my memory.

This particular example is more powerful than most jeopardy situations, of course, but it shows how jeopardy works. Jeopardy magnifies the stalker and the prey, just as pain magnifies the sufferer and the tormentor. Jeopardy also magnifies third-party characters who get involved trying to save the victim or help the stalker.

Remember the old man Sweet-Face in *Butch Cassidy and the Sundance Kid*? Butch and the Kid are upstairs in a whorehouse when the Pinkerton men ride in. Sweet-Face points on up the road—the men ride on. That act of helping the heroes makes him somewhat important. Then the Pinkerton men come back, and, terrified, Sweet-Face points at the whorehouse. The character probably doesn't have more than twenty seconds of screen time. But because of his involvement with jeopardy, he is far more memorable than time would suggest.

Bigger Than Life

Major characters must be extraordinary in some way. We must believe them to be special, even unique. That gives far more importance to their story, makes them far more important in the audience's eyes.

How do you make a character bigger than life? How do you establish this kind of heroic proportion? William Goldman's solution in *The Princess Bride* was simply to say so. In a marvelous comic passage, he tells us that the girl becomes the tenth most beautiful woman in the world at, say, age thirteen; by fifteen she is the second most beautiful. Later, as she falls in love, and still later, as she suffers pain, she becomes the most beautiful woman that ever lived.

But that's in a novel where the narrator's voice is intrusive. When the narrator's voice cannot simply state that she is beautiful, the task is quite different; in film it's harder yet, since you have to cast a real actress in the part. There's a limit to what makeup, lighting, and gauze on the lens can achieve.

It's not enough for the woman in the movie *Body Heat* to be pretty. She must be so beautiful that a sensible man could lose his mind over her. Now, it helped to cast Kathleen Turner in the role; but pretty women have been cast in other roles, and the audience hasn't found their beauty unforgettable. What worked in this case—and in every case where we believe a character is bigger than life—is that the other characters *responded* to her as the most beautiful woman imaginable.

Even in *The Princess Bride*, Goldman doesn't just leave us with his bald assertion that a girl is the most beautiful woman and a man is the greatest swordsman of all time. Instead we see how women and men respond to her beauty with envy or desire; we watch him in his obsessed struggle to acquire his skill, and see what happens when he meets the first opponent really worthy of his skill.

Why This Isn't Enough

What I've described so far—pain, jeopardy, and heroic proportion—is the stuff of romance. Not the commercial romance genre, of course. I'm speaking of the romantic tradition that began in western Europe with the Charlemagne stories and the tales of King Arthur. Fielding and Austen wrote partly to satirize the excesses of the romantic tradition; Louisa May Alcott, Charles Dickens, Mark Twain, and Margaret Mitchell arose from that tradition and in many ways epitomize it; Stephen King and William Goldman are, in my opinion, the best of our romanticists today. In fact, most contemporary fiction is romance in this sense.

But romance has gotten a bad name. This is because pain, jeopardy and heroic proportion are easy techniques to learn—and easy for unskilled writers to overuse. As they are used without restraint or inspiration, they become steadily less effective. When they are used again and again, the reader begins to recognize them the moment they appear. Ah, another "most beautiful" woman. Oh, here comes the car chase. Hack, spatter, slash—all the blood looks alike. Readers start longing for a woman who isn't the most beautiful. Let her be ugly.

And realism is born.

It's important to remember that writers in the realistic tradition—for instance, Updike, Bellow and Fowles—still use all the old tools. Pain, jeopardy and heroic proportion are still there. But they are more restrained, are used less often, and are better disguised.

By the end of Bellow's novel *Humboldt's Gift*, for instance, Humboldt is definitely bigger than life; he is as romantically "enlarged" as Captain Blood or Rhett Butler. The difference is that Captain Blood is bigger than life by page thirty, and Humboldt doesn't become recognizably heroic in size until near the end of the book.

Here is the delicate balance that you must find in realistic fiction: importance on the one hand and, on the other hand, belief. Your major characters must be unique and important if you expect your audience to care enough to keep reading; they also must be believable. And for that, you'll use two more tools: the character's past and the character's motive process.

Real People Have Memories

One of the things I noticed as I started working with science fiction was that so many of the main characters seemed to come out of nowhere. They had no families; they all seemed to be loners and drifters who had no roots. This is fine, within the romantic tradition: Does Dirty Harry have a mother? There's no evidence for it. But it doesn't matter, in romance, because the story *becomes* the character's past. That is, by the end of the story, you know all the things the character did earlier in the story, so that now he does have connections with other people.

To fully realize a character, however, you must give him a whole life *from the start*. He has a past, an elaborate set of meaningful connections to other people: family, friends, enemies, teachers, employers.

The most obvious way to tell a character's whole life is, of course, to begin with his birth. This is, however, the romantic tradition again. After all, no matter whether you're writing romance or realism, you have to begin the story at exactly the point where the main character becomes interesting and unique. If you start at his birth, then he must be bigger than life from the cradle. That's what John Irving did with *The World According to Garp*, but there aren't many stories whose protagonist is so interestingly conceived.

Instead, you will probably begin your story when your main characters are already nearly adults, with a wealth of experience behind them. How can you give a sense of the past?

The most obvious technique—and therefore the least effective and most overused—is the flashback. The present action stops for a while as the character (or, worse yet, the narrator) remembers some key event from days of yore. The problem with this technique is exactly that: the action *stops* for the flashback.

Time after time I have seen student stories or stories submitted to me as an editor that begin like this:

> Nora peered through her windshield, trying to see through the heavy snowfall. "I can't be late," she murmured. It took all her concentration just to stay at forty miles per hour. Yet the events of the last few weeks kept intruding, taking her mind off the road. She thought back to her last quarrel with Pete . . .

Cringe along with me, please. This flashback is not really giving the character a past, because the character has no present. The character has not yet been made important in the present moment—she is merely a stereotyped image, and a singularly dull one at that: woman driving in the snow. The flashback is not going to provide us with *additional* information about the character—it will provide us with our *only* information. We have no anchor in the present moment, so we are soon hopelessly adrift in memory.

Here's a good rule of thumb: If you feel a need to have a flashback on the first or second page of your story, that's a clear sign that your story should simply begin with the events being told in the flashback. In that case, don't flash back—tell the events in the order in which they happened.

Sometimes, many pages into a story, there is a need for the character to remember some key event. Then a flashback might be justified. But it still has a serious cost. It stops the present action. The longer the flashback takes, the harder it is for the audience to remember what was happening just before the flashback began. So flashbacks should be rare, they should be brief, and they should take place only after you have anchored the story in the present action.

The Past as a Present Event

Slightly more effective is having one character tell another a story out of the past. If you set it up properly, the telling of the story, besides conveying past information, can also *be* present action. Take, for example, the hiding-behind-tapestries scene in James Goldman's *Lion in Winter*. Each of King Henry's three sons has come to King Philip of France, trying to make a deal with him to destroy all the others. Now Henry himself comes, and his sons hide behind tapestries as the two kings confront each other.

Provoked beyond endurance, Philip tells Henry a story about his childhood. But the story he tells does not stop the action—it *is* the action. Philip tells how he was homosexually seduced by Henry's son Richard, and how he went along with the act, though he loathed it, in order to be able to tell Henry about it now.

With the pain that this revelation causes Henry—not to mention Richard, behind the curtain—the story is doing double-duty. It gives us some of the past of Richard and Philip, fleshing them out as characters; but it also causes terrible emotional pain in the present, which strengthens Henry and Richard as victims and Philip as tormentor.

Notice, though, that the story is not just any story. It is about pain in the past, Philip's pain. It isn't enough just to tell random stories from a character's past. They have to be stories that are important in the ways we have already discussed.

The Implied Past: Expectation

It is possible to give your characters a realistic past *without* stopping the action by giving them an *implied past*. There are several ways to convince the reader that a character has already lived a full life. One of the most powerful techniques is *expectation*. What a character *expects* will happen in the present tells us instantly what has happened in his past.

For example, if you're told that a child cringes when someone steps toward her with a hand upraised, you know at once that the child has been beaten often enough that she *expects* a beating. Without slowing the action, the author has given a sense of the child's past and told something of her pain.

Each of the following paragraphs implies things about a character's past:

The clerk repeated, "Cash or charge?" Nora looked helplessly at Pete. He spread his hands as if to show he wasn't holding a gold card. "You're the one doing the shopping," he said. "I can't afford this stuff." Still she made no move to pay. Finally he gave up and opened her purse for her. She had some cash. He used two bills to pay the clerk, put the change back into the purse, and snapped it shut. "You ought to use some of that to hire a bodyguard," he said. "The junkie who mugs you could O.D. and die, and then his family would sue you." She smiled and shrugged a little. As he left, he heard the clerk telling somebody, "And it was all hundreds! The whole purse!"

Pete watched for a gap in the speeding cars and stepped out into the road. Immediately drivers began swerving and slamming on their brakes. If everybody had kept going smoothly, he would have made it across the road easily; as it was, he barely made it back to the curb alive. How can people ever cross streets in America, if drivers go crazy every time they see a pedestrian?

As soon as Pete got in the door Nora began to cry. "I didn't mean to do it," she said over and over again. "I'm sorry, I'm sorry." It took fifteen minutes before she'd believe him when he said it was no big deal. "But it's completely smashed," she said. Hadn't she ever heard of insurance?

Pete noticed that Nora kept sliding the bills between her thumb and fingers. Finally he realized she was counting them, again and again, as if she had to make sure they were all there.

Nora was finally calm enough that she could talk to Pete again, but when she went into the living room, there he was, straightening the magazines, dusting, arranging the pillows, trying to make her feel guilty for being such a slob. It made her so angry that there was no way she could take part in a reasonable discussion. She rushed out of the apartment, ignoring him when he called her name, "Nora! Nora!" His wheedling tone reminded her of the way bratty children say *mommy*. "Maw-mee! Naw-rah!" In the elevator she remembered her mother-in-law's immaculate house, and realized that Pete's house-cleaning routine was probably what he had done as a child to placate the old bitch when she was angry at him. I'll never kill you, Pete, no matter how angry you make me—but I might just kill your mother.

Each of these vignettes reveals a character's expectations, implying a story from his or her past. Yet not one of them stops the action, or even slows it much. They add depth to the characterization without subtracting momentum from the forward movement of the story.

The Implied Past: Networks

Anyone who has been alive for any length of time has made many connections with other people. Unless we are torn from our normal milieu, those connections are going to show up. You can reveal much about a character through the way other characters react to her, (especially minor characters who behave predictably according to stereotype and don't draw undue attention to themselves):

Pete noticed the way people in the store looked at Nora. Quick, furtive glances. He couldn't see anything wrong with her—no run in her stocking, no underwear showing. He didn't catch on until he realized that the store detective was shadowing them. Apparently Nora was known here.

Nora knew that Pete was not the man of her dreams when the motel clerk took his check without asking for identification. She thought it might be classy to be recognized at the Hilton, but not at a motel that rents a room for ten dollars an hour. Still, a man who pays by check is probably telling the truth when he says he isn't married.

Everybody Pete and Nora ran into did the same thing. Just as they were about to ask her a question, they'd glance at Pete and then smile and say something noncommital. When they stopped for lunch at a diner called the White Trash Saloon, the used-up-looking waitress finally asked the question the others had sidestepped. "How's Joe Bob?" Nora smiled icily back. "He's home taking care of our seven children while Pete and I have a madcap, whirlwind affair." The waitress thought about this for a moment. "You don't have no seven children," she finally said. "Too damn thin."

Nora couldn't help noticing that all the unopened letters on the kitchen table had transparent windows on them, and a lot of them said FINAL NOTICE. Even through the closed door, she could hear Pete shouting into the telephone. "I'll make payments on that piece of junk any month that it runs! And if you send somebody to pick it up, I'll blast their head off!" A minute later he came back in, grinning. "An old girlfriend," he said.

Sometimes your characters' relationships will be important to the story, but sometimes they'll be there merely to add an illusion of a full life, or an

occasional comic touch. The main value of the technique is that your characters won't seem to be puppets, existing only to act out the plot.

Using an implied past makes your story like a group portrait in which one
of the subjects is looking toward something outside the picture and reacting
emotionally to it. You can't see what he sees, but you know it's there. It makes
the world of the portrait a larger, deeper, more believable place. In your story,
the characters will be received, not as artificial people acting out their assigned
parts, but rather as real people who live in a network of relationships. Though
only a small part of that network is explored in your story, the reader senses
that the rest of the network is there.

Complexity of Motive

Motive—the purpose the character has in mind when he takes an action—is
not something you *add* to a character. It is there whether you like it or not.
That's because readers will supply the most obvious motive wherever you
have not told them directly what it is.

If you are telling a straightforward romance, you can often leave out any
explanation of motive. In the film *Conan the Barbarian*, young Conan's mother
is killed before his eyes. He spends the rest of the film searching for the
murderer. It is not hard for the audience to grasp the idea that he is looking
for revenge.

Let's suppose that you want to write the same story, but you want Conan
to be a more believable human being. His relentless obsession with revenge
is not enough to sustain a realistic novel. So you would give him times when
he did not think of revenge. Perhaps you would make him even more complex:
he is searching for the murderer, not to kill him, but to serve him. In Conan's
mind the man's cruelty has been transformed into justice—he killed my
mother, thinks Conan, because she was weak and small. I will be strong
and large, and he will find me worthy. This kind of motivation borders on
pathological—but it is also intriguing and not at all unbelievable, given the
terrible trauma of seeing his mother's death.

The pursuit of ever deeper motives is not a trivial game played on the
surface of the story. Motive is at the story's heart. The only good definition
of *story* that I know is "the ordered presentation of causally related events."
The writer arranges the events in some order; whether the writer means it
or not, the audience interprets those events as having caused one another.
The cause or purpose of an action decides what that action means. That's
what the story *is*.

Nora tells Pete that the man who was in her apartment was just a salesman.
Pete reacts by saying cruel, vicious things to her, breaking a lamp, and storm-
ing out of her apartment. What does that scene mean?

At first glance, we might suppose Pete is insanely jealous. But what if we
then learn Pete knows the man—knows that he is a drug dealer and a former
pimp? Now we understand his rage. Nora's lie is a silent witness to him that

she is somehow involved with this man.

After a while, Nora confesses to Pete that the man in her apartment was her brother, but she hates him and doesn't want anyone she cares about to know that he has any connection with her. Now Pete understands why she lied, and is relieved.

Still later, the reader is shown a scene that makes it clear that the visitor was not her brother at all — he has been her husband for ten years, and they have never been divorced.

Each new revelation of a main character's motive is not a simple matter of adding more information — it revises all the information that has gone before. Events that we thought meant one thing now mean another. The present constantly revises the meaning of the past. Revelation of the past constantly revises the meaning of the present. This is the primary device of detective fiction, but all other fiction uses the technique as well.

The discovery of motive always requires examination of a character's thoughts, either through his dialogue with other characters, through direct telling of those thoughts, or by implication as new facts are revealed. All these examinations of motive come at the expense of action. A character who endlessly tries to understand his own motives seriously risks becoming a bore.

The Cost of Realization

The tools of realistic characterization are just as easily overused as the tools of romance. When romance is badly done, it feels melodramatic, formulaic, unbelievable. When realism is badly done, it feels pretentious, self-indulgent, boring.

This is because revealing the character's past and examining his motives takes time. The audience will expect that anything to which you devote a lot of time is important; it will amount to something in the story. There are only so many things in a character's past that are really important in the present story — if you keep going into the past, you are either going to repeat yourself, which is boring, or you are going to recall events that don't really matter — which, done to extremes, causes the reader to feel confused, disappointed or frustrated.

Too often, in the effort to make a character believable, an unskilled writer will go into elaborate detail about things that don't matter at all. Endless explorations of thought to discover motives about things that don't matter are the hallmark of bad literary fiction, just as formulaic repetitions of bigger-than-life characters who have no soul are the sign of bad romance.

But the best romantic writers and the best realistic writers are not far apart. The good romantic writer uses the realistic tools of motive discovery and revelation of the character's past; the good realistic writer tells stories about people of heroic proportion who suffer real pain and pass through genuine jeopardy.

The trick is to find the precise balance. Look at how Dickens does it. In *Great Expectations*, when we meet Miss Havisham we see only her eccentricity: She's an old woman who wears a tattered bridal gown and lives in a house filled with decorations for a wedding that never took place. This makes her instantly memorable. This is vital for Dickens's purpose, because he was writing a serial; the reader had to remember characters, not from minute to minute, but from day to day.

Once her eccentricity is established, however, he does not increase her importance by making her even *more* eccentric—that would make her comic, and she is too important to be farcical. Instead, he uses pain. Miss Havisham's niece treats the young boy Pip quite cruelly. Havisham sees his suffering with delight. "Does she make you cry? Does it hurt?" We realize that she is teaching the girl to be cruel, so that it is really Miss Havisham who is the tormentor. Pip's pain magnifies them both.

Later, Dickens fully realizes Miss Havisham by giving us the story of her past. Her bridegroom jilted her on the day of the wedding. Her trust in him had been so complete that his betrayal caused her extraordinary pain. She stopped all the clocks in the house and never let any of the decorations for the wedding celebration be taken down; the moment of betrayal becomes the center of her life from then on. She raises her niece to be beautiful and attractive, so she will have power over men, power enough to hurt them as deeply as Miss Havisham was hurt.

Now her motive is discovered, and though she is not altogether sane, she is understandable, believable, even deserving of some degree of sympathy. Dickens used her eccentricity to make her memorable for a day; he used her cruelty and Pip's pain to make her memorable throughout the novel; he used her past, her pain, her motives to make her memorable forever.

In my novel *Speaker for the Dead*, I used a similar pattern of development. My main character, Ender Wiggin, has been wandering from place to place for many years. Now he is forced by circumstance to spend time with a family that has recently lost its father—a man who treated his wife and children cruelly. I knew I wanted Ender to take the father's place in the family and, through his innate goodness, to transform the family into a whole and happy unit.

The trouble was the six kids. I knew their names and ages, but not much else, except for the oldest kid, who figured prominently in the plot. Time after time I'd be writing along and discover I had completely forgotten to mention one of the children for several chapters. I had to keep looking at my notes just to remember which kid was which. If I couldn't keep them straight, how could I expect the readers to tell them apart?

I couldn't solve my problem by simply eliminating any of the shadowy children's characters. To make the book do what I wanted it to do, they all had to be there. The family had to be large, and every member of the family had to be memorable and clearly differentiated. Each one had to stick in the reader's mind.

All those children shared the painful experience of an abusive father—but each one experienced him differently. Their responses would therefore be different, I realized, and when Ender Wiggin meets them, he would first notice their eccentricities.

The youngest boy is methodically violent and uncontrollable. He attacks Ender with a knife when they first meet, and when Ender constrains him, he urinates on Ender's lap.

The youngest girl watches even the most outrageous goings on without a sign of interest, and almost never speaks.

Another boy, who was blinded and therefore uses artificial eyes, copes with stress by switching off his eyes and blasting music through earphones, so that the rest of the world simply ceases to exist.

The next oldest boy is ardently Catholic, and views Ender—with some justification—as Antichrist; he resents the way Ender heals his family more than he would have resented it if Ender had done them harm.

And so on—each child with an eccentric pattern of behavior. The eccentricities help the audience to differentiate among the children right from the beginning. Gradually, though, as each child's individual past and motives are revealed, their eccentricities begin to fade. By then, I have given them new experiences with pain and jeopardy that will make them more memorable, and each child is found to have particular strengths that are vital to the family's survival and success, giving each child a heroic role to play.

By the end of the novel, if my skill was enough to do all these things well, the audience should believe in and care about each of these children as an individual. Then, when Ender Wiggin chooses to stay with the family he has healed, the audience sympathizes with his choice. It is the proper conclusion to that part of the story.

Which Tool Do You Use?

Not every storyteller uses all these tools, however. Most television shows and most novels don't use any tools of characterization more powerful than eccentricity, pain and jeopardy. Isn't that all that most action-adventure shows and situation comedies offer? Is there anything more powerful in the characters of most bodice-rippers, most commercial romance novels, most science fiction? That's why you forget such characters so quickly. Yet those techniques are obviously enough to *sell* the story—and to find plenty of readers.

So the basic techniques are a start; they're enough to make a story work. But eventually you will also want your stories to endure. One of the surest ways is to have characters that are so important and so believable to the readers that they can't forget them. They will tell everyone they know about your story; years from now, they'll give the story or show the videotape to their children.

You know characters like that: Miss Havisham and Uriah Heep; Tom Sawyer, Huck Finn and Nigger Jim; Macbeth, Othello, Shylock; Meg, Jo, Beth and

Amy; Scarlett O'Hara, Rhett Butler and Melanie Hamilton; Frodo, Samwise, Gollum — wouldn't you like to add your own unforgettable characters to that list? I know I want to.

We all have equal access to the tools. And for those of us who weren't born with the genius to do it instinctively, using the tools constantly and studying the results is the only way to learn to use them well.

Choosing Your Storyteller

by Joel Rosenberg

Who's going to tell your story? Yes, I know you're going to write it, but who's going to *tell* it? Whose eye will you be using? The protagonist's? A camera's? God's? What *point of view* will you use?

That's one of the most important decisions you're going to have to make for each and every fictional story; the point of view you choose will affect almost everything else in the story.

Before you begin any piece of fiction, you must, in effect, sit down with your reader and make a deal about what restrictions will govern this particular story, and then both of you must live with that decision.

Point of view is the major kind of restriction. It sets the boundaries of the story, defining what is possible. When you're writing in first-person point of view, for instance, you don't have to worry about whether readers will think you're cheating them when you withhold information from them that you're also hiding from your protagonist. When you're writing from multiple points of view, on the other hand, you *can* make readers worry about whether or not the present protagonist is going to get killed. But more on the specific restrictions later.

Your point of view choice is also important in that the point of view affects how much the readers can believe in the story being told. A proper choice can lead to the willing suspension of disbelief.

"Willing suspension of disbelief" is Samuel Taylor Coleridge's phrase. Coleridge was talking about poetry and the poetry reader, but the notion is crucial to what all fiction writers are really after: getting our readers to agree to *pretend*, just for a while, that these characters are real people with real issues in their lives. Adhering to whatever point of view you choose can help with that because you won't be giving the reader any unnecessary reminders that your story is, quite literally, a string of lies. It's much better to help them pretend, instead of making it difficult.

You have three basic choices to consider when choosing the point of view your story will be told from: *first, second*, or *third person*; me, you, or him (or her).

Well, you only have two real choices. We can quickly dispense with second person. Here's why:

It's late at night. You're sitting in the passenger seat of your 1969 LeMans convertible, watching the intertwined shadows slither across the blinds of the brightly lit house. Your mouth tastes like Pershing's cavalry has been camping in it, so you slump down further in the sweat-slick bucket seat and consider for a moment whether to try and clear it with a mint, or to just fire up another cigarette.

To hell with it, you think, as you shrug and pull another Camel from the battered pack, then fire a kitchen match with your thumbnail. The match flares like a torch; you inhale the thick smoke and lay your head back against the headrest, wondering. Wondering what?

Wondering what *you* are doing in this story, because not only does it sound like Raymond Chandler on a bad day, but you also know you're not a character in one of Rosenberg's tales, and *he knows* you're not a character in one of Rosenberg's tales—so what gives, eh, bucko?

Which is precisely the problem. You know that you aren't a character in one of my stories, just as your readers know that they're not characters in your stories. Right from the first line, I've strained the reader's credulity, and probably shattered my credibility. Which is why, except for an occasional *tour de force*, choosing second-person point of view is probably a mistake.

The First Person Is Not a Female President's Husband

One good way to write is from a *first person* point of view, where a character tells his or her own story. After all, it's the way we naturally tell others about what happens in our own lives.

"There I was, late at night, sitting in the car . . . " would have been a *much* better opening to the above scene.

The biggest advantage of *first person narrative* is that it can promote an almost instant identification between the reader and your protagonist—and that identification can quickly lead to the willing suspension of disbelief.

I used first person in *Emile and the Dutchman*, one of my science fiction novels. Here's part of the opening:

I hated the Dutchman at first sight.

"An officer is a model of courtesy and politeness, to subordinate officers as well as superiors"—it says so, right on the first page of *Contact Service Rules, Regulations, and Proprieties*.

Space aboard Major Alonzo Norfeldt's cabin was mainly lacking. And the atmosphere wasn't improved by the stench of cheap wine mixed with the nauseating smell of stale tobacco. The fat man was no visual thrill as he lay back on the rumpled linen of his bunk, scratching at his belly, just above the waistband of his shorts. If he had bathed in the past week, there was no solid evidence.

"Second Lieutenant Emile von du Mark, reporting to the Team Leader as per Regulation—"

He cut me off with a thump of his hand against the nearest wall. "Enough of that. I don't need Regs this early in the morning."

I wasn't aware that two in the afternoon was even part of the morning, but I let it pass.

"You heard of me?' He reached under his pillow, brought out a well-chewed cigar, and stuck the soggy end in his mouth.

"Yes, sir." I wanted to leave it at that, but he pressed.

"And what have you heard, Mister von du Mark?" A vague smile played across his lips; a childhood memory of my cat playing with a captured baby mole sprang up.

"That you are a competent—"

"Belay that. I asked you what you heard."

I shrugged. To hell with him, too. "That you are a tyrannical, overbearing Team Leader, with a record of four good, solid contacts—and two Drops—but an incredibly high fatality record among your teams' members. That you are a drunkard, and a smoker—both of which are obvious. That you are an officer, but you certainly are no gentleman. Sir."

The Dutchman threw back his head and laughed. "You got guts, Mark." He stuck out his hand; I accepted it automatically. I returned his pressure quickly enough to prevent his cracking my knuckles.

Barely.

"Of course," he went on, "I've always favored brains, myself."

For *Emile and the Dutchman*, deciding to use first person was easy. Since the stories are about Emile growing and changing, the obvious way to tell them was through his eyes, letting him every once in a while realize that yet another piece of his youth has been hacked away.

Besides, it helps with bringing comic elements into an otherwise serious tale: while Norfeldt's more unsanitary and antisocial habits might have seemed unbelievable were I to discuss them as the author, it's different when Emile is speaking: after all, we're all used to hearing people stretch things a bit. The soggy cigar under the pillow is something Joel-Rosenberg-the-writer couldn't have gotten away with; Emile-von-du-Mark-the-storyteller can.

First person has the further advantage of being straightforward: it's easy to tell if you're violating first-person point of view; mastering the subtleties of the different forms of third person isn't nearly as easy.

A useful variant of first-person narrative is *second-person address*—which is entirely different from *second-person narrative*. In second-person address, the reader is an important character, but not as a protagonist—as the *audience* of the story, being talked to by the first-person narrator. This isn't the same as making the reader a character in the story; as a matter of fact, when you think about it, the reader-as-listener really isn't much of a lie at all.

Mark Twain used second-person address in *The Adventures of Huckleberry Finn*, which begins:

You don't know about me without you have read a book by the name of *The Adventures of Tom Sawyer*; but that ain't no matter. The book was made by Mr. Mark Twain, and he told the truth, mainly. There was things which he stretched, but mainly he told the truth. That is nothing.

I never seen anybody but lied one time or another, without it was Aunt Polly, or the widow, or maybe Mary.

While getting away with so much fractured grammar requires Twain's master touch—and, like the dialect that comes later, it is not recommended for us lesser mortals—the choice of second-person address for this story is one that even a beginner could have made. After all, it's easy to see that a reader can much more easily accept Huck as a storyteller—and a fine one, at that—than as an author. Both second-person address and Huck's use of language add to credibility, instead of detracting from it.

Not every story should be—or can be—written in first person; *first-person narrative* does have limitations. There is no way to get information to the reader that the protagonist doesn't have access to—say, that there's a six-foot-two ax-murderer standing in the closet. And if the protagonist is someone that readers wouldn't be able to identify with—say, a six-foot-two ax-murderer who likes to stand in closets—the readers probably won't get past page one.

Another drawback is the difficulty in using first person when the protagonist is heroic and knows it. It's one thing for the *writer* to describe a character as bold and brave, but it's different when the character describes himself that way—it comes off as bragging, not as objective description. Imagine how Robert E. Howard's *Conan* stories would have sounded in first person—"I flexed my massive thews and hacked through the cringing vermin. . . ."

Now, there are ways around that. One method is to give the heroic protagonist/narrator something of a modest attitude, which is what Robert B. Parker does both skillfully and subtly with his introspective detective, Spenser. But that's tricky. Usually it's better to use the remaining voice: third person.

Third Person in Four Flavors

There are at least four kinds of third-person narrative: *omniscient, camera eye, single point of view* and *sigma character*. The difference between the four lies in the freedom the writer is allowing himself.

Omniscient is the least restrictive point of view; it's author-as-God. Not only can the writer comment on what's going on in the protagonist's mind or in a minor character's head, but also he or she is perfectly free to discourse on events happening offstage, or warn the reader that something is about to happen ("Unbeknownst to our hero, a horrid fate was about to befall him"). Why not? The narrator—make that The Narrator—is omniscient; The Narrator Sees All, Knows All.

The omniscient point of view used to be a lot more popular than it is now. Last century, a writer would often come out onstage and address the reader directly, saying something like, "Ah, dear reader, you have probably been wondering what happened to little Amanda who, as you may recall, we last saw hanging from a vine above the pit of crocodiles, lo, almost two hundred pages ago. Be of good heart; your questions are now to be answered!"

Nineteenth-century readers were willing to put up with a lot of nonsense from nineteenth-century writers, and while Edgar Rice Burroughs used to get away with this early in this century, we are now in the 1990s, and we must be more careful.

Omniscient is probably the trickiest of all voices, and it's dangerously attractive, simply because it allows the writer the most freedom. Why straitjacket yourself into a more restrictive voice when this one is available? Because while your readers may be wonderfully perceptive and warm-hearted individuals, they aren't omniscient. They never have been; they never will be. They aren't used to knowing what goes on in more than one mind at one time, or knowing what is simultaneously happening both where they are and in a dark room a hundred miles away, or what will happen in the future. By removing those familiar restrictions, that limitation to a single point of view, you may be endangering their willing suspension of disbelief.

We write fiction to manipulate our readers' thoughts and emotions for the few minutes that they're reading our stories; if by taking the easy way out and unnecessarily using omniscient point of view we alienate instead of move our readers, we've failed.

If you're going to use the omniscient point of view—if there's no way but omniscient to get information to the reader that the point-of-view protagonist doesn't have access to—the best way is to break into omniscient only sparingly, as an occasional break from a more restricted third-person point of view. Think of these as omniscient *digressions*.

And it's tricky; it requires a master touch. Robert A. Heinlein has the touch. *Stranger in a Strange Land*, *Citizen of the Galaxy* and *Orphans of the Sky* are each worth studying for their use of point of view alone. Heinlein sometimes slips into an omniscient point of view, but with almost agonizing delicacy; this presence as narrator comes in only when necessary—and most of the time he gets himself on- and offstage almost silently.

Here's one of Heinlein's omniscient paragraphs in *Orphans of the Sky*.

> Hugh accepted a *de facto* condition of slavery with no particular resistance and no great disturbance of soul. The word *slave* was not in his vocabulary, but the condition was commonplace in everything he had known. There had always been those who gave orders and those who carried them out—he could imagine no other condition, no other type of social organization. It was a fact of nature.

While I strongly recommend the whole book, you don't need to have read it or have any feeling for who Hugh is to realize that the above paragraph *couldn't* have been written from Hugh's point of view: if the word *slave* isn't in Hugh's vocabulary, it can't be used from his point of view. If Hugh isn't capable of imagining a freer sort of society, the only way for that to be explicitly pointed out is for Heinlein to come onstage and tell us.

But reread the last sentence of the paragraph: "It was a fact of nature." Heinlein is carefully preparing us for the return to a more restrictive point of view. Robert Heinlein knows that this sort of social organization isn't a "fact of nature"; you and I know it, too, but *Hugh* doesn't. The mistake is Hugh's, not Heinlein's—Heinlein is carefully slipping back into Hugh's point of view so he can continue with the story.

If there is some knowledge that your protagonist doesn't have that you *must* share with the reader, use third-person point of view with omniscient digressions, as in the Heinlein example. Plan on putting a lot of effort into this slipping in and out of omniscient voice; it's tough.

And if you find yourself using a lot of omniscient digressions, you're probably lecturing the reader. Cut it out.

Use omniscient passages only when necessary, and slide out of them carefully; you must step onstage and then slip offstage without bumping into any of the scenery.

No Camera Eye

Camera eye is the opposite of omniscient. The readers know only what is going on in front of them, never gaining any direct insight into what a character is thinking or feeling—just as though they were watching television or a movie.

Sometimes, the readers are in effect perched behind a protagonist's eyeball; sometimes the point of view isn't quite so restricted. Still, it is an awfully limited way to tell a story.

Which is part of the problem, and one of the reasons to avoid the camera-eye point of view. A strength of filmed fiction is its ability to suspend disbelief by showing—"Ethel, *look* at the Death Star!"—while the power of written fiction comes from its ability to put action in context, to explore the underlying meaning of what is going on.

That sounds heavier than has to be. Just take a look at any of the screen versions of *The Adventures of Huckleberry Finn*, and you'll see what I mean. Compared to the book, they're flat and emotionless, simply because the medium wasn't up to the depth and complexity of Twain's high-powered messages about human nature. The movie can show only what is done and said, not what is thought and felt.

Still, camera eye does have its uses, particularly for short stories where something that the protagonist knows is the key to surprising the readers. But if you find yourself using camera eye in a novel, reconsider. Camera eye automatically distances readers from the protagonist, and few readers will put up with that for a whole book.

Using Single Point of View Doesn't Mean You're Closed-Minded

A good compromise between omniscient and camera eye is to write in third person from a *single character's point of view*. The readers see the action through the eye of the protagonist, just as though it were a form of camera eye—but with an important difference: the readers are able to follow the thoughts and feelings of the character. If the character sees something or thinks about something, so can the readers—and if not, not.

That last is important. When you're using the single point of view, describing how the protagonist looks is *verboten*, unless he's looking at himself right at the moment.

Why? Because you have agreed to restrict the telling of the story to a single character's point of view, after all, and that would be breaking that agreement.

So what? you ask. *Readers aren't going to notice, are they?*

Well, yes and no. Maybe they won't, consciously. But breaking what is in effect your unwritten contract with them will bother them at least subconsciously, later on, say, when there's a bit of information that the character doesn't have and that you're not willing—yet—to share with the readers.

I want *my* readers to remain unbothered on all levels.

My favorite way to write in third person is to use what I call *first-third*, to write from a third-person point of view as though it were first person. The story proceeds from the point of view of the third-person protagonist almost exactly as though he were a first-person narrator, with access not only to what the character sees, hears, tastes, feels and remembers—but also to what that character, and *only* that character—can think or imagine.

This is one of the easier tricks of the trade to take to the typewriter; first-third makes it simple to see if you're slipping out of the point of view. When going over a passage, *translate it*—mentally or on paper—and watch the errors stand out.

I wrote *The Sleeping Dragon* from a variety of first-third points of view. It began this way:

> Karl Cullinane reached out his fork and speared the last stick of asparagus from the stainless-steel serving plate in the middle of the table, not bothering to set the asparagus on his own plate before taking a bite. It was cold and mushy, almost tasteless; he swallowed quickly.

To check it, I mentally translated it to this:

> I reached out my fork and speared the last stick of asparagus from the stainless-steel serving plate in the middle of the table, not bothering to set the asparagus on my own plate before taking a bite. It was cold and mushy, almost tasteless; I swallowed quickly.

Fine, so far. But what if the passage had gone on to say this (which it didn't):

> He was a lean, almost skinny man in his early twenties, dressed, as was common for college students, in a wrinkled blue workshirt and faded jeans, the shirt open to the third button, the sleeves rolled back.

Now that seems vaguely wrong, the point of view slightly skewed. But translate it—

I was a lean, almost skinny man in my early twenties dressed, as was common for college students, in a wrinkled blue workshirt and faded jeans, the shirt open to the third button, the sleeves rolled back.

—and it looks *dreadful*. Nothing would occur to a narrator that way; if I'm telling the story from Karl's point of view, and I want to work in some description of Karl, I'd have to do it more cleverly.

The classic way around this describing-the-protagonist problem, of course, is to have the protagonist look at himself in a mirror. I find that clichéd and awkward; the solution I favor is to do it by function and action, by *showing* him or her as someone who has to shave her legs/his face twice a day or twice a month, who can casually pick up an anvil or has trouble opening a jar, who can walk under a turnstile or must stoop to walk under the *Arc de Triomphe*.

This gives me a way to describe the protagonist without violating point of view, but there's another advantage: it helps in *gradually* building an individual picture in my readers' minds, one that they can identify with. To my taste, that's preferable to stopping the action of a story to draw a prose picture. Besides, when my protagonist is a sympathetic character, I want my readers to identify with him, to see themselves in his shoes—and I don't see any necessity of handicapping myself by reminding my readers of physical differences between themselves and the protagonist.

The Sigma Factor

If you can write a novel from a single point of view, you should; either first person or limited third. But life isn't simple, of course, and neither is writing. While it's a good idea to maintain a single point of view for a short story or novella, often a whole novel shouldn't or even *can't* be written from a single character's point of view. After all, even when the story is strongly centered on one character, you'll often have other characters off somewhere doing important things that readers really would like to be in on.

The obvious way to solve that problem is by using an omniscient point of view. Not the best way, but the obvious way; the trouble with an omniscient point of view is still the same as it was a couple columns ago: it can interfere with the reader's involvement in the story.

The best multiple point of view is what is technically called, for no good reason that I've been able to discover, the *sigma character* form. The name may be strange, but the idea is good: the story is told from a variety of points of view, but from *only one point of view per scene*—just as though it was limited third or first-third. The point of view can switch from character to character during scene breaks, or—as is more frequently the case—chapter breaks, but each scene is told from one point of view.

This lets readers get into the head of the present point-of-view character, the so-called sigma character, without having to commit themselves to living with one character for an entire book. That's particularly handy when you want to put the readers into the head of an unsympathetic character you don't expect them to put up with forever. And you can do this without forcing your readers to endure an omniscient point of view. (If you're writing your first novel, seriously consider using a sigma character with a *first-third* point of view, both on the grounds that it gives you a lot of freedom, and that it's easy to tell if you're violating point of view.)

A particularly strong use of the sigma character comes in Larry Niven and Jerry Pournelle's *The Mote in God's Eye*. Perhaps the entire novel could have been told—and a large portion of the story *is* told—from the point of view of Captain Lord Roderick Blaine, master of the INSS *MacArthur*. But had it been, we as readers would have missed the great pleasure of getting inside the heads of an unusually large and well-drawn cast of characters.

Which would have been a pity. After all, one of the reasons I read and write fiction is to meet new and interesting people.

The Things They Say

by Dwight V. Swain

The things a person says reflect and reveal his character. Couple his speech with that of other story people and you have dialogue, one of a writer's most useful tools for creating unique individuals, revealing relationships, building conflict and advancing a story.

There are a variety of other reasons for a writer to use dialogue, of course. One is that, well done, it makes reading easier. It isn't as silly as it sounds. Watch the browsers at any bookstore if you don't believe me. Thumbing through the opening pages of a book, more often than not they'll pause at a broken page, one with lots of white space.

A page with dialogue, specifically.

The solid, blocky pages, heavy with copy? They'll tend to pass those by.

There are more reasons for using dialogue than easy reading, of course. A major one is drama.

Ray Palmer, my old pulp editor and mentor, put this in the simplest possible form.

"Always open with dialogue," he told me. "Why? Because when two people are talking, they have to be talking *about* something—something your readers can understand without a lot of explanation. Like for instance a fight."

Well, that may be overstating it a little, but the principle's sound. Dialogue equals people, and people talking equals some sort of interchange of information or ideas or feelings. Chitchat isn't enough. Even two lovers exchanging sweet nothings in bed is a prelude to something about to happen.

In addition, the tone of that dialogue sets a mood for the scene, establishes a feeling. Witness our two lovers with their verbal foreplay.

Note, too, that one wrong word or phrase can change that mood and lead to someone getting up and going home or to the guest room.

So. Dialogue provides both mood and information.

Often, also, it can be used to contrast the difference between what a viewpoint character thinks and what he says. Again, consider two lovers—apparent lovers, that is:

"I adore you, Carolyn," he said, stroking her hand gently.

A nicely calculated move, it bared his wristwatch: 7:30. Desperately, he searched for some acceptable excuse to leave. He had to get to Deirdre's by eight. Yet he couldn't make it obvious. Not with Carolyn's inheritance in the balance.

An additional dialogue value is the way it lends an air of reality to a story. The things a person says, the way he speaks, are major factors in bringing him alive on the page. It's one thing to say your heroine's rival is amoral and less than literate, another to quote a line like "So he's on the take. Who cares? A buck is a buck. He can snag my nylons anytime."

What about dialogue's individualizing function?

The words you speak, what you say and how you say it, reveal you as a particular person. If you're bookish, you talk one way; if a sports fan, another. Intelligence comes through, and so does slow-wittedness or illiteracy. The cautious person speaks with restraint, the reticent as little as possible—perhaps to the point of limiting himself to monosyllables to a great degree. Garrulousness may indicate a pulsing ego. But then again, it may not; the rush and gush of words sometimes reflect embarrassment, and any police interrogator knows the value of silence at the right moment in pushing a suspect to confess. Most bartenders and airline hostesses have been conditioned to make conversation with anyone and on any subject.

These are things a writer must think about, be aware of. If the words he puts in his story people's mouths are out of character, he'll be hard put to rise above them.

Those words should reflect such factors as sex, age, occupation, status, and background.

A grandmother speaks: "I keep everything tidy."

Her housewife daughter: "I like a neat house. But quality time together beats spick and span."

Housewife's teenage girl: "So the joint is a mess. Who cares?"

Housewife's clerk-typist friend: "I try to straighten the place up, but it gets to be a shambles."

The manager's wife: "I have this wonderful Puerto Rican woman. She keeps our house spotless."

The Puerto Rican: "All the time clean, clean. I get so—how you say?—*cansada*. Sometimes I wish I go back to San Juan."

If the housewife's husband is middle management, he'll probably speak reasonably literate standard English. His mechanic may not. And his doctor quite possibly will salt his lines with medical terms totally out of range of his patients' experience. A soldier has his own vocabulary, and so does a sailor, and so does a miner and a carpenter and a farmer. It also goes without saying that Maine and Mississippi and California and Colorado and the Carolinas have their private speech patterns.

(It should be noted, though, that regional differences and area dialects are fading, thanks to television, education, and military service. Outside of an occasional phrase added for color, beware of throwing in chunks of Ozark or Cajun folk speech or the like. To have one urban gang character describe another as a "bad dude" makes your point. To inflict a page of "Like I mean ya know I doin' skag like I ain't not ready to wig out on no crystal" on your readers is something else.)

How do you learn to individualize with dialogue? The answer, of course, is that you listen and that does mean *listen*, to people of all sorts talking in all sorts of situations, insofar as you can manage it. Television and, in particular, the VCR are useful tools in this regard. By taping a program you can play chunks of dialogue that impress you over and over again until you get their pattern, their rhythm, their individualizing touches.

Beware, however, of putting too much trust in such. A TV performance is a carefully polished thing. The skill of writer, director and actors sometimes can throw you off-center.

One way around this is to do some private taping with your own recorder. Hide the instrument in some place where people talk — a teachers' lounge, for example, or an office smoking area, or a garage waiting room, or by a feed store cash register — and study the results carefully.

The results may surprise you. You'll discover that people seldom talk in a straight line, and that much of what they say is fragmentary, banal, and well-nigh meaningless. There'll be a lot of what's sometimes described as presymbolic utterance — words designed merely to evidence nonhostility and open contact on the "Nice day, isn't it?" and "What's new?" level: "Hey, Joe." "Yo, Mack." "Wife finally let you out?"

Men talk differently when there are no women present than when there are. So do women when there are no men. Teenagers hardly speak to each other in the same language they use around parents or other adults. Ditto for ethnics, drug addicts, doctors, soldiers — just about any group you can name. If you're presenting characters from such a category, they must speak with the flavor of their "in" patois. But beware long, unreadable passages of word-for-word phonetic transcription — such will tend to lose readers.

However intrigued with such you are, don't ever forget to assign your people individual tags of speech, special phrases and patterns and topics that help identify them for your readers. (Did I say topics? Yes. A character who never can forget the Mets or Dodgers or his beloved '66 Chevy is as clearly labeled as if he spoke Swahili.)

Listening to people, you'll encounter endless empty conversations — ". . . and then I said, and then he said" — that merely fill time. (This world is full of people who can't stand silence.)

All this helps you to grasp the flavor of speech. But beware of using it as more than spice when you write dialogue. So far as your story's concerned, it's "dead time" — waste space on the page that could be put to better advantage advancing your story.

Unless, that is, your object is to show how vapid and boring a particular character is. And even then, more than a little may prove too much. Putting readers to sleep is a cardinal sin!

On the other side of the coin, there are times in any story when you need what amounts to filler, in order to expand a moment of tension. Or perhaps you must provide your villain with some sort of cover to distract the hero while the bomb is planted or the files stolen, so you send in the villain's accomplice to hold the hero away from the action with chains of banality while the reader, who knows about the bomb or the robbery, is jumping up and down with panic-bred suspense.

Bear in mind, however, that the key to including empty words is to establish the time pressure and potentiality for disaster *before* you throw in meaningless, time-wasting dialogue that slows the hero.

Whatever the pattern you're trying to achieve, practice is your key to improvement. To learn to write good dialogue, write dialogue endlessly. Then commandeer friends to read it back into a tape recorder. Inevitably, no matter how you cringe at the result, the work will sharpen your lines.

What about the relation between story and dialogue?

Your story moves from one state of affairs and state of emotion to another state of affairs and state of emotion—in other words, from beginning to end. And from beginning to end it's a continuing process and reflection of change—specifically, the change of your character's state of mind and situation.

Each scene, each episode, must reflect this. It must play a role in effecting this change.

As an important component of said change, ever and always dialogue must advance the plot.

How do you make dialogue do this advancing? By having it give the reader information needed to understand what's happening.

In providing that information, most speeches should be designed to influence another character's attitude or behavior.

It also will help if this data comes in bits and pieces, rather than indigestible chunks:

"Where could she have gone?"

"The bar, probably."

"Thanks a lot. I doubt there's more than a hundred bars in town."

"Not on Denton Street."

"Denton Street! My God, she couldn't have gone there."

"It's Eddy's turf."

"Heimlich's too! And if he gets hold of her . . ."

"Oh, Lord, I read you! We've got to move."

"Like fast."

They hit the door running.

You understand, it would have been simple enough to say, "There are a lot of bars in town, but probably she's gone to one of the ones down on Denton Street. That's Eddy's turf. The only trouble is, Heimlich's moving in there too. And if he gets hold of her . . . well, we'd better move fast." But it wouldn't have been as effective. Short speeches, sentence fragments, broken phrases read faster and hold audience interest tighter most of the time.

It's vital, too, that in addition to conveying information, good dialogue should reveal and build emotion. It's not just weather talk, it's goal-oriented. The people who are talking want something: in the example above, to find the girl.

Further, finding her is important, and there's an implied time factor to drive the searchers.

You may even come to feel that it's not a bad idea to try, wherever possible, to center your dialogue around a character's efforts to accomplish something, change something. Then let the second character, to whom he's speaking, either agree or disagree, be set up to help or hinder.

If the second character agrees, hold down the bit. Why? Because dialogue of agreement is dull. If he disagrees, the passage probably calls for greater development because it reflects conflict, and conflict with its potentiality of failure for the first character evokes emotion.

Does this mean that dialogue must always center around action scenes? No. The issue is merely that, as mentioned before, most speeches should be designed to influence someone's attitude or behavior:

"It's a good job," he said. "I could go a million years and never get a better chance. Just because it means a move . . ."

"I know, John. Only . . ."

"Only—?"

"Mother."

"Stell, we can't tie our lives to her forever."

"But her home, her church, her friends. They mean so much to her. She'd be lost without them."

"Stell, we stay here with me in a dead-end job and our own lives are lost. Don't they count too?"

"Please, John. Can't we at least think it over?"

"All right, all right. We'll think it over."

Again, conflict. But a different kind of conflict. On a lower level at the moment, it paves the way for something more intense later on.

Note, too, how situation influences speech pattern. Urgent moments, bits loaded with action and tension, tend to be characterized by short words, short sentences, short speeches. An episode in which characters reflect, debate, try to decide what to do, or review past incidents, moves more slowly and draws forth longer, more thoughtful speeches.

So there you have it where dialogue's concerned: By the words your people say and the manner in which they say them, dialogue should characterize and individualize them, give information to advance the plot, reveal and build the emotion that galvanizes the story.

Beyond that, always strive for the *provocative* line. Hunt for at least occasional new, fresh, original ways for your characters to say whatever it is they have to say. In their proper places, slang, colorful analogies, personification, and the like can prove very effective.

How do you find the provocative line? Write whatever dull clichés come handy, then go back and rework. *Complex* may then become *as tangled up as a meatball in a can of spaghetti. Jumpy* is reworked to *jerking like a crawdad on a hook* or *wriggling like a barefoot boy on hot cement.*

Which is fine within limits. Just don't carry it so far that your readers label it as straining for effect.

Bear in mind also that only scientists and others trained to speak in facts do so. Others filter information through their emotional reactions. Most people think and talk more in terms of "great," "awful," "dumb"; "But Mother, everyone's doing it"; "I mean, it was the longest speech I ever heard"; "Hah, I wasn't scared, but he was *big*!" And ask any policeman how precise the drivers in a fender-bender are in their accounts of the accident!

Never forget as you write dialogue that the situation—the state of affairs, and the state of mind of your characters—is changing continually as your story progresses. Your story people's emotions are in flux. Their speeches should reflect this.

Try to keep reticence as common in dialogue as it is in life. Few of us will tell a woman how ugly she is save in a rage, nor lecture her husband on how badly brought up their children are. A well-bred man who flaunts his wealth shows poor taste, and so does a woman who brags about her promotion, or any of a hundred other deviations from propriety. Nor do we reveal intimate or embarrassing moments easily. Our pattern, if we're going to talk at all about such, is to divulge just a little, tentatively—wait for a reaction—then tell a little more.

Bad taste, bad manners, and rudeness have their place, however. Given the right character and situation, they may come through with truly shocking shock value.

Where do you use dialogue? In general, you may find it most effective when it reflects a certain tension, great or small, in at least one character. Thus, he's likely to resort to speech to break the ice when he meets someone new or feels nervous in a social situation. When he has a goal, wants something, or seeks to win information, dialogue is a device to help him get it. In moments of crisis he may lose control and lash out at opponents or bystanders.

Just *don't* use dialogue merely to fill space or substitute for thinking through your plot!

How much of it should you include?

That depends on your story, of course. But remember the value of white space and broken pages in helping to catch reader attention.

And don't be tempted to try for the story told 100 percent in dialogue or totally without it. They're literary stunts and not worth your time.

How do you make the speeches in a dialogue episode hang together? In general, the trick is to let each one acknowledge the one ahead of it.

Sometimes, the first speech may be a question, the second an answer:
"Where did you go?"
"Oh, downtown and around."

Sometimes the linkage is a repetition:
"I'm sorry, but I simply haven't got the money."
"You haven't got the money? What happened to it?"

An "empty" word or phrase may serve as a bridge:

"I hate to make a move this way."

"I know, I know. But there's Edna's sister to consider."

An action often may take the place of words in any conversation:

"Sarah, I simply can't understand you."

Sarah turned away as if Cecile hadn't even spoken. In wordless silence she looked out across the hills, the harbor.

There are all sorts of continuity devices such as these. Simply check the dialogue passages in any book or magazine till you become familiar with them, then practice using them in your own work. Soon they'll become second nature to you.

Remember, too, that silence can be golden, as in the case of Sarah, above, if someone doesn't want to discuss a matter further. And if you still want to introduce the information that the character walked away from, you can always have another person hazard a guess as to what the character thought or felt.

Finally, when it dawns on you that a dialogue sequence has bogged down, don't despair. Length quite possibly is the issue. Go back over the passage again and cut, condense, intensify, tighten. Believe me, another day will prove it was worth the effort.

Five Ways to Strengthen Fiction With Dialogue

by Loren D. Estleman

Pick up any three novels on this month's bestseller rack and you will find they have one thing in common: the characters talk to each other. A lot. This is because the authors know that dialogue should be approached not as a problem but as an opportunity, and should be put to work. They recognize the form's five strengths and have learned to take advantage of each as a key to sales. They are as follows:

Dialogue presents information succinctly. With this in mind, the writer can scrap paragraphs of exposition and establish essential information quickly and painlessly while making his characters live. Consider this exchange between the hero and a gun shop proprietor from one of my westerns, *Murdock's Law*:

"What's you business?"

"Page Murdock. I wired you last week from Helena looking for a Deane-Adams. You said you had one."

"Hell of a long ride just for a gun."

"I was coming anyway."

His eyes narrowed. "You some kind of law?"

"Does it show?"

"You could be on one side or the other, from the look of you. In this business I see my share of both."

"Maybe you've seen Chris Shedwell lately," I said. "My boss got a report he's on his way here. He's wanted for a mail train robbery near Wichita ten years ago."

Here, in scarcely more than a dozen typewritten lines, I have explained who and what my hero is and why he is there, and I have set the scene for the book's central conflict. Without this passage, I might have clogged three pages with dull background. Note how each line advances the action. Never lose sight of the reason for this kind of exchange in the first place, which is to bring certain information to light. Don't wander.

Dialogue brings immediacy to the prose. After thirty years of live, on-the-spot television broadcasting, audiences are no longer content to be told what happened. They want to feel as if they are part of the action. I went for that "You are there" effect in this scene from "The Used," a short story that appeared in *Alfred Hitchcock's Mystery Magazine*. Charlie Murch, on the run from the Mob, has gone to his friend Bart Morgan looking for a getaway stake:

Murch said, "I need money, Bart."

"I figured that." Morgan's eyes dropped to the table. "You caught me short, Charlie. I got bit hard on the last three at the Downs Saturday."

"I don't need much, just enough to get out of the city."

"I'm strapped. I wish to hell I wasn't but I am." He removed a quarter from one stack and placed it atop another. "You know I'd do it if I could but I can't."

Murch seized his wrist gently. "You owe me, Bart. If I didn't lend you four big ones when the Dodgers took the Series, you'd be part of an off-ramp somewhere by now."

The "now" feeling is achieved by the characters' simple statements and by a minimal use of narrative. The actions that are described—moving a coin, seizing a wrist—meaningless in themselves, assume importance because of the conflict inherent in the dialogue. Murch's desperation and Morgan's uneasy reluctance are experienced firsthand. Simplicity is the operative word.

Dialogue is informal. For better or worse, the average person hears far more than he reads, and what he hears in everyday conversation is rarely phrased as eloquently as written narrative. Good dialogue pleases him because it's not above kicking off its shoes and getting familiar without being hindered by the rules of usage. It creates an illusion of real speech, while turning its inadequacies into assets. In *The Midnight Man*, I capitalized on one such imperfection during a tense encounter between my private eye and his female client:

"It looks as if I hired the wrong man," she said stiffly. "Perhaps I should have gone to this Bassett person."

"In the first place," I sighed, "you hired me because the price was right. In the second place, Bassett's not the kind of man anyone hires, and in the third place, you came to me in the first place."

I had an English professor in college who would have boiled me in oil for echoing like that, but the effect is genuine without sacrificing clarity. Furthermore, you can't help but *like* Walker for his ability to get his point across so forcefully whilst thumbing his nose so blatantly at the Queen's English. Shatter the rules if they get in the way, but above all make yourself understood.

Dialogue provides a change of pace—in most fiction, anyway. Some writers use it to tell most or all of their story, but to me this is as artificial as using all narrative and no dialogue. No one talks *all* the time. Often, I will insert a scrap of dialogue between long descriptive passages just to kick the reader out of his stupor, as in this from another of my private eye novels, *Motor City Blues*:

It was one of those places where you had to tip the guy at the counter fifty cents before he'd let you in. In this case he was a bony young black seated on a high stool behind a display of latex breasts and plastic phalluses. He had an afro you could lose a shoe in and invisible eyes behind mirrored glasses and needle tracks all over his mahogany wrist where it stuck out of his cuff as he reached for my two quarters.

"Cold out there," I ventured.

"So's the world, man."

Like a pitcher's change-up, the brief colloquy induces alertness. Also, in just two lines I have managed to say something about the man on the stool that might otherwise require at least a paragraph. Which brings me to:

Dialogue creates character. This is as noble a reason for existing as any device can claim. Examples of how a character's speech reveals his inner workings have appeared in each of the passages I have quoted. The suspicious gun-shop owner in *Murdock's Law*, nervous Charlie Murch in "The Used," the brash detective in *The Midnight Man*, the grim vest-pocket philosopher in *Motor City Blues*—you learned something about all of them without having to be told. Introspection, that word-eating process by which the writer explains his creations to the reader, is far less popular than it was in Charles Dickens's day. Partly, this is because it consumes too much time in this hectic age, but it is also unrealistic, as no man may read another's thoughts or know him as he knows himself. Since dialogue is the means we most often choose to express ourselves, it is the means most readily accepted by readers.

Hearing Aids

When used as an instrument instead of decoration, dialogue can be the most important item in the writer's kit. But like all instruments, its use requires knowledge and skill. To the writer who would develop an ear for dialogue I suggest five steps:

• *Write plays.* Even if you never try to sell them, the emphasis on verbal interaction between characters forces you to exercise speech usage. Best of all, you will learn to draft only lines that will advance the action. All else is dross, and lean, muscular language skills will result.

• *Listen to people.* Much can be learned about an individual by his conversation. Listen for favorite idioms of speech—the manner in which (for example) someone born in Germany constructs sentences as opposed to how a lifelong resident of the Bronx does the same—the conflicting verbal patterns of the young and the aged, etc.

• *Read a lot of dialogue.* Choose a writer or type of writing that interests you and see how the experts do it. American crime and mystery writers seem to have established a patent in this area. Raymond Chandler started it with the salty repartee that makes his Philip Marlowe series crackle. Gregory McDonald's *Fletch* books are highly recommended for their deft use of brittle conversation to advance the plot, as is anything by George V. Higgins, who seems to get by on almost no narrative at all.

• *Read your dialogue aloud.* Awkward phraseology, longwindedness and unrealistic structure come to the fore when read aloud, and they demand fixing. Having someone read for you is also effective, but beware: Very good readers can make bad writing sound better than it is.

• *Relax.* Good dialogue is delicate, and tends to collapse when leaned on too heavily. If you're fatigued or concentrating too hard on the deft phrase, the snappy comeback, your results will sour. Tackle it fresh, and once it starts flowing—and it will, if you have followed at least two of the previous steps—don't tamper with it. You can do up the seams later.

Develop an ear for dialogue as a musician develops an ear for rhythm and tone. Once you have learned to make its five strengths work for you, your fiction will live. And sell.

Setting Your Novel Straight

by Helen Haukeness

When I worked as a first reader at Avon Books, I picked up each new manuscript eagerly, hoping that *this* one would achieve that indefinable sense of vitality that makes a successful novel. Frequently I found memorable characters, an engaging plot. But too many books, particularly first novels, missed the third member of that basic triumvirate: setting.

A simplistic definition of setting is a backdrop against which your characters perform. A sense of *place*, and all that it suggests, is essential to a novel. A successful novelist calls into play every aspect of environment. A lack of visual scene will leave your characters and their interactions suspended in limbo; but setting also denotes time, establishes mood, and provides that necessary component — atmosphere. Atmosphere, in fact, often assumes as much importance as character and plot. Would Davis Grubb's novel, *The Night of the Hunter*, give us the same shiver of horror if it were set in a sleepy midwestern town rather than a remote, dark, forested area? I doubt it.

Setting doesn't imply paragraphs of flat description, or assertions, say, about the mood of a place. The background of your novel must be interwoven with your characters and what they are doing at any given time. Each element, in fact, should enhance the other two, and all three should be as tightly meshed as the finest Irish lace. It's no accident that the phrase "spinning a yarn" found its way into our language — a good storyteller twists all the fibers of his tale together into a whole that is stronger than the sum of its parts.

Oddly, some writers who know the importance of plot and character overlook the significance of setting. But even those who do pay attention to it sometimes have difficulty weaving in just the right backdrop for characters in action. Here are a few frequently encountered problems, and ways in which they can be rectified.

Failure to Understand the *Depth* of a Setting

A story's setting comprises more than buildings and roads and flora and mountains in the background. Setting involves an entire environment: furniture, weather, people, tools, toys, clutter, lighting, odors. In a word, *details*. The ambiance you seek to create comes from carefully selecting telling detail. All in all, the word to keep in mind is *specificity*.

Realism is not a representational photograph, although it has representational elements. A novel is designed to have a certain effect on the reader, and the novelist's job is to elicit the desired response by selecting and rearranging aspects of reality. Segments of *real* experience are intensified, isolated, arranged in a pattern unlike that of life, so that the reader is given a new, plausible experience.

I'll discuss these points more specifically throughout this article.

Using Stereotyped Descriptions

If you haven't traveled widely, if you feel the life you know is a circumscribed one, don't let it worry you. All small towns are not alike, nor are all city blocks. A rather ordinary environment, seen through observant eyes and put down by a creative mind, can take on a vitality that gives a novel life and breath. Furthermore, what seems commonplace to you may well be unusual to most of your readers.

All of us have specialized knowledge of *something*. There's plenty of atmosphere to be found almost anywhere. Have you ever worked in a science lab? Bred racehorses? Even if you married young and had four children in rapid succession, perhaps you collect ceramic elephants or maintain a passionate interest in boating. Dig deep. Keep a notebook or file folder of brief descriptions, observations and evocative images, even if what you jot down can't be utilized in your current project. Later, when searching for a bit of life-giving detail, a few minutes browsing through your notes may present you with exactly what you need. Even if your notes go forever unused, you will at least get into the habit of listening and observing.

Setting an entire novel in a locale you have never visited can be risky, though skillful authors have done it with great success. For single scenes, you can research, look at pictures, *imagine*. The Tolkien trilogy is a good example of a fantasy world — and let's not forget *Gulliver's Travels*. Obviously, historical novels wouldn't exist at all if authors were too timid to summon up a life they had never experienced. However, even here your mind should be put to work to come up with specifics, to provide the necessary sense of place.

(Be wary, though, of using backgrounds that have been overdone. I've had my fill of novels set in academia, thank you, and as for hospitals, television seems to have sapped the drama inherent there.)

Failure to Use Words as Symbols of Atmosphere and Mood

Make the sentences in your narrative do double, even triple duty. A room, for example, can evoke both mood and atmosphere by the deft use of detail. Using the detail to suggest something more than appearance is sometimes overlooked.

F. Scott Fitzgerald was a master in the use of symbol. In the first chapter of *The Great Gatsby*, we not only are shown the Buchanan's mansion in East Egg, but also are subtly immersed in the affluence and excitement of the twenties — in other words, the *atmosphere*.

Note how magnificently Fitzgerald uses color to signal affluence: "red-and-white Georgian Colonial mansion whose windows reflected gold." Inside the mansion, the living room is a "rosy-colored space" with "gleaming windows."

The rug is "wine-colored." A few pages later: "Inside, the crimson room bloomed with light." Rosy hues and the gleam of gold — unmistakable symbols of wealth and fortune.

Take a close look, too, at how Fitzgerald builds excitement and restlessness throughout the chapter. The two young women's dresses are "rippling and fluttering." Daisy is "winking ferociously toward the fervent sun." Later, as Nick Carraway stands alone on the lawn, we are told, "The wind had blown off, leaving a loud, bright night. . . ." Nothing passive here. Fitzgerald's portrayal of *motion* — rippling, fluttering . . . wind blowing — gives the scene's mood: turbulent emotions, promising cataclysmic events to come.

Often, Fitzgerald brings the elements of affluence and excitement together in a single sentence: "The two young women preceded us out onto a rosy-colored porch, open toward the sunset, where four candles flickered on the table in the diminished wind." This isn't a photographic scene; it vibrates with life.

A note of caution: Don't use, for the sake of evocation, symbols that jump away from the narrative, no matter how apt you think they may be. They may well be apt, but they may also jar. Your reader is intelligent; there's no need to use a cudgel.

Failure to Evoke *All* the Senses in Descriptions of Setting

A setting is sometimes thought of as a kind of picture we see in our minds. True enough. But the visual image is only part of the material we have at our disposal to create a sense of place. There are sounds that can be evoked, smells we can be reminded of. References to taste can make us recall similar gustatory experiences. Nudging all the reader's senses can make the difference between a black-and-white still life and theatre-in-the-round.

Most of us would rather attend a dinner party than listen to a blow-by-blow account of the event after it has occurred. In this passage from James Joyce's *The Dead*, note how the sounds and tastes, as well as the visual images, make us feel that we are sitting right at the table as the aunt's dinner party draws to a close.

> Gabriel having finished, the huge pudding was transferred to the table. The clatter of forks and spoons began again. Gabriel's wife served out spoonfuls of the pudding then passed the plates down the table. Midway down they were held up by Mary Jane, who replenished them with raspberry or orange jelly or with blancmange and jam. The pudding was of Aunt Julia's making and she received praise for it from all quarters. She herself said it was not quite good enough.

Joyce also allows Aunt Julia to reveal her diffident pride without interference from the author.

I've known some fine authors who go through later drafts of their work to insert phrases that evoke all the senses in passages where such evocation is missing. If you're the kind of writer who simply gets the story on paper as quickly as possible in the first draft, indulge yourself in this most creative stage; critical appraisal can come later, when you may decide to add sensual images here and there. But temper your additions: A hint is more effective than overkill. Remember the psychological truism that to entice anyone, make the person want more, not less.

Failure to Write Scenes Through the Character's Eyes

To paraphrase Dickens: When you have created people you're going to write about, it is their business to play out the play, and not yours. A character's perception of his setting can convey a state of mind far more sharply than any assertion by the author. Look at this passage from Nathanael West's *Miss Lonelyhearts*:

> Suddenly tired, he sat down on a bench. If he could only throw the stone. He searched the sky for a target. But the gray sky looked as if it had been rubbed with a soiled eraser. It held no angels, flaming crosses, olive-bearing doves, wheels within wheels. Only a newspaper struggled in the air like a kite with a broken spine. He got up and started again for the speakeasy.

Gray sky rubbed with a soiled eraser . . . a kite with a broken spine. These images elicit our empathy with Miss Lonelyhearts's mood much more effectively than if West had simply told us that Miss Lonelyhearts was tired and depressed as he walked to the speakeasy.

Failure to Change Setting Throughout an Entire Novel

Major characters must show many facets, and something must change in their lives to bring your novel to a satisfactory resolution. A good novel avoids monotony by changes of pace and of mood—and of setting. Move around a little—give your readers a glimpse of color on a rainy day, a breath of fresh air when they've been in the house for too long. Contrast in setting not only sharpens your main focus, but also adds interest similar to that of conflicting emotions within a character.

Some authors rarely use the same setting in two consecutive chapters. Gail Godwin opens her novel *Glass People* in a starkly modern California apartment, the sterility of which reflects Francesca's lifeless marriage. Chapter two flashes back to Francesca's life before her marriage on the other side of the continent, where she and her mother led a sumptuous life of parties, travel and spending, spending, spending. Chapters three (a short one) and four take us back to the California apartment. Chapter five leaps ahead to an airport hotel room where we discover Francesca and her new lover. Chapter six finds Francesca in a simple mountainside dwelling, with Francesca's mother urging her to buy vitamin pills instead of jewels—a sharp contrast to the world of fashionable clothing, exotic skin creams, and expensive restaurants we found them sharing earlier. Here, the physical setting is rustic and earthy, with a landscape allowed to grow wild and a vegetable garden growing produce to enhance physical well-being rather than titillate over-refined appetites. The story line threads the scenes together, and the contrast in scene whets our appetite to read on.

Using Fictionalized Geographic Names That Don't Sound Authentic

Readers want to glimpse a "real" (albeit illusory) world; you would do well to avoid names like "Centerville High," which bring to mind a prototype rather than a specific locale. (No doubt there are towns called Centerville, but thousands of other names are much more interestingly imaginative.) If you worry about choosing the name of an existing place, for the sake of your own or others' anonymity, consult your atlas and mix and match—that is, take a town or a city with a name that appeals to you and set it down in a different state: when writing about a metropolis, that problem often doesn't occur, and actual city names are used because the characteristic flavor of a particular city is essential to the novel's life. Can you imagine Nelson Algren's *The Man With the Golden Arm* set anywhere but in Chicago? Or Henry James's *Washington Square* set in Colorado?

Isolating Descriptions From the Narrative Line

Let the background of your novel come to life through your characters' thoughts, dialogue and actions. No matter how beautifully you describe a room, a season, a day, or whatever, your reader is apt to skip over it in order to pick up the thread of the narrative—thereby losing, of course, much that is essential to your story. (A playwright once told me, "You can risk three minutes without advancing the play's climax; more than that, and you've lost your audience." I doubt most novelists can risk as many as three paragraphs.) Consider, for instance, this passage:

> Castle pushed his bicycle up King's Road. He had bought his house with the help of a building society after his return to England. It was similar to the houses on either side of him, set row upon row in a middle-class neighborhood. Even the rather gaudy stained glass of the Laughing Cavalier over the door was repeated in his neighbors' houses—at times it reminded him of the stained glass in doors opening into provincial dentists' offices.

All right, we do glimpse the street on which Castle lives, and even learn something about Castle's tastes. But how much more is told the way it was actually written by Graham Greene in *The Human Factor*:

> Castle pushed his bicycle up King's Road. He had bought his house with the help of a building society after his return to England. He could easily have saved money by paying cash, but he had no wish to appear

different from the schoolmasters on either side—on the salary they earned there was no possibility of saving. For the same reason he kept the rather gaudy stained glass of the Laughing Cavalier over the front door. He disliked it; he associated it with dentistry—so often stained glass in provincial towns hides the agony of the chair from outsiders— but again because his neighbors bore with theirs, he preferred to leave it alone.

In a single paragraph, Greene gives us three pieces of vital information. We learn the economic and social level of Castle's neighborhood; we briefly glimpse the exterior of his house; and—most important, in terms of plot—we see the extent to which Castle does not wish to appear different from his neighbors (although he could afford more, he will live with something he dislikes rather than draw attention to himself). The latter point, which Greene underscores in different ways, is essential to understanding the character (and therefore, the actions) of Castle, the novel's major figure—and we discover that point through a few sentences about Castle's house. Plot, character and setting are skillfully meshed.

And that's what spinning a yarn is all about.

The Question at the Core of Your Story

by Ronald B. Tobias

L et's consider the Egyptian architect who first thought of the idea of the true pyramid, and equate the process of building the Great Pyramid of Khufu with the equally difficult task of constructing a good story.

First, an *idea*. But ideas are like the wind; they have force, they have energy, but they rarely have much shape. The architect knew he wanted to build something on a grand scale, something that had never been done before (or since), something that would last forever. A tomb for his pharaoh. Something first-rate, something that would wow the world.

Second, an *audience*. He was building for his pharaoh, and if he couldn't convince him, then he might as well go home. He had to know his audience, he had to know how to surprise and intrigue him, so he developed a *strategy*.

"Listen, Khufu, when the day comes for you to die (may the gods forbid), you want to be *ready*. You want your cousins in heaven to know you've *arrived*. You want them to know you were the greatest king Egypt ever had. Impress the gods. Impress *everyone*."

"How?" asked Khufu.

The architect knew then he had hooked the pharaoh. But he hadn't landed him yet. "With this," he whipped out a sketch of the pyramid and showed it to him.

"Impossible." Khufu shook his head. "It can't be done."

"Yes, it can," tantalized the architect.

"How?"

Now the architect really had the pharaoh's attention. "I'll show you how," he promised, as he laid out the drawings in front of Khufu.

"How are you going to build this?" Khufu wasn't one to give in easily.

The architect explained each phase of construction. "First we quarry about six million tons of stone . . . ."

"What do you mean, *we*?" demanded the king.

"Not you and me," clarified the architect. "We put to work all the people hanging around in the off-season between crops, let them do it."

And so it went. From idea to strategy to sketch (the structure) to working drawings (the plot) to construction plan (the action) to manpower (the characters).

Then came the difficult question: *Why*?

The question of *why*? is at the core of every story. Why are you telling this story? What's the point? The question of *why*? separates the physical act of construction from the philosophical reason for doing it. It moves us into a completely different and much more subtle (but just as difficult) realm.

Why? isn't just icing on the cake. Nor is it something you figure out after it's done. The nameless Egyptian architect who told the pharaoh Khufu why the king needed such a grand tomb ("You want your cousins in heaven to know you've *arrived*.") wasn't really giving the king the real *why?* of such a massive undertaking. He was only making an argument he thought would sway the pharaoh. The real *why?* is much more profound than a simple appeal to one man's vanity. It has to do with a spectacular convergence of culture and science, combining elegant expressions of religion, philosophy, sociology, mathematics, architecture and manual artistry into a single object that represents boldly the vision and strength of its builders. So strong is that expression of idea that to this day it still grips our imagination. The pyramid is an impossible feat made possible, and it survives, only slightly battered by history, as a monument to a king and a testament to a people.

The Egyptian architect could have answered truthfully, when he was asked *why?*, that he wanted to build the Great Pyramid because he saw it as the crowning achievement of Egypt, persuasive testimony for future generations that this was a great nation.

And how do you make that testimony? By heaping together six million rocks in the middle of the desert? No, of course not. You make it by the elegance and the precision of its statement.

The builders knew from Rock One what they wanted to say and how they wanted to say it. But the architects already had a thousand years of pyramid building behind them: this was hardly a new invention. It was a refinement of an old idea.

Writing is a tradition thousands of years old also, but any similarity between pyramid construction and writing ends there. We enter our works much less absolutely and less certainly than the architect enters his. Our ideas are subject to change. They grow; they wither; they change from one state into another, from a catepillar into . . . what? A Viceroy butterfly? A death's-head moth? An ugly black beetle? Words are not rocks, and neither are ideas.

How then can you control the ideas in your work? How can you give them shape and direction so they don't run all over the place like ants in panic? How do you focus a process as slippery as writing so that the ideas mesh, so they unite like the stones of the pyramid, into an elegant and precise whole?

We're back at *why?* Why am I doing this? One motive: to get rich and become famous. Another motive: to write a work of literature that will keep people marveling for decades. Two entirely different motives, each of which will affect what you write and how you write it. Well, you say, why can't I have both? Fine, that too will affect what you write and how you write it. Any motive will.

Examine your motives. Be honest with yourself. Decide which road you want to travel. Answer the question *why?* Your answer will help you decide how to develop the pattern of thought in your work, which is *theme*. Up to this point we are like the architect who has concentrated only on the technical problems of construction. The time must come—and it should come early in your work—when the aesthetic side of the work must express itself. Writers who ignore the *why?* either end up with a garbled version of the answer or no answer at all.

The word *theme* makes people nervous. Maybe it's because most of us have bad memories about the themes we had to write in high school. (Remember your teacher handing out assignments? "Write a five-hundred-word theme about your most embarrassing moment.") The theme I'm talking about isn't the theme the teacher was talking about.

We should begin with a kind of working definition in order to clear up the air about what theme is and how it works. Theme, for our purposes here anyway, is the *central concern* around which a story is structured. Sometimes you hear that theme is the "message" of the story, the point, the central idea, or the statement of the story, but that's too confining and doesn't always work.

Theme is your inertial guidance system. It directs your decisions about which path to take, which choice is right for the story and which choice isn't. As we write, we only start to understand the actual meaning of the work, but with theme, we actually structure the work on a *concept* that guides us from the start.

Theme shouldn't be some fuzzy, in-the-back-of-your-mind idea, but a viable, working pattern. There are several types of patterns into which all works fall; choosing the theme that best suits the story you want to tell will help you express your idea clearly.

The idea of theme comes from what we may call priority of technique. Almost every work contains the major elements of storytelling: plot, character, style, idea and mood, or emotional effect. These five elements do not always have the same priority in the work. Sometimes plot is more important than character, and sometimes character is more important than plot. Any one of the five elements of plot, character, mood, style, or idea can dominate the others. The element that does dominate the work is said to be the work's *theme*.

Let's examine each major pattern of theme more closely.

Plot As Theme: Goldfinger Meets Miss Marple

We are action junkies. We like to have things happen, and we like for them to happen fast and furiously. We like to escape the humdrum pattern of everyday life. So a lot of us read books to escape the drabness of our workaday world. The theme of escapist literature is just that: escape. We can, on the turning of a page, go on the hunt, join the chase, stalk the prey. These works aren't serious works of literature, and they aren't meant to be.

In these works everything, including character, becomes secondary to action and plot, all of which moves to the final outcome, *the grand finale*.

The pattern is typical of everything from the James "007" Bond novels to the Conan series. Even stylist Agatha Christie novels fall into this pattern of theme.

Because such little premium is placed on people or ideas, we categorize these works as popular literature. The author makes no serious attempt at social comment, no real delving into the human condition. Outside the context of the story, the people and events have little meaning in our own lives. However much we enjoy these works and look forward to the next one, their effect is momentary. We read, we enjoy, we forget, and we read another one.

Obviously these books comprise a big chunk of the commercial market. Success for some is measured on the bestseller list; these books make money—a lot of money. Ripping yarns have always held us hypnotized from the days of fireside storytellers to the computerized book clubs. They have an important place in the spectrum of literature, but success depends on understanding the basic function of the work: to allow readers to escape into a world they ordinarily would never otherwise know.

Effect As Theme: *Friday the Thirteenth, Part XXII*

Another very large section of the commercial market belongs to the effect category. The main focus of the pattern changes from events to emotional effect. Certain types of books and films strive primarily for a certain emotional effect that the reader or viewer expects to experience in the work. That effect may be terror (as in the case of any Stephen King or John Carpenter work), suspense (as in the case of the works of Robert Ludlum, Robin Cook, or Alfred Hitchcock), love and romance (as in the case of any Harlequin or Silhouette novel), or comedy.

Comedy has never done as well in literature as it has in film. We expect humorists from Charlie Chaplin to Mel Brooks to be funny and so we look forward to their works as such. If they try to step out of character we tend to be very intolerant. Charlie Chaplin once made a movie in which he played a serial killer (*Monsieur Verdoux*), and audiences couldn't deal with their sweet Charlie playing a serious dramatic role as a man who marries women for their money and then murders them. The film, actually one of Chaplin's better ones, was a box-office flop, and to this day is still obscure.

Look at the problem Woody Allen had, converting from his early silly films (*Sleeper, Bananas, Everything You Wanted to Know About Sex but Were Afraid to Ask*) to his later serious films (*Manhattan, Interiors, Hannah and Her Sisters*). We resisted the change because we want Chaplin and Allen and Stephen King to write what we expect of them. We want them to make us laugh or to scare us the same way they did in the past.

If you choose *effect* as your theme, then concentrate on that effect in your work. Study your successful rivals and see how they did it. It is also possible to combine more than one effect in a work. No doubt by now you've heard the word *dramedy*—Hollywood's buzzword for stories that are half drama and half comedy, in films such as *Silver Streak* and *Midnight Run*.

Combining effects has its dangers. One shouldn't work at the expense of the other. Note the way horror and comedy were mixed in *An American Werewolf in London*. It shocks *and* it makes us laugh, all in the right places. It's a precarious balance, because the audience could end up laughing where it was supposed to be frightened, and that's a death blow to any work. John Irving combines drama and comedy effectively in *The World According to Garp*. As in Plot As Theme, make sure you understand the expectations of your audience before you write your story.

Style As Theme: Poetry in Motion

This category departs sharply from the mainstream commercial market and focuses on a small minority of books in which the author's *style* becomes the focus of the work. The work may still include all the basic elements of good storytelling, but plot, character and action take a backseat to this expression of style.

Of course every novel has its own style, but in this case the style of the piece has such a profound effect that everything else is seen through it. It acts as a colored lens through which everything is shot.

The bulk of American readers and moviegoers have limited patience when it comes to tolerating such an elevated artistic technique. John Hawkes, considered by many to be one of the best living authors in the United States today, has been writing for forty years and is virtually unknown in this country except in universities and by other writers. In France, however, where style is appreciated by a larger segment of the general public, Hawkes is very popular. Books like *The Lime Twig* and *Second Skin* are the perfection of individualized style over stock-in-trade elements of plot and character.

Character As Theme: The Making of Mr. and Mrs. Right

Literature is full of books about people. When a work concentrates on a person (or persons) so that he or she (or they) become the center of plot and action, then the theme of the work is *character*. *David Copperfield*, *Madame Bovary* and *Anna Karenina* are just a few examples. (Just look in your library for books with people's names in the titles.)

We are fascinated by other *people*. Nonfiction biographies have always sold well, and so do fiction books and films about unique people who capture our imagination. These works delve into the core of character, into an examination of the human spirit. The character is at once the plot and the action.

Writing about people (as the theme) is richly rewarding. As opposed to Plot As Theme and Effect As Theme, which don't ordinarily lend themselves to serious literary treatment (but do offer larger audiences), this theme pattern manages to combine both if you wish.

The perfect example in American literature, said to be "The Great American Novel" (the one we always hoped to write, right?) is *The Adventures of*

Huckleberry Finn. Part of the reason for its success is that Twain, the consummate storyteller, combined penetrating characterization with serious literary treatment.

We are often told that if a book is literary it won't sell, and if it does sell it's not literary. If there is any truth to that statement (and there is some), the problem lies more with the author's belief that it's true than with any actual truth of the matter. It's certainly more true of Plot As Theme, but less true of Character As Theme. A book worth reading that was a huge international bestseller, which has the character of several generations of a family as its theme, is Gabriel Garcia Marquez' *One Hundred Years of Solitude*. Garcia Marquez went on to win the Nobel Prize for literature; proof that you *can* both write and sell well.

The earlier theme patterns we've discussed are more limiting than Character As Theme, which opens up all kinds of possibilities in the full range of writing.

Idea As Theme: It's the Thought That Counts

Of the other four theme patterns, none succeeds as well as the *idea* pattern in creating events and characters of significance that reach far beyond the words printed on the page. These are the works that affect us profoundly, make us think, perhaps even change our lives. Over history, works from this category have been the ones to change the world: start and stop wars, cause revolution and incite riots, expose cruelty, abuse and stupidity in government, in the marketplace, and in the privacy of our homes. They are found on the shelves of every library and bookstore, including the children's sections. We flourish on ideas, new and old. They make us reach beyond our grasp.

A book like *Robinson Crusoe*, for example, is a book of ideas. Because of the title you might think that the character of the shipwrecked sailor was the theme of the novel, but *Robinson Crusoe* is more about ideas than it is about a person who gets stranded on an island. The same is true of *Don Quixote*.

(It is worth pointing out here that film adaptations of novels—including *Robinson Crusoe* and *Don Quixote*—routinely alter the theme of the original work for the screen. While the plot pattern remains the same, and the characters more or less stay the same, the theme pattern often shifts from the more difficult and less cinematic Idea As Theme to the easier and more exciting Plot As Theme. This is the reason why so many people who have read the book are disappointed with the movie version: the ideas have been wrung out of the original.)

Ideas can take many different forms as they shape the thematic content of your work. The list that follows includes only the major themes, all of which you will recognize. These ideas can't always be expressed in a single word or a sentence. They are often complicated concepts that affect characters and plot on a continuing and changing basis throughout your work.

In *Billy Budd*, for instance, whose theme falls under this category, there are two common interpretations of the work, *and they are at complete odds with each other*. Some readers believe the story is about the cruelty of the system (the British navy, society in general) that will slaughter innocence (represented by the character of Billy) in order to protect itself. It's a cynical view, but one that can be argued powerfully.

On the other hand, someone not quite as cynical could come back with an argument just as powerful—that in order for a system to survive (we're back to talking about society) it must make rules to protect itself, and in the long run it is best for all, even if, from time to time, a person gets caught in the cracks and is sacrificed by the system to make it work. This is the cost of civilization, and perhaps this is closest to what Captain Vere himself believed.

Is the cost too expensive? Some will say yes and others will say no. Which is the correct interpretation for the story, the first or the second version? Or maybe there's a third way or even a fourth way of looking at the story. What did Melville think? Does it really matter?

No, it doesn't. *Billy Budd* contains ideas, and the whole point of ideas is to think about them, discuss them, and reach our own conclusions. As an author, you can't force your audience to think a certain way, but you can make your audience think *about* your ideas.

Here are the major categories into which most Ideas As Theme fall:

• **The moral statement.** Any work that spends the major part of its energy to persuade us to accept a certain moral principle would fall under this category.

The danger here is that too many writers love to get on a soapbox and preach. They'll do anything to wax philosophical and talk about the meaning of good and evil in the universe. They use the fiction as an excuse to tell the world what they think. Their characters never come to life, and their plots are flat and unconvincing.

These writers ought not to be writing fiction. If they feel so strongly about their ideas and want to put them to paper, they should write nonfiction, which is much more suited to sermonizing.

Of course there is nothing wrong with sermonizing in either fiction or nonfiction. The problem is that in the case of fiction the author methodically promotes a point of view at the cost of storytelling; this is the definition of propaganda.

But if the plot is gripping and the characters believable and sincere, and if you're interested in telling a story (as opposed to using fiction simply as a format for your ideas), then the *moral* of the story should hit home. But the writer must be more interested in the characters than in the moral message itself. The ideas and the morals must be the *result* of the story. In propaganda, the story and the character are the result of the idea. They become a means rather than what they should be: an end in themselves.

• **Human dignity.** Suppose you were a bit odd. Not dangerous, not crazy, at least not in the clinical sense, just offbeat. You don't fit comfortably into the role of a John or Jane Doe. And suppose you suddenly find yourself locked in a mental ward so your behavior can be "observed." Around you are some of the truly sick, mentally unbalanced people who cannot cope with the real world. And suppose still that the nurse in charge of your ward is intent on making you conform—perhaps the word should be *submit* rather than *conform*—to her tyrannical system of care?

An absolute nightmare. Ken Kesey wrote the book, *One Flew Over the Cuckoo's Nest*, a powerful and harrowing story of one man's fight for dignity and the right to be who he was in the face of a system that set out to destroy him.

The struggle for *human dignity* is one of humankind's basic conflicts, one that we think and write about a lot. We have a base, animal side to us: brutal, selfish and powerful. We also have a higher spiritual side: caring, giving and intelligent. Works in this category explore both sides, and costs of both. Usually the central characters, like McMurphy in *One Flew Over the Cuckoo's Nest*, are put at a disadvantage and have to struggle for their right to be what they want to be.

The struggle may be external, as in McMurphy's fight against dehumanization in the institution, which is usually a metaphor for society as a whole. Or the struggle may be internal, as in a character who recognizes his or her own weaknesses as a human being and has to confront those demons that live inside. Anyone who's ever seen Marlon Brando play the down-and-out boxer Terry Malloy in *On the Waterfront* will never forget his speech, "I coulda had class . . . I coulda been a contender . . . I coulda been *somebody*!"

● **Social comment.** We live in a huge kettle of people. Our society, however much we're attached to it, has its problems, and writers like to address these problems in the hopes we will pay attention to them and perhaps even do something to make this a better world. American literature has many great examples, among them novels like *The Grapes of Wrath*, *Elmer Gantry* and *The Octopus*.

As with the Moral Statement, writers get tempted by the urge to preach when it comes to talking about the ills of society. The golden rule of writing, *show, don't tell*, is never more true than here.

There is a famous story about a French Impressionist painter and a famous French Symbolist poet that underscores the problem writers have when the idea becomes more important than the story. The Painter and the Poet were in a cafe arguing:

"You writers have it easy," scoffed the Painter. "All you need is a few good ideas and a pen." He waved his hand in a wide arc as if to dismiss the Poet. "Now, *painting* is hard. Every brushstroke is one-of-a-kind, not like words—they're always the same."

"If it's so easy, why don't you write some poems?" challenged the Poet.

"All right, I will." The Painter accepted the challenge, downed his absinthe, and steamed off to his studio to write his great poems.

Several weeks went by before the Poet bumped into the Painter at their favorite watering hole. From the Painter's sheepish grin, the Poet guessed things weren't going so well for his friend.

"Written any good poems lately?" the Poet taunted.

"I don't understand it," confessed the Painter, still puzzled by his aborted attempt to write poetry. "I had good ideas. They just wouldn't turn out right on paper."

"That's because you don't start with ideas," the Poet smiled knowingly. "You begin with words."

The Poet was saying that strong stories generate their own ideas, not the other way around. The story and the characters always come first. Abstract intellectual concepts for ideas will put a story back on the poisoned path of propaganda.

So if you want to criticize our society, if you want to wave a red flag or suggest change, then find the story to tell it. The author of *The China Syndrome* wanted to warn us about the dangers of a nuclear meltdown, and at the time we weren't too interested in the message, at least not until real life stepped in—as it does at the oddest times—and we were reading headlines in the newspaper about Three Mile Island. Suddenly the message was urgent and the warning of *The China Syndrome* was very real.

And yet the story line of *The China Syndrome* held its own. The author wasn't crusading. The plot was intriguing, the characters were reasonably interesting, and the tension and suspense kept our interest. The author resisted the impulse to use one of the characters as his own mouthpiece; he let the characters speak for themselves out of their own roles in the story. True, the character played by Jane Fonda, and to an extent the character played by Jack Lemmon, make speeches about the dangers of nuclear energy, but those speeches come from the characters' moral and social consciences rather than directly from the author's.

This lesson is the key to writing successfuly if you feel the urge or the need to make social comment in fiction. Steinbeck makes us care about the Joad family in *The Grapes of Wrath*, and the Joads, through their anguish, teach us about America during the Depression, about the poor and the displaced, the wandering homeless in search of the American dream.

Too much propaganda has been written in the guise of fiction. And readers don't like propaganda because the story and the characters lack sincerity. Argue from your characters' convictions, not your own. Don't let the message get ahead of the medium.

• **Human nature.** What is Man? A question as much for writers as it is for philosophers; a forum for fiction as much as it is for the treatise, the monograph or the essay. As writers, part of our job is to explore the nature of humanity, either through individuals (Character As Theme) or through a broader view of people and humanity in general.

The difference between Character As Theme and Idea As Theme (Human Nature) is that in the former category, the character in the work is particularized. One-of-a-kind. We don't see anyone we really recognize, but we are intrigued by the character's uniqueness.

In this category of theme, however, the main character or characters of the story represent *universal human types*. We do recognize the people, although we may not recognize their circumstances.

These characters, and their crises, reach beyond the page because they represent our view of civilization, of humankind in general. William Golding's gripping novel, *Lord of the Flies*, takes a group of very proper British schoolboys and strands them on an uninhabited island without adults. Before long the children, forced to create their own society, drop any pretense of a polite genteel society and revert to a savage, brutal system in their struggle for power and survival.

Robinson Crusoe, a story about a shipwrecked sailor who must confront the difficulties of a solitary and primitive existence, also explores what it means to be human, and what it means to be civilized. Note that in both works, the characters are isolated, cut off from others without any real hope of help.

The same is true for the cast of characters in James Dickey's *Deliverance*. Isolated in the Appalachian backwoods, several men from middle-class suburbia suddenly find themselves confronted by a harsh, cruel environment that forces them to confront truths about themselves (and perhaps about us all).

● **Human relations.** This theme pattern is akin to the previous one. In that pattern, the author is concerned with understanding who we are as people, whereas in this pattern the focus shifts to examining the difficulties people have when it comes to getting along with one another, *especially* when it comes to complex, intimate relationships that occur in love, in marriage and in the family.

These stories hit close to home. We all know to some degree the difficulties of developing, keeping or dissolving relationships. We've read a ton of books and seen as many movies about starting up or starting over, of marriages under fire, of working through all the domestic crises that trouble us.

Sometimes the stories are painful, as in *Ordinary People*, as a family tries to cope with the death of a son and finds that it has to redefine itself. Larry McMurtry's *Terms of Endearment* also explores the strained relationship between mother and daughter and how the daughter's terminal illness forces them to deal with the problems they'd been avoiding.

The stories don't have to be tragic in order to contain the truth. The basic premise behind the play *The Odd Couple* examines the relationship between two men, one compulsively neat, the other compulsively sloppy.

As in the Human Nature category, in Human Relations theme patterns we are brought close to the ideas because of their universality. We all know Oscar Madisons, just as we know Felix Ungars. These stories talk about us as a class of people, as a society, and as a civilization. If you should decide to write a work that has as its theme a study of the pains and/or the rewards of relationships, then you should concentrate on the characters themselves rather than the relationship itself. The relationship comes from character; don't force characters into relationships.

Avoid clichés of character and action, like the story of the brilliant but alcoholic brain surgeon who falls in love with a woman who saves him from his own self-destructiveness, or the story of the mad scientist and his forbidden experiments that result in the creation of a monster. And please, no more vampire stories, unless you can do what Anne Rice does in her *Vampire Chronicles* by throwing out all the clichés about vampires and creating characters and situations that are totally new.

Make the people interesting but don't make them bizarre, for that will make our identification with them difficult or even impossible. These should be people we believe we could be ourselves if we found ourselves in a similar position. This theme was the foundation for *The Big Chill*, exploring a web of relationships between college classmates who reunite several years after graduation. Somewhere in those characters we no doubt recognize ourself and our friends; we recognize their problems; we recognize their joy and their grief. In the end, it is just as much a story about us as it is about the fictional characters.

The appeal of universality is that the story works within the realm of possibilities for all of us. If your characters are too much out of the mainstream of people as we know them, then they are apart from us, different, at most entertaining oddities. For this Human Relations theme to work as an idea, you must reach out and speak to us, your audience, and make us feel the pain and the joy of living with other people.

• **Innocence to experience.** How often have you heard someone older complain that youth was wasted on the young? We look back to our childhood and remember the awkwardness, the confusion, and best of all, the magic moments of discovery, those "firsts" — our first love, our first sexual experience, our first apartment — as we traveled the rocky road to maturity.

Writers like to explore that road and its various stops along the way — not simply the events, but the effect of the events on people. These stories are often called "coming of age" stories or "loss of innocence" stories. *The Summer of '42* and *American Graffiti* are well-known examples.

This theme pattern is much more common in film than in literature, perhaps because there is no real book market for people "coming of age." The Young Adult (sometimes called YA) market does address these questions of maturity, but in the same shallow, formulaic way that romance novels explore love. This kind of reading is meant to be light, entertaining and escapist. If the questions are demanding and tough, and if they relate too closely to the discomfort of daily living, then they break the illusion of a world in which our problems always find perfect solutions.

Theme is an element in the heirarchy of technique that develops during the course of the work. We may think we know what our work is really about, but the experience of writing usually changes all our preconceived notions. Picasso pointed to the process of discovery and said that what you actually accomplished during the act of creating was what was important, not what you intended to do. Rarely are the two the same.

As you write, the horizons of your work will constantly open up. You will see new things, think new thoughts, find new directions. The road through the dark forest of confusion is never clear, and we make our choices about which road to take at every juncture, never sure where that road is going to take us. But if you decide on a pattern of theme, you decide on a kind of roadmap that you want to follow and it will guide you. Your decisions won't be nearly as blind, and like Dante, who must negotiate the road through Hell in the *Inferno*, you too will have a guide, your Virgil, to help you through the endless maze.

Scene and Sequel: The Two Keys to Strong Plots

by Jack M. Bickham

I f you understand *scene* and *sequel*, you can write well-plotted stories. If you don't, you can't.

Scene and sequel are two fundamental story components that have a definite, unvarying structure — and that structure is what gives fiction coherence, forward pace and suspense. Once you understand scene and sequel, you will never be at a loss to know what sort of "move" you should make next in your story, and your readers will be constantly worried and entertained.

Failure to write proper scene-sequel structure will result in confusion at best, story chaos at worst.

Lets' start at the beginning and go through the steps you'll need to know to master construction of scenes and sequels.

Establish a Story Goal

What readers like in stories is curiosity and suspense. They like to worry about what's going to happen next — how things are going to turn out.

To make your readers worry, you must establish a *story question*. This is the main thing the reader will be concerned with throughout the story, whether the story is twenty or two thousand pages long. The story question needs to be introduced early, the key elements of the story must relate to it, and the ending must answer the question you posed at the outset.

You establish a story question by having your lead character state a *goal* that's essential to his or her happiness. Readers will take this goal statement and turn it into the story question.

If your hero, Joe, says, "It's vitally important to me to get a better job in this company," readers will worry: "Will Joe get a better job in the company?" Or if Milly, your lead character, desperately wants to win the 5-K race, your readers will worry: "Will Milly win the 5-K race?" Whatever the stated goal, readers will turn it into a story question and worry about it.

Once readers have started to worry, however, you can't expect to worry endlessly about the same situation. Stories must grow and move; readers must be kept on tenterhooks as the lead character tries and fails and tries again. You need twists and turns in your plot — smaller but intense dramatic situations that pull readers through the pages — that affect your hero's path to the story question's solution.

Which is where scene comes in.

Create Scenes With Goals

Scenes are those parts of your story where the excitement is, where the hero struggles against opposition to move forward in his quest, where winning moves him closer to his story goal, or losing sets him back from it. A scene is always a fight in some form: sometimes physical, more often verbal, and always external—acted out and shown.

The pattern of scene is *goal, conflict, disaster*.

A scene begins when your hero sets out with a specific, short-term goal—something he wants to accomplish or attain that he thinks will bring him a step closer to his long-term story goal.

Perhaps our hero, Joe, mentioned above, has the story goal of getting a better job at the company. (Story question: *Will* Joe get a better job?) To attain his goal, he decides that his first step is to become better educated. But to get better educated, he has to take a class. And to take a class, he has to get off work every Thursday.

Joe's thought processes in deciding he has to get off Thursdays are important to your story, and the reader must understand them. But they are essentially nondramatic—because they are internal.

To involve the readers in something exciting and significant, you must create a scene: Joe marches into the president's office to ask for Thursdays off.

"Mr. President," Joe says, "I have come to convince you to let me have Thursdays off. If I can get Thursdays off, I can go to school, improve myself, and win a better job here in your company. I must ask you to give me Thursdays off."

The readers, hearing a secondary goal—one obviously a stepping-stone to the story goal—now have a short-term question to worry about: "Will Joe get Thursdays off?" So—just as you have a story question—you now have a *scene question*.

The question must always deal with whether the hero *can* or *can't*, whether he *will* or *won't*. It cannot be a vague thematic question ("Is education a worthwhile goal?") or one that asks how somebody is going to feel. It must always be a question that appears answerable with a simple *yes* or *no*.

To make sure your readers understand your scene question, you must state the goal clearly and specifically.

Often, as in the example just above, you can have the character state the goal for you. Sometimes you will paraphrase it for the character, writing something like, *Walking into Mr. President's office, Joe felt nervous. He simply had to persuade the boss to give him Thursdays off*. This is no place to be subtle. The readers must know the goal in no uncertain terms, so they know what's at issue—and what scene question they're supposed to worry about.

Unclear story goals probably cause more of the vague and unsatisfying fiction that's being written than any other factor. Sometimes, reading such stuff, you can see the author just bumbling along in search of something dramatic, not knowing what the scene goal was.

Just because you have a scene goal, however, doesn't automatically mean you have a scene. Even with a good short-term goal that is stated and specific, you still have only a potential scene. You don't have a scene until you have *conflict*.

Give the Scene Conflict

Conflict is the heart of a scene, and without it there can't be one.

What if Joe makes his plea and Mr. President says, "Okay, Joe, you've convinced me. Take Thursdays off, and God bless!"

Good for Joe—bad for you.

Suspense is built through setbacks, not through good news. Whenever things are going well for Joe, the reader relaxes. You don't want that. To make your story work, Joe must not get a happy answer from Mr. President right off the top. He must instead get conflict—exciting, involving, suspenseful conflict.

If Mr. President gives Joe what he wants, Joe walks out happy, closing in on his story goal—the reader isn't worried anymore—and the suspense and excitement just went out of your story like air out of a punctured balloon.

Joe must encounter conflict with Mr. President.

Mr. President must say that he isn't convinced Joe needs time off for a class. Then—since he is committed to his quest—Joe must argue, try to convince him. Mr. President must throw out new objections. Joe must try to counter them. The two opponents must struggle, maneuver, perhaps misunderstand one another, escalate, try different tactics, possibly get mad at one another.

This conflict section of the scene—the bulk of it—must be played moment by moment, with no summary. There are two reasons for this. One is that scenes are the most important and exciting parts of your story, and if you give them short shrift, your story will turn out dull and flat. The second reason is more fundamental: the scene is the part of your story that must grip and enchant your reader, so you make it as much like real life as you possibly can—and there is no summary in real life.

The conflict must be external, onstage, dramatized through actions. Many beginning writers want to write about internal conflict—warring impulses within the character. So do I. But I—like all published novelists—have learned that the conflict inside is essentially nondramatic: it can't "play" onstage now.

To make the conflict dramatic, you must have another character (or, in rare cases, some other clear obstacle), you must have a goal, and you must have an exterior struggle the audience can visualize and follow. The conflict might be verbal, it might be physical, it might involve bullets flying in a western novel. Whatever it is, it must be faced and developed—externally. Then if the outer conflict exacerbates the character's inner conflict, great. But first we must have the external fight readers can see and enjoy dramatically.

End the Scene

A scene must end with a development that answers the scene question. Your answers can be *Yes*; *No*; *Yes, but*; or *No, and furthermore!* Let's consider each of these.

As already noted (but it bears repeating), a *yes* answer is fatal. If Mr. President answers *yes*, Joe gets his Thursdays off. He leaves the office happy, and well along on his quest for a better job. He relaxes. So does the reader. Suspense dies. So does your story.

Your scenes must always end in a disaster.

The disaster at the end of a scene must always be organic—it must grow out of the conflict that just took place. For our imagined scene, we could not have an alligator drop through the office transom or somebody run in to say the factory is on fire.

A disaster must be honest. It must also be a *No*, a *Yes, but* or a *No, and furthermore!*

Of these, a *No* answer is the weakest.

Suppose at the end of the scene Mr. President says, "Joe, for the last time, the answer is *No*. Now get out of my office!"

This is definitely bad news for Joe. But he is really in no worse shape than he was when he went into the scene. He started without the day off and he ended the scene without the day off. In that sense, nothing has "happened." He hasn't made any progress and he may feel a bit more desperate, but he hasn't been set back, either. So in this sense your story has become static— the plot has ground to a halt.

That's why a *No* answer may be okay sometimes—but as a writer you should strive for something worse, something dynamic.

Let's try *Yes, but.*

Joe enters with his goal. Mr. President opposes him. They argue and struggle. At the end Mr. President says, "All right Joe, you can have Thursdays off, *yes, but* you will have to take a cut in pay." (Which means Joe can't pay his rent or afford tuition for the class.)

When Joe leaves the scene, he's gotten what he wanted, but he has two new problems: paying his rent and paying his tuition. He's in worse shape than when he entered the scene—and as a result of his own well-intentioned, goal-motivated struggle.

This is good for you. The readers have worried about the scene question because it relates to the story question. Joe has struggled through conflict, fighting to attain a worthwhile short-term goal, and the readers have rooted for him. Now, at the end of the scene, instead of getting something nice for his efforts, Joe has gotten himself into a worse pickle! This creates more reader worry and tension, more suspense—more sympathy for Joe.

The *No, and furthermore!* disaster ending is even better for your scenes.

Let's play our office scene again. Same goal, same conflict. At the end Mr. President shouts, "Joe, you have strained my patience past the breaking point.

I hate pushy employees. For the final time, the answer to your question is *no, and furthermore*, you're fired!"

This is great! Now when Joe staggers out, he's really lost something and he's in far worse shape than when he entered the scene. He's further from his story goal than ever. He's created new problems for himself. He seems to be moving backward in his quest. He's unhappy and so is the reader—and we have suspense, the readers turning the page to see what happens next.

What happens next, for Joe, is reaction to the disaster. And that's where the other story component—the *sequel*—comes in.

Create the Sequel

If the nature of scene is questing and excitement, the nature of sequel is feeling and logic. The sequel is where your character responds, emotionally and intellectually, to the action of the scene, and then tries to figure out a next step.

Our character, Joe, may walk out, strike his palm to his own forehead, and say, "My God, I feel terrible! What can I do? Nothing looks very good. But I guess I can go down the street and ask for a job at the shirt factory." And he then walks down the street and goes in to ask for employment.

In a nutshell, that's a sequel. With fiction sequels, just as in real-life ones, there is a pattern: *emotion, quandary, decision, action*.

In real life, when we are hit by a terrible development, our first reaction is emotional. We weep or lose our tempers, are filled with sadness or rage or dismay or humiliation. But whatever the feeling, it is emotional. Before we start to think, we go through a period of raw feeling where we aren't capable of thinking much at all.

At some point—again, in fiction as in real life—we stop reeling emotionally and start trying to figure things out. We look back on what just happened, try to see why it happened and what it means, start thinking about what we must do next. This process—review, analysis and planning—is the quandary section of the sequel.

Finally, we reach a new decision. We decide what to try next. And then (if we are in a well-plotted story) we put our plan into action.

So should your hero act. It's important to remember that your hero's decision must require him to *do something* to try to get closer to his story goal. Sympathetic characters are active: they always try again (in a new scene); they do not get stuck in sequel, wearing a hair shirt or endlessly weeping. They get moving and pick a new short-term goal (the story goal shouldn't change) without waiting for someone to bail them out.

Once your character has chosen a new short-term goal, you are ready to create the next scene.

In this way, scenes cause sequels, which lead to new scenes, which cause new sequels. The two structural components link like sausages, each supporting the others behind and in front.

Unlike scenes, sequels do not have to be told moment by moment—so it's here that you build in transitions, time passages and summaries.

Sequels slow the pace of your story because readers aren't so caught up in moment-by-moment conflict; their sense of tension and haste eases, and they'll accept a summary such as *For two weeks she felt paralyzed by sadness, but then on a Wednesday* . . .

Control the Pace

Through your handling of scenes and sequels, you control the pace of your story.

Conflict makes up the bulk of "typical" scenes (if there are such things). The statement of the scene goal might be only a few lines; the disaster may fall at the end of a single sentence.

In your story, however, a complex character might start into a scene with such a complicated goal that you need a page or two to present all its subtle nuances. Or you might delay the conflict for a moment—to give a related story-event time to happen "offstage"—by having the protagonist and the antagonist discuss the goal before arguing.

Or, to reinvigorate a slowing story, you might increase the amount of conflict in a scene. You accomplish this by raising the stakes, by giving one or both characters more reason to be desperate or angry, by introducing more issues to fight over—or all of the above.

How you develop your sequels also depends on what kind of story you're telling, what kind of character you're dealing with, and what sort of pace you wish to create.

Scenes are swift and exciting, sequels slow things down. So in a slam-bang action adventure story, you want swift pace, and such horrendous, pressurized disasters that the main character doesn't have much time to think before acting. An entire sequel might consist of something like this:

Stunned and angered, Bart knew he had to get moving at once if he was to escape the trap. He decided to try to climb the cliff, grabbed a rock outcropping and heaved himself upward.

In a psychological novel, however, where the thought process of the character *is* the point of your story, you might devote many pages to the quandary section of the sequel, providing careful delineation of your character's every thought.

Or in a romance novel, your heroine might spend an entire chapter in the emotion section of a sequel, going over and over her emotional reactions to the disaster that just affected the course of her romance.

In a spy story, the decision section might be greatly expanded, as your operative starts carefully working his way toward his next overt goal—setting up false leads and confusing signals as he edges nearer the next inevitable confrontation.

Character affects your sequel pacing, too. A college professor is not likely to have the swift-moving, thoughtless sequels that the cowboy in your next story might have.

My scenes usually run from four to eight typewritten pages, and my sequels, somewhat shorter—because I'm writing suspense, which has a fairly fast tempo. However, the latest hero I've been working with tends to think more than most action heroes, so I've been writing longer sequels lately. (But every time I start an expanded sequel, I judge how long I can develop the section without slowing my story pace too drastically.)

Play With the Presentation

Of course, not all fiction we read is composed of a scene following a sequel following a scene. Experienced storytellers sometimes vary the pattern when presenting their work—but all fiction must be *plotted* and *planned* using scene-sequel construction.

In other words, you must create your plots using this construction, but you don't always have to show readers each step.

For dramatic reasons, you can withhold information from your reader for a while, leave out a sequel to get readers right into the next exciting, fast-paced scene, or play with the order of the information you reveal.

In a novel of mine, *Tiebreaker*, I presented a long sequel by my hero, Brad Smith, to a scene that took place before the novel opened. In feeling and thinking about the scene that took place in the back story, Smith presented vital background information about himself to the reader. He also characterized himself emotionally.

Although I didn't show it in the novel, I meticulously plotted that earlier segment of Smith's life—scene-sequel, scene-sequel—to know how Smith had gotten to that point of the story.

Elsewhere in that same novel, Brad planned (in a sequel) a meeting with a friendly contact to obtain information. But I worried that the story's pace was slowing, and I wanted to get to the next big scene, involving physical threat, as soon as possible. Also, I didn't want the reader to know yet what Brad was going to learn: I wanted the reader puzzled and mystified.

I planned—and even wrote—the meeting scene, but in my final draft I left it out, jumping readers past the entire scene and the sequel. The books picks up Brad in a much bigger and faster-moving scene later in the day, doing stuff the reader doesn't understand right away.

The overall story pace speeded up, and skipping the scene and sequel created temporary confusion about what was happening—making the reader more tense and worried. (Later in the book, in another sequel, Brad recalled the details of the scene and sequel I'd skipped.)

One of the most common variations writers use—especially in suspense novels—is to bring a character to the opening of a big scene, or to the disaster at the end of a scene, and then change viewpoint to another character. The readers, with curiosity at a high pitch, read pellmell through the second viewpoint section to get back and find out what happened with the original character.

Obviously, this device works only if you're employing multiple viewpoints. But in one of her early novels, *The Trembling Hills*, Phyllis Whitney shows how to accomplish a similar switch in first-person, single viewpoint fiction.

Whitney has her young heroine enter a room where she is to tell an aged and intimidating matriarch, "I am your granddaughter." In the previous sequel, the coming scene is set up as terrifying and vital. The frightened heroine opens the door of the room to enter the big scene—and the chapter ends.

I still remember the pleasure, tension and curiosity I felt as I whipped over to the next page, intent on seeing this scene unfold.

The next page began a chapter set later that evening at the family dinner table.

Puzzled and tense, but dragged on by curiosity about the scene I'd expected, I read several pages of this less dramatic—but necessary—scene. Finally, the narrator mentioned her afternoon experience. In a sequel to the dinner scene, Whitney revealed the young woman's recollections of the skipped scene.

This was much more effective than playing the scene in normal sequence:

- The delay in presentation whetted my curiosity and tension.
- I'd been drawn through a dinner scene that otherwise might not have engaged my attention.
- By describing the scene in the context of a sequel recollection, the author was able to omit anything that might have been dull (impossible in scene's moment-by-moment structure), and to add thoughts and feelings about the scene that wouldn't have fit the quick flow of the scene itself.

That's craftsmanship of the highest order.

You probably shouldn't scramble your presentation of scenes and sequels until you understand the technique completely. With deviation comes the danger of confusion. And perhaps you'll *never* deviate: many writers complete fine stories with textbook scenes and sequels following one another in straightforward order.

Making the Scene

Learning to use scene-sequel construction takes practice. Here are two ways to explore the technique:

• *Watch for the scene-sequel pattern in other writers' stories.* What you've previously been unaware of will leap off the page; in most good narrative fiction, almost every encounter is made into a scene or presented significantly in a sequel—even encounters with hotel doormen, parking attendants or other minor characters.

Deliberately searching for the structure will alert you to juggled scene-sequels. When you come across a reordering, search the story for the missing component—and try to determine why the author so arranged the story. (Once you're familiar with scene-sequel, you'll be able to see structures even in stories that depart from the pure form.)

• *Work with the scene-sequel pattern in* your *stories*. This is the best way to master the technique—and you'll improve your stories while learning.

On an old story, or one you're now working on, mark off the scenes and sequels—or places where you're missing one of the components. Then summarize each on an index card; cards for missing components should be identified with keywords (*fistfight sequel*, for example).

Arrange the cards in the order of your story. Then arrange the cards in the actual order of the events. Is there any difference? Why? Does the difference enhance your story? If not, return to the real-time order.

Look at the cards for missing components. Now, fill those cards in with a few paragraphs. What happens in that missing time? You don't have to include that information in your story (although you may want to), but you *must* know what happened.

Some writers, of course, are dismayed that craft is necessary in writing. Literary devices or structures such as scene-sequel make those writers worry about being less "free" or "spontaneous." They claim that their stories are "different" or something.

When we refuse to accept structure or technique, what we're really saying is "I don't understand the beauty of the concept," or "It sounds too hard and I'd rather be a dilettante."

Nothing is restrictive about scene and sequel writing—anymore than any art form has restrictions. You are free to do anything you want within the confines of the structure.

I'm reminded of the old story of the small child put out with his ball in the front yard, only a few feet from heavy traffic, because Momma wanted him to feel "free." The scared child had no fun at all; he had to be too careful the ball didn't roll into the street. But when put in the backyard, with a fence to keep both him and the ball in safe territory, he ran and kicked and had a grand time, feeling completely free because of the fence.

If you free yourself to run and kick within the limits of scene-sequel construction, your plotting—and your ability to grab and hold readers—will be better than ever.

Keeping Your Fiction Shipshape

by Lawrence Block

T here are really only three things you have to do," I heard a man say. "First of all, you have to get them on board. Then you have to make sure you keep them on the ship. And finally, you have to kill them at the end." I thought at first that I was overhearing a declamation from *Every Boy's Guide to Piracy*, and my head swam with visions of peglegged parrots wearing eye patches and Hathaway shirts, brandishing cutlasses and leaving no swash unbuckled. But I was not tossing on the high seas, or tossing 'em back in some waterfront dive. I was at a party in Greenwich Village, and there was not a pirate in the room. (There were, however, a couple of agents, and the distinction between the two is a narrow one indeed.)

But the speaker was neither pirate nor agent. He was Donald E. Westlake, the prominent mystery novelist and occasional screenwriter, and the violent criminal activity he was advocating was strictly metaphoric and to be perpetrated on dry land. He was talking about writing, and the intended victims were readers.

"First you've got to pipe them aboard," he explained. "You've got to hook them good and get them into the boat. Then all you have to do is provide enough shipboard activity to keep them there. Decent food, plenty to drink. Entertainment in the evenings—a juggler one night, some played-out operatic soprano the next. Remember, you've got an essentially captive audience here. They'd just as soon stay put.

And then, at the end, you've got to kill 'em. Or the whole cruise is a failure."

For years I've watched speakers stand up in front of rooms full of writers and explain that every story has a beginning and a middle and an ending. While I've never had occasion to argue with this bit of wisdom, neither have I ever seen what good it does anyone to know it. A story has a beginning and a middle and an ending. Terrific. A person has legs, a trunk, and a head. So what? Now that we know that, what do we know?

Listening to Mr. Westlake, however, it struck me that dividing a story like Gaul into three parts might be of value in detailing what we must do to make the fiction we write satisfying to those who read it. Our obligation would seem to vary with the portion of the story, and we have to focus on different considerations depending on whether we're dealing with the beginning, the middle or the end.

To depart from our nautical metaphor, the beginning of a story is a snare. We have to engage the reader's attention. We have to draw him in and trap him, and the more effective is our trap, the more likely we will be to have him with us for the duration.

The middle of the story is a joyride. We don't have to be so competitive now because there's less competition out there. With every paragraph, the reader considers himself to have a greater investment in what he's reading. It's easy for him to quit on the first or second page, much harder to jump overboard and start swimming when we've had him with us for half a dozen chapters.

The ending of the story is the payoff. It's the promised destination that drew him onto your boat in the first place. (The nautical motif seems inescapable, doesn't it? I can't manage to shake it.) If the ending doesn't deliver, the reader feels cheated by the entire experience. He may have enjoyed himself all along, but he's apt to forget that now; all he'll recall later is that he finished with a feeling of considerable dissatisfaction. "The first chapter sells the book," Mickey Spillane has said of his own work. "The last chapter sells the *next* book."

Let's talk about beginnings.

Piping Them Aboard

The first chapter sells the book. The first page sells the story.

And it is there at the beginning that good salesmanship is most important.

In the introduction to one of his books of poetry, e.e. cummings explained that his poems were in competition, not only with other poems but with flowers and balloons and mud puddles and train rides and, indeed, with everything that might occupy a prospective reader's attention. Our fiction is similarly competitive, and it is essential for me to remember that nobody has to read something simply because I had to write it. A couple of people—my agent, my editor—have to go through the motions, but if their eyes glaze over, they can turn the pages without paying too much attention to the words contained thereon. Nobody else even has to turn the pages. No one has to print what I've written; once it has been printed, no one is obliged to buy it; the person who buys it can stop reading after a paragraph and pick up something else instead, or watch television, or go out and mow the lawn.

It is my job to keep this from happening, and I can best assure this by starting out right.

Sometime last year I picked up *A Study in Scarlet*, Sir Arthur Conan Doyle's classic novel of Sherlock Holmes. I blush to admit that I had never read it before. (I do a lot of this sort of blushing. The list of acknowledged literary masterpieces that I have unaccountably missed is a lengthy one. The books could fill a library—and, come to think of it, often do.)

The first thing that struck me about *A Study in Scarlet* was that it could never have been published today in the form in which it appears. The book takes forever to get underway. Watson talks about how he met Holmes, describes their lodgings, and provides a wealth of admittedly absorbing detail before anything happens. That a novel should take so much time getting started seems incomprehensible to us a century later, and it becomes even more remarkable when we recall that *A Study in Scarlet* first appeared as a magazine serial. I don't know just where the first installment ended, but it's unlikely that it could have contained more than a bare hint of the story itself.

Would a contemporary editor reject Conan Doyle's novel? Not necessarily. The writing is so good and the characterization so engaging that a good editor might well stay with the book through its desultory opening, and then get wholly caught up in the book's narrative flow. But that same editor would certainly insist that the author refashion the opening in order to make the story more accessible to the reader.

Ought the book be revised today to accommodate the tastes of modern readers? No, certainly not. *A Study in Scarlet* has been in print since its first appearance, and it seems likely to remain in print as long as people read books in English—or in any of the dozens of other languages into which it has been translated. It does just fine in its present form, and it would be a travesty to alter a word.

But today's reader knows what he is getting when he picks the book up. He knows, for openers, that the book is a classic, that it has delighted generations of readers, and that he can be certain of a rousing tale and a fascinating cast of characters. He knows who Holmes and Watson are, and knows that at least half of the pleasure of the book will be the delight of their company during its reading. He is presold. The book could open any damn way and he's going to stay with it.

You and I are not in that enviable position. (Neither, when the book first appeared, was Conan Doyle, but he lived in different times. Readers were less hurried, and they very likely had fewer alternate pastimes available to them. Even so, he would not have been ill-advised to get the game afoot a little closer to page one.)

In a couple of my *Writer's Digest* columns over the years I've written about opening paragraphs and their function in getting things off to a good start. But the beginning of a novel amounts to more than a couple of paragraphs. It is, indeed, as much as it takes to pipe your readers aboard, to get them hooked even as you get the story going.

You have to manage several things at once. First, of course, you have to attract their attention and draw them in. You may try to accomplish this by beginning with the action already in progress; later on, you and they will both have time to take a breath and put your feet up, and you can then fill them in on the whys and wherefores of what they've been watching.

This is a handy device, but it's not the only way to start quickly. You can open with a provocative statement about the story or one of its characters. ("Most people take a lifetime to learn life's most important lesson. Jack Bayliss learned everything he had to know in five minutes one September afternoon on the leeward side of a West Virginia Mountain.") You can use a background anecdote. ("When Audrey was a baby she was always a picky eater. Years afterward, her mother would tell anyone who listened about the day she tried to get the child to eat an artichoke . . . ")

At the same time that you engage the readers' attention, you want to let them know what kind of a story they're reading. This task is not a burden to be carried exclusively by the beginning of the text. The title will share the load, along with the blurbs, the jacket copy, the cover art, the promotional campaign, and whatever reputation your previous work has earned you. All of these elements have combined to give readers an idea of what to expect from your book, but they will still not entirely have made up their minds when they read your opening, and it can either increase their appetite for what follows or put them off altogether.

Some years ago a friend strongly urged me to read *Another Roadside Attraction*, Tom Robbins's brilliant first novel. I dutifully picked up the book in a store, read the first two pages, and put it back. A few weeks later my friend asked if I'd read the book.

"I started to," I said, "but I could tell it wasn't my kind of thing."

"It is absolutely and unequivocally your kind of thing," he said. "I'll bet you got bogged down in the first two pages, didn't you? I should have warned you about that. Pick it up again and bull your way past the first two pages, or skip them if you have to. They're false advertising, because the book's completely different from what they'd lead you to expect."

A further chore of the beginning is to make you care about the story, to convince you that you ought to give a damn how it turns out. I had a slight problem in this regard with my novel, *Out on the Cutting Edge*. While the beginning was smooth enough, and while there was enough movement to keep the reader from dozing off, the book seemed to my editor to lack a sense of urgency. She felt the reader would wonder why my detective hero, Matthew Scudder, would care all that much about the fate and whereabouts of a young woman he's hired to find. We've never seen the woman, and neither has he, and we're thus not all that concerned about her, and wonder why he would be.

I solved this problem by adding a prologue in which Scudder imagines the woman's last day. The chapters that follow are unchanged; we still don't see her, and neither does Scudder, but we've had a strong hint that something terrible will turn out to have happened to her, and we've established that there's some kind of psychic bond between her and the detective. We believe that he feels as though he knows her, and we even feel as though we've met her—but of course we haven't.

Keeping Them on the Ship

Once you've got the readers on board, how do you keep them there? Of our three sections of this discussion, this has been the most difficult for me to prepare. And that seems appropriate, because for a great many writers, the middle of a story presents the greatest problem. This is less noticeably the case with short fiction, where there's simply less ground to be covered between the start and the finish. (The shortest of stories may be said to have no middle; the beginning leads almost directly to the ending.) In the novel, however, most of the book is middle. A chapter or two gets the book underway, and a chapter or two later on will finish it off, but between the two stretches an endless tunnel, a bottomless abyss, a vastness beyond measure. Page after page of innocent paper has to be filled with words, all of them well-chosen and placed in some presumably agreeable order.

The most self-assured of writers is apt to suffer a crisis of confidence during a book's lengthy midsection. His nightmare tends to be two-fold. First, there's the mounting concern that the book will never be done, that the middle will extend forever, that each new page he writes will bring him farther from the beginning but not a whit closer to the end. (There is, incidentally, an alternative to this concern. The writer becomes anxious that the middle will be too short, that he cannot possibly pad it out long enough to fulfill either the general requirements of the fiction market or the specific ones of his own contract. I have on occasion had both of these worries at the same time, and have sat at the typewriter simultaneously alarmed that my book was going to be too long and that it would wind up too short. It is, let me assure you, a curious matter to write scene after scene not knowing whether you should be padding them or cutting them short. If you induce a comparable neurotic state in a lab rat, he sits down in the middle of the maze and chews off his own feet.)

Besides worrying over the long and short of it, the writer is typically concerned that what he's shouting is going to fall on deaf ears, or on no ears at all. The readers, cunningly hooked by the book's beginning, will dislodge that hook and swim off into the sunset.

And, indeed, this happens. I don't finish every book I start reading, and I somehow doubt I'm unique in this regard. While I once felt some sort of moral obligation to wade through every book I picked up, somewhere around age thirty-five I outgrew this foolishness. In this world, one of many books and little time, I feel comfortable occasionally leaving another writer's book unfinished.

But the thought that someone—anyone—would abandon one of *my* books . . . well, that's another matter entirely.

Some of my concern in this regard may derive from my own literary apprenticeship. I started off writing softcore sex novels, and the experience left me imprinted with the notion that, if I ever let a whole chapter go by without someone either making love or getting killed, I was waving a beige flag at the reader's attention span.

While this left me with some bad habits that I had to learn to break, I think I was probably luckier than some writers who emerge from an academic background and start off writing thoughtful, introspective novels in which there is not a great deal of dramatic incident. All things considered, I would rather give too much than too little attention to holding the reader's interest.

How do you keep the readers aboard? How do you keep them reading?

The first thing to remember is that they *want* to keep on reading. They picked up the book in the hope that it would engross them utterly. The most compelling blurbs in ads and on book jackets are those that assure you that the book, once begun, cannot possibly be set aside. I know any number of people who read books in order to get to sleep at night, yet no one would try to sell a book by hailing its soporific properties. "This book kept me up all night" is a far more effective promotional claim than "This book lulled me right into a coma."

More than they want insight or laughter or tears, and far more than they want their lives changed, readers want something that will keep them reading. Once hooked by your opening, they have an investment of time along with their investment of money in your book. Every additional page they read increases their investment and commits them more deeply to finish what they have started.

So you have a lot going for you. The readers would prefer to stay with you, to see the book through to the end, to have a good time on the way. All you have to do is keep them amused.

And how do you do that? Here are a few ways:

• *Have interesting things happen.* Most of the books I've written in recent years have been detective stories. While the category is broad enough to embrace a wide range of novels, a common denominator exists in that a lead character is almost invariably called upon to do a certain amount of detecting. This very often involves going around and talking to people.

When my detective hero, Matthew Scudder, goes around knocking on doors and asking questions, he's acquiring information that serves to advance the plot. But if these scenes did no more than provide him with data, they would make very tedious reading indeed. It is not enough that they be functional in terms of the book's plot; it is also essential that they be interesting.

In *Eight Million Ways to Die*, for example, Scudder is hired by a pimp to investigate the murder of one of the pimp's girls. He pursues the investigation by interviewing each of his client's surviving girls. Writing these scenes, I took pains to make each interesting in and of itself. I did this by letting the women emerge as individuals, with their own separate histories, personalities and current life-styles. Their different perceptions of the pimp enlarged the reader's understanding of that enigmatic character, too.

Every scene you write can be more or less interesting depending on how you write it. Not every scene deserves full treatment, and there will be times when you'll hurry things along by summarizing a scene in a couple of sentences. But the more space you give to a scene and the more importance you assign to it, the greater is your obligation to make that scene pull its weight by commanding the attention of the readers and keeping them interested and entertained.

• *Keep the story moving.* The readers will accept a lot of tangential scenes, if they're diverting enough. But you don't want to do such a good job on this that they forget the point of view of the whole thing.

In the broadest sense, fiction is about the solution (successful or not) of a problem. If the readers lose sight of that problem during the book's vast middle, they cease to care. They may keep reading out of inertia if you provide enough entertainment along the way, but if anything comes along to break their attention, they may not get around to picking the book up again. Even if they do keep reading, you may lose your hold on their emotions.

Several times in recent books I've stopped along the way to rewrite a chapter, cutting scenes down or chopping them out entirely. They were entertaining enough as written, and I had to chop out and throw away some nice snappy dialogue that I felt rather proud of—because it was slowing the book's narrative flow. I feel the need to do this as I go along because I'm not comfortable otherwise, but many writers find it works better if they let their scenes run on and do their cutting after the first draft is finished. In either case, the same considerations operate.

• *Pile on the miseries.* One thing you want to do in the book's middle is turn up the gain on your narrative. You do this by making the problem more of a headache. This makes its solution more essential.

In suspense fiction, a standard way to do this is to toss another corpse on the floor. The readers are already committed to the idea that the initial murder must be solved and the murderer apprehended. When someone else dies, such a resolution becomes even more imperative. Furthermore, you've introduced an element of urgency; the hero must act not only to restore balance to the universe, but also to prevent the death of other characters, including some who may by now have become important to the reader.

Similarly, you can raise the stakes for the readers by making the problem's solution more difficult. In *A Ticket to the Boneyard*, another novel about Scudder, he is trying to apprehend a particularly vicious killer. While he is struggling to track the man down, several things happen to heighten the tension and raise the stakes. There are additional murders. Scudder gets severely beaten. And his closest friend on the police force turns on him, denying him support he'd come to take for granted.

• *Enjoy the trip.* Some people enjoy writing. Others hate it. As far as I can tell, there's no real correlation between the pleasure the author takes in a book's composition and the pleasure a reader will take later on.

Even so, I suspect we're well advised to have as much fun with all of this as we possibly can. And it's the middle of the book that is most apt to appear burdensome when we're bogged down in it. If writing a book is driving across America, the book's middle is an endless highway across Kansas, and there are days when every sentence is as flat as the unvarying landscape.

There are, to be sure, a lot of interesting things in Kansas. But you won't enjoy them much if you spend every moment telling yourself you can't wait to get to California, and if you're twitching with anxiety that the book will be too long or too short or just plain lousy.

Forget all that. Stay in the now. Enjoy the trip.

Speaking of trips . . .

Killing Them at the End

A while back a friend of mine was flying from Los Angeles to New York. He was in the first-class section, a luxury to which he is not much accustomed, and the chap seated beside him was some sort of yuppie businessman, on his way to or from some sort of hostile takeover. The little swine had a clear enough conscience to lose himself altogether in the inflight movie, a pleasure my friend was willing to forgo.

The yuppie laughed immoderately all through the film. When he unplugged his earphones even as they rolled the final credits, my friend asked him how he'd liked it.

"Not so great," the young man said.

"But you laughed your head off," my friend protested. "If you hadn't been belted in you'd have fallen out of your seat."

"Oh, I'm not saying it wasn't funny," the little shark replied. "There were some great laughs in the thing. But, you know, it just wasn't a very good picture."

Now this story might do little more than illustrate the perversity of the Young Undeservedly Prosperous, but for the specific film involved. It was *Burglar*, the Whoopi Goldberg vehicle based (more or less) on a book called *The Burglar in the Closet*, a mystery novel written by, uh, me. And the chap seated beside the chortling little chiseler was my agent, the redoubtable Knox Burger.

And, worst of all, the damned whelp was right. *Burglar* was a million laughs, but it just wasn't a very good movie. And virtually everyone who saw it reacted much the way Knox's seatmate did. They roared while they were in the theater, and then they told their friends not to bother going. This was true of the insider audiences; laughter was riotous at the large Manhattan house where I saw the film screened, and the very people who laughed the loudest then went home and wrote scathingly negative reviews. The reaction was the same at the theaters in suburban shopping malls. Everybody had a good time for ninety minutes and went out shaking the old head in disgust.

Why should a film — or fiction in any form — provoke this sort of contradictory response? How could audiences have such a good time with the picture while it was going on and respect it so little once it was over? In the particular case of *Burglar*, I think there are several answers. The gags were too easy, the characterizations were shallow, the relationships were too hard-edged — there were lots of things wrong with this movie, and most of them need not concern us here. But one factor that I'm sure contributed to the film's failure to generate good word-of-mouth was the relative weakness of its ending. The ending was soft, and it left the audience unsatisfied.

Mickey Spillane's dictum — "The last chapter sells the *next* book" — is very true. But there's even more to it than that. The last chapter sells the next book by convincing the reader that the book he's just finished was terrific. That doesn't just make him a customer for your next effort, but it makes him a powerful salesman for what he's just finished reading. The stronger your ending, the more likely he'll be to recommend the book to his friends. It is word-of-mouth ultimately that creates bestsellers. Nothing else, no amount of advertising and publicity, can sustain a book that does not get touted by those who read it. And a book with an unsatisfying ending just cannot generate strong word-of-mouth on a broad scale.

During the past year I've read a pair of unusually well-written first novels, both of them suspense yarns, one set in Michigan, the other in the Florida Keys. Both books have generated a lot of favorable comment among mystery pros, no doubt because of the genuine excellence of their writing. Neither did as well with the public at large, and I think I know why. The ending of one was improbable, almost silly, while the other ended very inconclusively. I enjoyed both immensely while I was reading them, but ended feeling somehow cheated and unsatisfied.

I know I've hurt my own sales in the same fashion in at least one book. *Ariel*, a novel I published ten years or so ago, was a story of psychological suspense featuring a twelve-year-old girl who may or may not be evil, and who may or may not have murdered her baby brother in his crib. And the ending is inconclusive. You don't find out for sure what the girl is and what she did. A few reviewers liked the enigmatic ending, but more than a few did not, and I don't blame them. It was vague because I was vague—I didn't know what had happened. I would have greatly preferred a less uncertain ending if only I could have come up with one.

What makes an ending work?

Maybe the best way to answer that is to listen to a Beethoven symphony. By the time the last note of the coda has sounded at the end of the fourth movement, you damn well know it's over. When that last ringing chord hits you, every musical question has been answered, every emotional issue has been resolved, and you don't have to wait for the folks around you to start applauding in order to be certain the piece is done. If Ludwig van B. had set *Ariel* to music, there wouldn't have been anything enigmatic about the ending, believe me.

It's generally a good deal easier to write an ending with impact if you have that ending in mind from the onset. The more clearly you are able to perceive it as you go along, the more you can shape the various elements of the story so that the ending will resolve them in a satisfying fashion.

Does this mean that you must have the whole book outlined, in your mind or on paper, before you write it? As one who almost never uses an outline, I'm hardly inclined to advance such an argument. It is possible, however, to know your ending without knowing just how you're going to reach it.

Several novelists, most recently E.L. Doctorow, have likened the writing of a novel to driving at night. You can see only as far as your headlight beams reach, but you can drive clear across country that way.

Very true, and I've written any number of books in just that fashion. But I've been most successful when, while I could not see past the range of my headlights, I nevertheless knew my ultimate destination in advance. If I just hop in the car with no goal in mind, I may have an enjoyable journey, but I run the risk of not getting anywhere, or not even really knowing when the trip is over. (In point of fact I travel that way all the time in real life, but it doesn't work as well in fiction.)

Dorothy Salisbury Davis, who does very well indeed with beginnings and middles as well as endings, has said that she can't comfortably write a mystery novel unless she knows from the onset who did it. She may change her mind in the course of the book, she may wind up hanging the murder on someone other than her initial choice, but she always has a solution in mind as she constructs the problem.

I haven't always done this, but I certainly have an easier time when I do. It seems to me, too, that a substantial portion of the books I've abandoned over the years have been ones for which I did not have a strong ending in mind from the beginning. I ran out of gas on those books not specifically because I wound up painting myself into a corner or wandering in an insoluble maze, but simply because each book sort of wobbled to a halt. I think it may have been the lack of a concrete destination in the form of a foreseen ending that brought this about.

The most satisfactory endings resolve everything. Like that Beethoven coda we just heard, they answer questions we never even thought to ask.

Most of my books are mystery novels, concerned with a crime and its solution. Find the murderer and you've found the ending. Mysteries, however, are frequently concerned with more than crime and punishment, and sometimes an ending has to do more than name a perpetrator and clap the cuffs on him.

Eight Million Ways to Die is a good case in point. The book begins with the murder of a call girl, and the stakes are raised when two other prostitutes die, one an apparent suicide. And, finally, Scudder brings the killer to justice. He does so by making himself a stalking horse, a move that almost fails when the killer waits in Scudder's hotel room with a machete. But Scudder and justice prevail, and the bad guy gets what's coming to him, and the ending is dramatically satisfying.

But the string of murders is not all that the book is about. It's also about life and death in New York, and it's very much about Scudder's attempt to come to terms with his alcoholism. He struggles to stay sober as he chases the killer through the city's terrible streets, and the book follows him in and out of ginmills and detox wards and AA meetings. After the book has seemingly ended, after the killer has been found out and dealt with and the solution explained to Scudder's client, there is a final chapter in which the detective is brought face to face with his own illness and has to confront himself or back down.

The first ending, the unmasking and apprehension of the killer, is dramatically effective but not everything it might be. Because of the story itself, the killer is not someone we have met before. (Hollywood can't bear this sort of thing, and in the film version the killer is the sneering villain we've met early on.) But the second ending more than makes up for it. A considerable number of people have told me, in person or through the mail, how much impact the ending had for them. Many of them have assured me that they cried, that they were moved to tears.

And that is what an ending ought to do. It ought to move readers. It need not move them to tears—although that doesn't hurt. But it ought to leave them knowing that they've been in a fight and that the fight is over. You don't have to leave them feeling happy—although a downbeat ending is usually hard to bring off effectively. But you do have to leave them feeling complete. They may finish wondering what will happen to the characters afterward, and that's all right, as long as you leave them feeling that the issues raised in this part of the characters' story are resolved.

Not every successful book has an ending that works in this sense. Some people break the rules and seem to get away with it. The example that comes to mind is John le Carré, who has made an occasional habit of endings that I can only assume are intentionally obscure. Both *The Spy Who Came in From the Cold* and *A Small Town in Germany* have ambiguous last pages; you have to read them over a second or third time to be certain what is taking place. The author's writing is so clear elsewhere that it is puzzling his ending should be so murky. I can't seriously argue that this weakness, if that's what it is, has hurt le Carré with readers or critics. He's doing just fine, and for all I know maybe I'm the only one who finds his endings opaque.

Any questions? Yes, Rachel?

Why "kill them at the end," sir? Why such a violent image?

I don't know, Rachel. I've asked myself the same question, and originally looked around for a way to paraphrase Donald Westlake's original observation that triggered this discussion. But I can't find an alternative that works as well. Comedians, and performers in general, use that metaphor. "I killed them in Keokuk," the vaudevillian would say. "I knocked them dead. I beat their brains in. I slaughtered them."

I guess the implication is that members of the audience—and in our case the readers—are overpowered by the material. It overwhelms them, and killing is the ultimate way of being overwhelmed because it is undeniably final. What you may be objecting to, Rachel, is the implication of hostility between the comic and his audience, the writer and his readers. If you're trying to kill your readers, doesn't that mean that you hate them?

No, not in this case, not when they pick up the book hoping to be killed in just this fashion. Even if you continue to dislike the metaphor, I'd urge you to strive for fictional endings that seem to fit it. Because this kind of metaphoric death is anything but final. Unless you kill them at the end, they won't keep coming back for more.

Giving Order to Your Fiction

by Jack M. Bickham

You happen to meet a friend on the street.

She says, "Hello."

You say, "Hello."

You're heating water for coffee, and get too close to the flame.

You jerk back from the pain.

The telephone rings.

You answer it.

The doctor taps your knee with his little hammer.

Your leg jerks.

Simple transactions like these happen all the time. They illustrate the basic principle of *stimulus and response*, the mechanism that makes your fiction make sense and move forward in a straight disciplined line.

Seeing how straightforward the pattern is, one wonders why so much fiction is unpublishable because it's screwed up in terms of stimulus and response. Maybe it's because most of us don't like to think that humans are really so mechanistic and predictable. The idea of a knee-jerk existence repulses most of us. But money-making writers believe in the principle for ordering their fiction, whether or not they accept the theories of such psychologists as B.F. Skinner in real life. Fiction must be *better than life* in many ways, and this is one of them.

The principle is simple. For every stimulus: a response; for every response: a stimulus. When you show a stimulus in your story, you must then show a response. When you want a certain response, you have to provide a stimulus that will cause it. Following this simple pattern, you'll begin to write copy that makes good sense and steams along like a locomotive.

Stimulus and response works whether you are trying to get someone to duck his head (you throw something at him!) or plan his next step in a complex plot. It works in writing dialogue and dramatic action, and it works in planning the architecture of a novel. Some S&R transactions are simple. Others are complex. Let's look at some of each.

The Simple Transaction

The simple transaction is one almost like the knee-jerk reaction. Someone calls your name and you turn your head. Thunder crashes and you jump. "Catch!" someone says, tossing you a ball, and you either catch it or drop it, but in any case you react. Or maybe it's dialogue like—

"Will you marry me, Cindy?" he asked.

"Yes, oh, yes!" Cindy sighed.

So when the response seems straightforward and easily understood, all you have to do as a writer is make sure both the stimulus and response are presented:

√ clearly,

√ in the proper order, *and*

√ close together, so the relationship is not obscured.

Which, believe it or not, some people manage to mess up.

Clearly: Problems with clarity come when the writer assumes that the reader will understand a cause-and-effect relationship when such a relationship is not at all obvious.

Suppose you read a fictional incident in which a single man meets a lovely and unencumbered young woman. They go out together, then wind up spending a wonderful night together. After which the man bursts into bitter tears and attempts to take his own life. This transaction—wonderful night spent with a lovely young woman causing the man to be plunged into abject despair—is not clear on its face. If the author were to tell you what he *forgot to provide*—the fact that the man is a devout Catholic priest—perhaps his tragic response to the adventure would make more sense.

Sometimes clarity can be lost even more simply. Again the problem is that the writer forgot to put down on paper all his assumptions about what was going on. In this case, the transaction fails not because we are unclear about the background, as above, but because the writer forgets to make the stimulus clear and complete:

Joe walked up to Archibald.

Archibald ducked violently.

Seeing this, the reader is confused. How does Joe's walking up cause Archibald to duck? It doesn't make sense. But the close juxtaposition of walking up and ducking clearly imply that one caused the other.

You ask the author of the transaction. "Oh!" he says. "Well, you see, Joe was mad, and he took a swing at Archibald.

"I guess," the author adds lamely, "I forgot to put that detail in."

In the proper order: Let's cite an example:

Bob hit the dirt, hearing the explosion.

This is presented backwards. The syntax makes the reader aware of the response before he knows about the stimulus. The sentence should be recast:

Hearing the explosion, Bob hit the dirt.

That makes sense.

Similarly, don't use such constructions as "while . . . ," "as he . . ." and "at the same time as . . ." because all these connote *simultaneity*, and in good S&R writing that just doesn't happen: you show the cause, then you show the effect.

Close together: In plotting long works such as novels, writers often get in trouble not only by skipping plot developments that should follow one another in S&R fashion, but also by putting so many developments between plot stimulus and plot response that the cause-effect relationship is no longer apparent.

Not long ago I read some student copy that illustrated the problem. There was a sequence in which the wife hurled a vase at her husband, konking him on the head. The expensive vase broke and the husband got a bad laceration. The author then presented a long scene between the wife and her mother in which the marital relationship was discussed. Then the author followed the wife to an art restorer, where she talked about getting the vase repaired. In the course of this scene, the author gave me a "core dump" of research stuff on art restoration. Then—finally—we had a scene where the husband was getting his scalp stitched up. But by that time so much else had happened—more than fifteen pages of copy—that I got confused and momentarily forgot what stimulus had brought him to the emergency room.

Unless you're plotting a big multiviewpoint novel, your stimulus-response components must be closer together than that.

The Complex Transaction

All stimulus and response transactions, you will note, are not as conveniently simple as those we've dealt with so far. What if, for example, we have something like this?

"Will you marry me, Cindy?" Bob asked.
Cindy hit him with her beer bottle.

Or, instead of having someone touch a hot stove and jerk back in reflex, as we did in an opening example of a simple transaction, what if we have a sequence in which two men face each other across a restaurant table, and one of them extends his hand, putting it in the flame of the table candle, and then, instead of jerking back, *he leaves his hand in the flame, cooking*?

What we have discovered is that in every transaction, no matter how simple and straightforward, there is always a step between the stimulus and the response, and it takes place inside the mind, heart and body of the person receiving the stimulus and preparing a response.

That process between S&R, we call *internalization*.

In a simple transaction, internalization needn't be presented. In the case of "Hello"—"Hello" or the knee-jerk—it's machinelike and predictable. But when Cindy hits her suitor with a bottle, or the man feels the pain and ignores it, cooking his hand, something more is going on.

To make such complex transactions make sense, we must show the emotions or thought processes that go on inside the character between the stimulus and the response—what hidden workings make the unexpected response logical. In other words, we have to "play" the internalization.

How would insertion of internalization make our examples make sense? Consider:

(*Stimulus*) "Will you marry me, Cindy?" Bob asked.

(*Internalization*) THE QUESTION SHOCKED HER. SHE HAD PRAYED FOR JUST SUCH A PROPOSAL FOR TWO YEARS. BUT NOW—ON THE SAME DAY SHE HAD ACCEPTED REGGIE'S PROPOSAL, IT WAS HORRIBLE FOR BOB FINALLY TO ASK HER. INSTANT RAGE FLOODED THROUGH HER AND

(*Response*) She hit him with her beer bottle.

Now the transaction makes some kind of sense.

I leave it to you to write an internalization for the man holding his hand in the cafe candle. It might just be that he'll feel the agonizing pain but remember that he must prove to his colleague that he is fanatically tough and self-disciplined, so he fights the pain, fights the impulse to jerk his hand out of the flame, and sits there, cooking himself. (If that sounds farfetched, you weren't around for Watergate.)

Understanding and acceptance of the need for internalization, incidentally, provides an answer to a question often asked by fledgling writers: "When do I go inside the character's head?" One part of the answer: *When you must, to explain a complicated and unexpected response to a stimulus.*

So if you want to drop in a bit about the character's thinking or feeling process, or even a tiny bit of background, set up a complex stimulus. The character is then forced to pause an instant and react internally to formulate the unexpected response.

There may be times, of course, especially in mystery fiction, where the experienced craftsman will purposely leave out the internalization in order to create a puzzling transaction—in order to heighten reader tension and curiosity. That's a somewhat advanced technique. If you're new to the idea of S&R in fiction, I strongly urge you to handle such transactions straightforwardly for a while, until you absolutely have it down pat. Only then can you risk tinkering with the norm.

Background Information Is Not Stimulus

Stimulus is specific and immediate. Background is not stimulus.

For example, if Carolyn goes into her medicine cabinet to take two aspirin, and I ask you why she did this, in terms of S&R, *don't*—please—say something like, "Carolyn had a headache all day." To work well, a stimulus must be *specific* and it must be *immediate* and it must be *external*—something the reader can see or hear in the outside story world.

The fact that Carolyn had a headache all day is *background information*. The reader, at some mysterious level, will not believe the transaction.

In other words, it's all well and good to let me know that the headache had persisted all day, but as a reader, I demand to know: "Why didn't she take aspirin earlier? At noon? Five minutes ago? Or why didn't she wait another five minutes? *Why right this instant?* Because stimulus-response actions like this must be specific and immediate if they are to work.

To make it work, you must show a transaction like this:

Carolyn's headache pulsed, as it had all day. (*This is background.*)

Thunder blasted loudly outside. (*Here's the stimulus.*)

The noise intensified her headache. (*Internalization.*)

She got up and went to the bathroom and took two aspirin. (*Response.*)

In one of my classes I pass out a sheet listing a number of actions. The students' assignment is to provide a *stimulus* for what's presented, and then provide a *response* to what's presented:

One action is:

Sam dropped the lighted match into the gasoline.

What would be the immediate stimulus for this? *Not* something like "Sam wanted to blow something up," or "Sam had been angry at the gas station owner for days," or "Sam didn't know fire would ignite gasoline." All that stuff is background.

Rather, it must be something like the following:

"Drop that match, fool!"

or

The match burned Sam's fingers.

or

A car backfired, scaring Sam badly.

Now suppose you get the match hitting the puddle of gasoline. What *response* do you put in next?

Before reading another word here, take out a sheet of paper and complete the transaction.

Stimulus: the match falls into the gasoline.

Response . . . ? (You write it down.)

Done? Fine. Now please *don't* tell me you wrote something like any of the following:

The fire trucks came. (*This skips steps, right?*)

Sam was horrified. (*This is not an external response to the match. It isn't specific to the match. It's a skip because Sam doesn't have anything external happening to horrify him yet. If you want to have Sam realize what he has done, and be horrified as the match falls, fine. But you're just temporizing between stimulus — the match hitting the fuel — and the response to that event.*)

The owner raced out of the station. (*This skips steps and is not immediate and specific to the match hitting the gasoline.*)

No, the response to Sam's dropping the match into the gasoline almost has to be some variation of an orange flash, or an explosion, or flames sizzling across the tarmac. Fire trucks may come, Sam may be horrified, etc., etc. But the *first thing* that happens—the next step—must show the immediate, specific result of that match hitting the gasoline.

Also, please notice that Sam's horror—even if it takes place as he realizes what he has done before the match hits the pavement—*should not be presented in that order* because it puts too much between the outside stimulus and the outside response. The next thing that's going to happen is a hell of a fire. That will be in response to Sam's match, not his horror. So you shouldn't put the horror in because it only confuses the issue.

One more point has to be made about stimulus and response.

KEEP IT SIMPLE!

Follow the rule of *one stimulus—one response*. You should seldom if ever send "stimulus clusters."

Most of us have witnessed world-class tennis at some time or other, watching as a great player blasted a forehand, saw the opponent's return going crosscourt, raced over to hit a backhand, sensed his opponent in retreat, and rushed to the net to hit a winning volley.

Great stuff. Pure stimulus and response, possibly with a little internalization-anticipation thrown in.

But even that great player we just watched would have been reduced to utter confusion if, *instead of seeing one ball come across the net, he had been forced to try to react to six.*

That kind of thing results in chaos in tennis, as well as in writing.

Look at this little bit of action:

Ralph exploded into the room. He threw his wrench at Ted. He yelled, "I'm going to kill you, Ted!" He raced across the room and hit Ted with a haymaker. "Are you going to confess or not?" he screamed.

Now you tell me what Ted's response is going to be!

It's at times like this that writers often lean back from the keyboard and say, "Geez, I'm stuck."

Why? Too many stimuli. We ganged up on poor Ted and bombarded him with several tennis balls, not giving him time to react to them in turn. So now that we've finally decided to give the poor guy a response, we're as confused as he is, trying to figure out what he'll respond to.

So maybe we make a desperate try at Ted's response like this:

Ted ducked the wrench. "Why do you want to kill me?" he replied. He reeled back from the force of the blow. "Never!"

And of course that doesn't make sense either. There is no way Ted can logically and clearly respond to a barrage of stimuli sent all at once. Send one ball over the net. Have it hit back. Send another ball. Have that one returned.

And each time you conclude a stimulus, ordinarily, hit the return key. *Make a new paragraph.* The stimulus goes in one paragraph, the response in the next separate one.

But what about dialogue, you may ask. There, characters can be talking, thinking and stage-acting all in a moment. Won't a moment's activity by a talking, gesturing character provide more than one stimulus sometimes?

Of course. Still, you keep it as simple as possible. And if you must have "stimulus packages," just remember:

- All parts of one stimulus package go in the same paragraph. When the stimulus ends, the paragraph ends.
- If more than one stimulus is sent, *the responder will always react to the last stimulus sent.*

Suppose Bill feels sorry for something he has done, goes to Ronald, says he's sorry, and offers to shake hands.

You *cannot* write it this way:

"I'm sorry, Ronald," Bill said, holding out his hand. He felt sorry.

Why is this impossible? Because the last thing you've put in the paragraph is internalization, and Ronald can't conceivably respond to *that*. So if internalization is involved, it can't go last in the paragraph.

You *can*, however, write it two other ways:

Bill felt sorry. He held out his hand. "I'm sorry, Ronald."

or

Bill felt sorry. "I'm sorry, Ronald," he said, holding out his hand.

Which will you choose? The answer depends on which stimulus in the package you want Ronald to respond to. If you want Ronald to speak, you put Bill's words last. But if you want Ronald to dash Bill's hand aside, or stare contemptuously at it, you'll put the hand last.

Your Response

Consider, analyze and practice your own S&R presentations. Carefully take some of your own copy and mark it up, putting stimulus and response markers in the margins, and noting whether you are following the rules. Do you find internalizations? Are they where they should be? Have you inadvertently skipped some steps in a chain of S&R transactions?

Take your time. After analyzing your own copy, log your observations in your journal. Make a note to analyze your own copy again in six months to see how you're doing after more practice.

Don't assume you're perfect in this area. The time you take may make all the difference between clear, dramatic copy—and a mess.

Just Say No

by Gary Provost

Hard-working Ted had a crush on Patty. One night at the Moose Lodge, Ted—though limping slightly from a hockey injury—asked Patty to dance and she said yes. Then he asked if she'd like to go candlepin bowling sometime and she said yes, that would be splendid. Ted got more and more infatuated with Patty, so he asked her to go steady and Patty said yes. Before long, Ted and Patty were in love. On a drizzly Tuesday afternoon at the coin laundry, Ted got down on his knees and asked Patty to marry him. Patty said yes. Ted said he wanted to live in Elgin, Illinois, and he asked Patty if that would be okay with her. "Yes," she said "Yes, yes, Ted, I love you more than I love anything, including chocolate-covered cherries, and I want us to have three babies, Okay?" Ted said, "Yes." So they moved to Elgin, where Ted applied for and got a job at the rope factory, and they had three healthy kids and lived happily ever after.

Pretty exciting stuff, huh?

Of course not. It's dull. Ted has no opposition to his goals. He wants a dance and gets it. He wants a date andgets it. He wants a job in the rope factory and gets it. Watching Ted move through life is like watching a football team pass and run its way down the field with no opposition. Nobody tackles them. Nobody intercepts a pass. The outcome is never in doubt because nobody scores against them.

It's great, when things come easily in real life, but in fiction it's a real snore.

The Ted-and-Patty story is dull because nobody ever says *No*. Without *No*, there isn't any tension, any conflict, any excitement—and there isn't any story, at least not a publishable one. For your fiction to work, continuous opposition must be trying to push back your character as he tries to push toward his goal. This resistance can be seen as a series of people, things and situations saying *No* to your character, or your character saying *No* to them.

Take a pencil and cross out any one of my *yes*'s in the Ted-and-Patty story. Replace it with a *No*, and watch what happens. Your interest level rises. You ask questions. How is Ted going to get Patty to change her mind and go out with him? What if Ted doesn't want kids? Are Ted and Patty going to end up getting divorced over this Illinois thing?

Your novel shouldn't be about a character getting everything served to him on a silver platter. It should be about a character who scraps and struggles and argues and overcomes, a character who damn near kills himself trying to beat down all the *No*'s between him and his goal. Every time he slays a few *No*'s, another battalion of them comes over the next hill. The whole reason for telling a story is that somebody or something said *No*. So if things are going swell for your character, keep it to yourself. Nobody cares.

The compelling story is made up of one big *No* and many smaller *no*'s, most of which will melt into *Yes*'s along the way. Most new writers seem to understand the big *No*. It is the impending hurricane that says, "No, you can't have a nice little town anymore." It is the assassin who says, "No, the president can't live past the tenth of August." It is the prospect of divorce that says, "No, Sheila can't have the happy marriage she always wanted." Any one of those can be the big *No* being shouted at your character all the way through the story, and we must wait until the end to see if our hero will turn it into a resounding *YES*.

But readers don't turn pages to get to the end. They turn them to get to the next page. And so there must be dozens, even hundreds, of *No*'s along the way that create hurdles for your character to jump, problems for him to solve. Let's take for example Susan Isaac's novel *Compromising Positions*. The novel could be about Judith, living a dull suburban life as a housewife. She hears about the murder of a local dentist and decides to investigate. She tells her husband this and he says, "Great, go ahead." When the police find out she's investigating they say, "Keep up the good work, Judith." When she becomes attracted to a policeman investigating the case, she tells herself, "Wonderful, I think I'll jump into bed with him."

Isaac's novel could be like that, but it's not. Isaac uses the essential *No* throughout. When Judith's husband, Bob, finds out that she's investigating the case, he says *No*. He doesn't want her doing that, endangering their children, making a fool of herself. His opposition, his continual *No*, creates tension between husband and wife all through the story. By page 193, when somebody has warned Judith to keep out of the murder, Bob's *No* has divided them.

"... if you are going to continue this insane quest of yours, if you are going to continue to subject the family to jeopardy, then I will simply do my best to protect my children and leave you to your own devices. You can do what you want."

"Bob." I walked to his side of the bed and touched his shoulder.

"Don't touch me, Judith. Don't touch me until you get your head screwed on straight again. Do I make myself understood?"

He turned over and reached for the light. I undressed in the dark and climbed under the cold cover to lie on even colder sheets. "Bob," I whispered, easing over to his side of the bed. "Bob." He shook his body, as though ridding himself of a pesty mosquito. I inched away, fluffed my pillow into a high soft mound, pulled the quilt over my ears and, eventually, fell asleep.

When the police find out that Judith is investigating, they say *No*. You're an amateur, they tell her: you're putting yourself in danger, impeding the investigation.

And when Judith and detective Nelson Sharpe start making bedroom eyes at each other in her kitchen, she tells him *No*.

"And you're goddamn insensitive," I replied harshly, trying not to cry and feeling my throat tighten with the effort. "Can't you understand that when I say no I mean no? I'm not being coy with you. If and when I decide I want to sleep with you, I'll drop you a line. Okay? If you're still interested, fine. If not, you're under no obligation. But right now I can't get involved."

All of these *No*'s melted into *Yes*'s as the story went along. Judith's husband grudgingly accepted that she needed some excitement and would continue to investigate the murder. The police eventually welcomed Judith into the investigation, even asked her to help. And both Judith and Nelson Sharpe finally said *Yes* to lust, and ended up in a motel together.

The *No* principle works at every level of the story. In your story, Joel has a big goal, such as stopping a computer virus from reaching a computer that controls nuclear missiles. Joel also has many important intermediate goals, such as convincing the President that his plan to kill the virus will work. And he has more even smaller goals, such as getting in to see the President, or even finding a cab so that he can get to the White House on time. Just as there are goals at every level, there is opposition at every level. Make it difficult for Joel to get in to see the President. When he finally gets in, make it more difficult for him to convince the President. When he finally convinces the President, make it almost impossible for Joel to kill the virus. Etc. Never let things go smoothly for long.

You can't have major goals and major *No*'s on every page, so the little *no*'s along the way will keep the reader on edge. For example, in a *Compromising Positions* scene, a detective hands Judith an envelope full of pornographic pictures of women, taken by the murder victim. If Judith can recognize some of the women, they might have clues to the murderer's identity. Judith opens the envelope, finds the pictures disgusting and says, *No*.

These are women who might be my friends—even me. They have kids, they squeeze cantaloupes in the supermarket. And suddenly, I'm looking in on their inner life, which they never thought would go public.

She hands the photos back.

Later, she does look at the photos, identifies one woman, and the story moves forward. This is just a little *no*, and Judith looking at the photos in the first place would not have sabotaged the story. But these little no's along the way create reader commitment by putting the big goal and the intermediate goals in jeopardy. Little *no*'s are the immediate concern of the readers. Little *no*'s make readers worry, and turn pages.

Reversals

The trick is getting from *No* to *Yes* in a believable way. If a character says *No*, *No*, *No*, then changes his mind for no apparent reason, the reader will feel cheated and the story will wilt. One major way to get a character from *No* to *Yes* in a way readers will accept is to raise the stakes.

No's create tension because something is at stake. If the character can't turn the *No* into a *Yes*, the company will be destroyed, the bunnies will lose their home, or the perfect husband will end up in the arms of another woman. So one common way of making a believable transition from *No* to *Yes* is to raise the stakes. A person who says no for a dime might say yes for a dollar. To raise the stakes:

• Increase the potential gain for saying *Yes*. For example, a beautiful woman walks into a private detective's office and asks him to take on a case that requires him to go to Cleveland for two weeks. He says *no*. By the end of the scene she has made it clear that she will go with him, and make herself romantically available. He changes his mind.

• Increase the potential harm from saying *No*. In *Tootsie*, for example, Michael Dorsey (Dustin Hoffman) pretends to be an actress so he can earn $9,000 to produce his roommate's play. By the time the film is half over, Michael has certainly earned that much from starring in a soap opera, so now he's ready to say *No* to the female impersonation. How do the writers raise the stakes to make him say *Yes*? Michael, as Dorothy, falls in love with Julie (Jessica Lange), who keeps talking about how much she admires Dorothy for her honesty. Now if Michael says *No* to the impersonation, the consequences are greater: he will lose Julie's respect.

Blackmail is a device for increasing the harm from saying *No*. If your character says *No* and then learns that something terrible will happen to him if he doesn't change his mind, he might change his mind. A typical example: Willy the Weasel says he won't testify against the mobster. Then he learns that the DA has evidence that Willy robbed a liquor store last year and will prosecute unless Willie testifies. Willie says *Yes*.

• Increase urgency. Make the character more aware of or more concerned with the stakes you've already established. For example, you might start a clock ticking: An unexpected deadline can often persuade a character to go from *No* to *Yes*. For example, a young diabetic has been kidnapped, and your policewoman character says *No* to an illegal search of a suspect's house. She wants to wait for a warrant. But then she finds out that the victim has enough insulin for only three days. Now the clock is ticking. She says *Yes* to the illegal search.

• Reduce the potential harm or risk from saying *Yes*. Sometimes a character will go from *No* to *Yes* if you make the *Yes* a little easier. Maybe your ex-sheriff, Marvin, has said *No* to hunting down the bank robbers because there are too many of them for one man to handle. Then he turns to his old pal Trigger Maddox, who is looking for a little excitement and offers to go along with Marvin. Marvin has help now, so he says *Yes*.

Raising stakes is effective, but the best and most subtle way to get your character from *No* to *Yes* is to exploit personality. Before the character ever says *No*, reveal, through story events, some aspect of his nature. Something in his past prompts the character to a new understanding, provides a new insight or presents a new challenge that makes him say *Yes*.

Perhaps he was a coward years ago and vowed he'd never be one again. Somehow he's shown his *No* was cowardly, so he changes it to *Yes*. Maybe a successful businesswoman has said *No* to running an important charity because it would mean a cut in pay. Then she realizes she's sold out her principles for money, something she swore she'd never do. She says *Yes*.

In my short story "Big Brother," Scotty—a lonely middle-aged man abandoned by his wife—decides to become a Big Brother. Here he talks to Neil Feirstein, a counselor trying to find the right kid for Scotty.

> Now another week had passed and here I was sitting across from Neil Feirstein, wondering: if I had a son, would I want him being influenced by a man like me?

Here is Scotty saying *No* to the whole idea. Even though he's applied for Big Brother, he is still resisting. They talk for a while about what kind of kid would be best for Scotty.

> Feirstein looked at me for a long time and then he said, "Cub."
> "Cub?"
> "His real name is Charles. Charles Banks. Everybody calls him Cub. Eleven years old."
> Without looking at the names, Feirstein reached into his stack and pulled out the third manila folder. I suspected that he had been planning to foist this one off on me even before I came through the door.

Scotty is still saying *No*, he's still resisting by getting into a negative frame of mind about this kid.

> "Cub's a funny kid," he said. "He comes to all the events even though he doesn't have a Big Brother yet. He keeps asking me, 'Have you got someone yet, huh, have you got someone?' He can be a pain in the ass sometimes, they all can. But he's Okay. He's got some rascal in him, but he's likable."
> "What kind of rascal?"

Dodging or procrastinating is another way of saying *No*—in this case, asking questions instead of agreeing is procrastinating.

> "Oh, I don't mean he's lifting Pontiacs or anything. But. Well, let me put it this way: if you leave your lucky rabbit's foot and your wallet out on the table when Cub's there and you go out of the room, don't look for your rabbit's foot when you get back. Cub will pocket it. But he won't touch your cash."
> "A kleptomaniac?" I said. "You want to match me with a klepto?"
> "These kids are not perfect," Feirstein said. "A lot of them have been abandoned by fathers and then again by stepfathers or maybe some boyfriend of the mother that the kid got attached to."

They go on for a while, with Scotty asking questions about Cub's interests. Scotty is getting closer and closer to *Yes*, but he is still resisting.

I was having a hard time just saying "Yes, Cub will do fine." This was important. Would I hit it off with this kid? Would we have fun together or would he be obnoxious? Would he like me?

"Was Cub abandoned?" I asked.

Feirstein glanced at the folder. "Father took off when Cub was six."

"I'll take him." I said.

Scotty's *No* has melted into *Yes* when he realizes that Cub was abandoned, just as Scotty was abandoned by his wife. He identifies with the boy. He cares about him. In the scene, Scotty has grown to the point where he can believably give up his *No*'s and turn to *Yes*.

While I have emphasized the *No*'s coming from characters, keep in mind the other kinds of *No*'s—those from *situations*. A locked door says *No* to the man who wants to get in. An alcoholic past says *No* to the woman who wants to run for Congress. Terminal cancer says *No* to the priest who wants to live long enough to find his brother. Situations, generally, shouldn't change character's minds; characters should change situations. For example, if the situation is a hot, dry and hostile desert saying to your character, "No, you can't survive, you can't have water," and then an oasis suddenly appears, there is little reader satisfaction. On the other hand, if the character changes the *No* to a *Yes*, by finding an oasis through his own cleverness, instincts, courage or whatever, readers are satisfied.

Also, keep in mind what I said about revealing the needed character information *before* the *No*. Don't get your character into a locked closet and then, in effect, write, "By the way, Joe is an expert on locks." Decide what tools, qualities or history the character requires for his *Yes* and give them to him before he says *No* (the private detective had an eye for the ladies before he said no, the policewoman had compassion before she said no, and Willy was a weasel before he said no).

Keep those waves of opposition coming all through your story and you'll find that a lot of editors who have been saying *no* to you will now say *yes*.

What a Coincidence!

by Nancy Kress

Writers are often admonished to avoid the use of coincidence in their fiction. And with good reason: coincidence (defined as "a remarkable concurrence of events, apparently arranged by chance") weakens a plot by making it seem unrealistic. But when used correctly, coincidence can actually *enhance* the tension and interest of your stories.

To understand how coincidence can be used effectively, we must first understand why and when it will not work.

Readers will reject coincidences that resolve plot difficulties. Let's say your protagonist, a successful businesswoman in her late forties, has spent thirty pages berating a female private detective for not finding the protagonist's daughter, given up for adoption twenty-five years earlier. Then, on page thirty-one, both characters learn that the detective *is* the daughter. You want readers to think, "Oh, wow!" but because this is an implausible, out-of-the-blue coincidence (*billions* of other people are the right age to be the daughter), readers are more likely to think, "Oh, come on now!" Writers use coincidence to resolve plots when they are desperate for an ending or cannot create events that grow logically from earlier events and characters' choices.

"But," the well-read will protest, "great writers have often used coincidence in just that fashion. Charles Dickens did it." Yes, he did. In *A Tale of Two Cities*, for example, Solomon Pross, informer for the French Revolution, turns out to be both the brother of the heroine's governess *and* the turnkey of the French prison at the very time that Sydney Carton needs to enter the prison to make his famous exchange with the condemned Charles Darnay. Nineteenth-century readers loved it. But nineteenth-century readers, devouring novels as a relatively new art form, were more credulous than twentieth-century readers—or editors. Coincidences that looked like unforeseen and startling surprises in 1859 would look like sloppy plotting today.

Acceptable Coincidences

You *can* use coincidence effectively in these four situations:

- *When coincidence sets up a plot complication instead of resolving it.*

Suppose our young detective is researching another adoption history and accidentally learns the identity of her own biological mother. This is a coincidence—"a remarkable occurrence by chance"—but the reader will accept it because the story itself is yet to come: what the detective *does* with her knowledge. Subsequent events, not the coincidence, deliver tension, character development and a satisfying resolution. The coincidence is not the story's target, but only its launching pad. You are allowed a remarkable take-off.

This principle holds true for all kinds of fiction. In my fantasy novel *The White Pipes*, the protagonist, Fia, discovers in chapter one that she has accidentally brought her young son to the one place where he can be discovered by his father, whom Fia fled ten years earlier. Readers accept this pure coincidence because the meeting between Fia and Brant (the father) only triggers the action, much of which grows logically out of their struggle for the child. Had I brought Fia to the city at the end of the book, let Brant recognize his son and then help Fia out of difficulty, the novel would have failed.

• *When the events seem remarkable or contrived at the time, but are logically explained as more information is revealed to the reader and/or the protagonist.*

This creates tension because readers wonder, "How on earth could *that* happen?" Espionage thrillers often use this structure: seeming coincidences of identity turn out to be the result of elaborate plans laid by double or even triple agents.

My science fiction novel *Brain Rose*, which centers on reincarnation, features two characters who remember being related to a third character in previous lives. This seems a preposterous coincidence—out of the billions of people who ever lived, why should three people in the same hospital happen to have known each other centuries ago? The coincidence is so great, in fact, that one of the three, a logical man, refuses to believe it at all. As the novel progresses, however, all three learn that certain factors of reincarnation memories account for the coincidence (which is not a coincidence at all, but a logical outcome of forces they didn't understand when they first learned about then mnemonic connections).

A word of caution: For this surprise-now-justify-later strategy to work, your readers must trust that you will eventually provide an explanation worth waiting for; you must handle the rest of your story authoritatively enough to convince readers you aren't a writer likely to commit an unwitting coincidence blunder.

• *When the story is humor not intended to represent any reality whatsoever.*

Comedy has its own rules. If it is outrageous, funny and fresh enough, it doesn't have to be plausible. Coincidence—the more blatant the better—only adds to the skewed view of reality that is part of the fun. Consider that stew of coincidences and improbabilities, Douglas Adams's *The Hitchhiker's Guide to the Galaxy*. When Arthur Dent meets his old girlfriend, Tricia McMillan, aboard an alien spaceship, the probability ratio of their having met in this way turns out to be exactly the same as her phone number. Similarly, if slightly more soberly, the romantic comedies of Georgette Heyer feature improbable parallel switches of affection. Just as Sophy in *The Grand Sophy* declares her love for Charles Rivenhall, Rivenhall's fiance Eugenia has formed an attachment to the man who was courting Sophy. Not likely—but a lot of fun.

• *When the point of the story is that life is more mysterious and unpredictable than we think.*

This is the most sophisticated use of coincidence. Improbable concurrences deliberately push at the edges of readers' beliefs, not to be amusing, but to dramatize a specific stance: we don't understand the workings of the universe. To support this point, the story must make coincidences seem plausible and logic seem absurd. However, unlike the events of absurdist or surreal fiction, these coincidences *might* just happen—*maybe*. Such a story unsettles readers by blurring the line between the expected and the possible.

In my short story "Craps," Charlie Foster encounters a series of coincidental "miracles": He chokes on a piece of broccoli but is saved when the ambulance hits a Mercedes and the impact dislodges the broccoli; he is nearly hit by a brick falling from a cathedral but is saved when a pigeon flies into and deflects the brick; an elevator accident kills two co-workers by Charlie walks away without a scratch. Charlie becomes obsessed with the need to know whether what happened to him was indeed random or whether some larger pattern operates in the universe. Before he comes to any conclusion, he is hit by lightning and recovers in a hospital that catches fire without any loss of life—"a bloody miracle," says one of the firefighters.

The danger in this kind of story is that it may become such an abstract intellectual exercise that readers don't *care* if it's full of coincidences or not. To prevent this, characters must seem real amid the strangeness, sympathetic amid the improbabilities.

User's Guide

Are there any "remarkable concurrences of events apparently arranged by chance" in your recent work? If so, test your coincidental scenes against our four types of situations: Is your coincidence the result of cleverness or laziness—does it advance the story or destroy realism?

If you haven't used coincidence effectively, you have two options for improving the story.

The first, of course, is to eliminate the scene. If the coincidence is used within the story to move the plot along, with only minor revision you probably can replace it with a scene that provides similar movement—and more believability. However, replacing a coincidental scene used as your story's climax or ending will require considerable rewriting.

You also might try shaping your coincidence to fit one of our first two effective uses (the last two you'd need to have in mind when beginning a story). Be prepared to alter your story's structure if you reshape; in our first example, we changed the young detective's original client from unknown mother into ordinary client, and brought in the mother as another character.

However you decide to use coincidence in your fiction, don't write as my "Craps" character Charlie Foster lived: not knowing if your coincidences are accident or intent. For your story to succeed, *you* must be in control.

Using the Flashback

by Nancy Kress

Y ou can't go home again, Thomas Wolfe tells us, and legions of others
mournfully agree with him. What's over is over. The moving finger
writ. The past is in another country, they do things differently there,
and besides, the wench is dead.

As a writer, however, you're a privileged creature—at least while you're
inhabiting your fictional worlds. You *can* go home again, or back to 1962, or
into your character's childhood—with the flashback. A flashback is a literary
time machine with strong headlights, illuminating background events and thus
making the fictional present clearer and more interesting to your readers.

However, there is a risk in driving this time machine. Use it too much, and
the reader will react like any passenger on a trip with too many changes of
destination and direction: Where are we now? Didn't we already pass this
monument? Aren't we ever going to get where we're going?

Using flashbacks successfully requires that you recognize what they offer,
how they should be integrated into story-time events, and when they have
become tedious detours rather than fascinating side trips.

Three Steps Back

Flashbacks can be categorized according to their length. Longer flashbacks
offer different advantages—and raise different problems—than do medium or
short ones.

The longest type—and the easiest to handle—is the flashback that lasts
nearly the entire length of the story or novel. Also called a *frame story*, this
construction opens with a scene that occurs after the main action is over.
Often the point of view is that of a character recalling events of many years
ago. The recollection slips into the main story, and then *stays there* until the
last few pages, at which time the story may or may not revert to the time frame
of the opening scene. Thus, virtually the entire tale becomes a flashback.

Readers are seldom confused by this structure because they're asked to
make only one shift in time, after which the story proceeds chronologically.
Examples are John Knowles's *A Separate Peace* and Herman Raucher's *Summer of '42*. Both novels open with adult men revisiting places important to
their adolescence. Memory becomes story time, and the adolescent protagonists take center stage until the last few pages of each book, when once again
the adult voices take over the narrative. And this is the main advantage to the
long flashback: At both ends of the book the adult voices can lend perspectives
their younger selves could not possibly possess. In using this technique,

149

Knowles and Raucher gained the richness of double viewpoints in single characters.

Remember, however, that any gain made through flashback must be paid for. *Any* use of this method distances readers from the action; flashbacks shatter the illusion that readers are witnessing events as they happen, *right now*. The flashback, by definition, is already over. Before you use it, think: are you more thrilled by today's kiss or one you remember from yesterday— or does the memory of the latter sweeten the former?

What about the *medium-length flashback*, which interrupts the main story? The readers just became interested in the startling meeting of the President and his illegitimate teenage son. Should you distract readers with a scene about the President's adolescence?

Maybe. The medium-length flashback, lasting one or two scenes or chapters, can serve several purposes: It can provide necessary background. It can explain motivations more dramatically than can blocks of exposition. It can allow you to start *in media res*, when things are interesting because conflict has surfaced, and then—after your reader is hooked—you can drop back in time to explain how the conflict came about.

The use of an opening crisis followed by a medium-length flashback is the most traditional form of this technique. Because it's been around a while and because genre fiction such as the western often employs it, the technique has earned a reputation for being hackneyed. The reputation is not deserved: In the hands of a writer telling a strong story and not merely trying to inflate a mediocre one, this kind of flashback still works.

Consider, for instance, Scott Turow's *Presumed Innocent*. The novel opens at the funeral of murdered prosecuting attorney Carolyn Polhemus. In the next scene, still in story time, narrator Rusty Sabich examines criminal evidence, including some brutal pictures of Carolyn's body. A flashback chapter comes next, in which we learn of Rusty's sexual involvement with the dead woman. Even though the flashback interrupts the criminal investigation that forms the main story line of the novel, we don't mind the interruption; the flashback adds tension (How will the affair affect the investigation?), emotional complication (Rusty is married) and complexity (Rusty is revealed as not as hard and rational as he'd like to be).

The medium-length flashback is sometimes, as in *Presumed Innocent*, given its own chapter; this tells readers when they are in story time and when they are visiting the past. The flashback may even extend over two chapters. Gail Godwin's *Violet Clay* opens with her protagonist living in New York and painting, rather unhappily, covers for paperback gothic romances. Chapters two and three flash back to detail Violet's earlier life: one chapter set in South Carolina, one in New York before the story itself opens. Clear transitions tell the reader where she is, and when:

> Nine years ago I had arrived in New York. It was spring and I had a
> few more months of being twenty-three . . .
> As I walked down Madison, past the galleries, nine years later . . .

I looked at my reflection in each plate-glass window I passed and recalled every detail of that younger version, getting dressed by herself in the Martha Washington Hotel. . . .

Such transitions become even more important when the medium-length flashback is not set off in its own chapter(s) but instead is a scene within a chapter. Readers are put off when they picture three pages of events occurring on the same day and later discover two of those pages occurred a year earlier.

The third type of flashback occupies only a few paragraphs. Because it is so short, it hardly interrupts the story at all. Still, like its longer cousins, it can deepen characterization and clarify situation. In Rumer Godden's *A Candle for St. Jude*, for instance, the young ballet dancer Hilda is showing Madame, a former ballerina who is Hilda's teacher, a new dance Hilda has choreographed. Madame is skeptical:

"What is your music?" she said, and she added sarcastically, "Scriabin?"

Hilda said with dignity that it was not Scriabin, it was Zedek.

"I never heard of him."

A smile flickered at the corners of Hilda's mouth. "He is a contemporary Czech composer," she said gently, but Madame had seen the smile and she did not forgive her.

"Mr. Felix helped you with that."

"No," said Hilda truthfully. Mr. Felix had refused to help her. "If you want to find out music you must find it out for yourself. That will teach you!" said Mr. Felix, though whether he meant it as a threat or a fact Hilda did not know. "If you want to do these ballets, do them by yourself," said Mr. Felix to her later. "Don't let anyone else lay a finger on them."

"I only want advice."

"Advice is the worst kind of help. It is pernicious, and if you don't know what that means," said Mr. Felix, "you should go and look it up in the dictionary." Hilda looked it up and was surprised to find how strong and final its meaning was.

"Once . . . I showed him some music . . ." she hesitated and said to Madame, "It was recorded. I found it and showed it to him. He said he thought it should make a good ballet. That was a year ago but I couldn't forget it . . ."

Notice that Godden starts the flashback in line nine with no transition at all. Although this is a little confusing (at least to me), it works because the subject of the mini-flashback, Mr. Felix's musical aid to Hilda, is also the subject of the story-time conversation surrounding the flashback. This commonality of topic compensates for the switch in time, weaving the miniflashback tightly into the narrative. The flashback wouldn't have worked if it had concerned, say, Hilda's math lesson rather than Madame's assertion about Mr. Felix.

Mini-flashbacks don't slow the story down much, and they allow for multiple forays into different aspects of a character's history. However, if you use them too frequently, the readers may feel they're following a temporal tennis ball volleying between past and present. You don't want to give them a pain the neck.

The Graceful Flash

How do you get in and out of a flashback plausibly? After all, if you just plunge in with *Two days earlier, Marcia had been eyeing some veal in the butcher shop* . . . the reader is likely to think, "Huh? A Butcher shop? Veal? I thought we were riding in a taxi toward a business meeting." Sometimes this discontinuity is exactly the reaction you want, but usually you should build a bridge between the main scene and the flashback.

The bridge can be an object. In the Godden example quoted above, the bridge is a piece of music. In Turow's *Presumed Innocent*, it is the set of photographs of Carolyn's corpse. As the protagonist views the pictures, it's entirely natural that his own affair with Carolyn comes to his mind.

The bridge can be a place, as it is in *A Separate Peace* and *Summer of '42*. Revisiting a locale important in the past evokes memories—and flashbacks.

The bridge can be an incident. In Sloan Wilson's *The Man in the Gray Flannel Suit*, Tom Rath is asked to fill out an employment application that asks him to complete the sentence "The most significant fact about me is . . ." He thinks of several possible answers, all of which tell us something about his character. One answer he bitterly considers is "The most significant fact about me is that I have killed seventeen men." This provides a plausible— even compelling—transition to a flashback about Tom's experience in World War II.

The bridge to a flashback could also be an overheard snatch of conversation, a song, a smell, an unusual color—anything that logically recalls the past to the protagonist, and thus to the reader.

When Not to Flash

Must fiction use flashbacks to convey events previous to story time? Of course not—and you may decide not to use any flashbacks at all. Some writers dislike them because they interrupt the story. Some editors dislike them because it's fatally easy to replace tight plotting with flashbacks. And some readers don't like them because they want to barrel through the story like a phobic running through a graveyard at night.

If you decide that, for *your* story, the disadvantages of flashbacks outweigh the gains, consider alternative methods for portraying the past. Here's a scene between Allen Strand and his son Jimmy, from Irwin Shaw's novel *Bread Upon the Waters*:

Jimmy took a wrinkled pack of cigarettes from his jeans pocket and lit up. Strand watched disapprovingly as Jimmy inhaled and blew the smoke out of his nostrils. He was the only one in the family who smoked.

"Jimmy," Strand asked, "do you ever read what scientists say about the relationship between smoking and cancer?"

"Do you ever read what the scientists say about atomic pollution?"

Strand sighed, the third time since he'd come home that evening. "Okay," he said resignedly. "You're old enough to make your own decisions." Jimmy was eighteen and made enough money at odd jobs he never explained so that he never had to ask Strand for any. He had finished high school, not disgracefully, a year ago, and had laughed when Strand had suggested college.

"Tell me, Jimmy," Strand said, "I'm curious — just what is this new music sound you keep talking about?"

Here — not in a dramatized flashback but in two sentences of description, four of dialogue, and two of exposition — we learn quite a bit about the past of these people. This includes both the factual past — Jimmy's age, scholastic history and employment record — and the emotional past, as implied in Jimmy's answer to his father, in Strand's sighing resignation over the cigarettes, and in Jimmy's refusal of college (especially telling because his father is a teacher).

Whether you choose to portray the past through flashbacks or through a combination of exposition, description and dialogue, the past is always implied in the present. In that sense, we can *all* go home — but flashbacks let fiction writers go home in style.

Using Foreshadowing to Keep Your Stories On Track

by Louis E. Catron

Your creative writing teacher taught you that foreshadowing is a hook. A storyteller's device aimed at the audience. A suspense-builder. Writing books say foreshadowing makes the reader or audience member look forward to discovering what will happen next. My *own* book says that, but recently my writing classes have taught me that although foreshadowing is effective for the reader, it is an even more significant tool for the *writer*.

The most-recognized use of foreshadowing is *writer-talking-to-reader*. In effect, the writer is saying, "Dear Reader or Audience Member: Pay careful attention, because this foreshadowing indicates that soon events will turn dramatically." Foreshadowing engages the reader's attention and, better, stimulates the imagination. For example, when a character in the movie *Gremlins* announces sternly, "Never, never, never feed them after midnight," that's foreshadowing, a suspense-building hook to make the audience wait anxiously to find out what will happen when the cuddly creatures are fed.

But a second important, often-ignored aspect of foreshadowing is *writer-talking-to-self*, in effect saying, "Dear Self: You are making a promise to yourself about the plot's development." It is your instruction to yourself about where to take the story; it keeps you on track. For example, consider a well-known struggling writer at work: "It was a dark and stormy night." Snoopy starts his famous novel. To the reader, this sentence suggests a mood. But as a "writer's IOU to the writer," the foreshadowing tells Snoopy (if he ever finishes his book) that he must write about a downpour of trouble.

Foreshadowing, in this sense, is an IOU you make to yourself. Every time you use foreshadowing, you are forced to follow up with conflict, complications, plot reversals and character evolutions. Foreshadowing is not a mere hooking technique for readers; it is a compelling demand that writers place on themselves.

Each instance of foreshadowing is the first of two stages in your story. First is foreshadowing's promise; then must come fulfillment. Foreshadowing is like an appetizer before the meal; the fulfillment is important—the main course, if you will.

Foreshadowing that isn't followed up is a red herring, a distraction that destroys the unity of the whole. Many writers forget fulfillment. Foreshadowing forces you to serve the main course: it forces the screenwriter of *Gremlins* to write a later scene in which someone gives that cuddly creature food and drink, with predictable disaster.

Incurring Your Self-Debt

You can experiment with writing yourself an IOU by assigning yourself to put foreshadowing in the beginning and middle of your story, novel or play.

If you have a story already in mind, using foreshadowing will help you move it forward. It demands movement and action, gives your story a sense of urgency and strength, and maintains the story's direction.

On the other hand, if you don't yet have a clear idea of what you want to write, use foreshadowing as fodder. Introduce character quirks, props that can be used to get the protagonist out of or into a tight spot, special conditions of environment or weather, strange or mysterious sounds, and the like. Asking yourself where these may lead can create a sort of serendipity, a fortuitous discovery of enriched ideas that will enhance your story, novel, or play.

Think of this experiment as a preliminary draft; don't handicap yourself by insisting that the foreshadowing be subtle. Disconnect your critical "self-censor," because this is no time to worry about hiding your craftsmanship. Instead, work in the foreshadowing as best you can, and let it force you to develop your story. Later, when you polish the piece into final draft, you will want to make foreshadowing more subtle, because art consists of hiding technique.

In this experiment, make each unit of foreshadowing refer to a different aspect of the story. For example, on the first page you can use foreshadowing to hint at the story's theme; on the next page let foreshadowing introduce a device the protagonist can use to help solve the story problem; and on the third page use foreshadowing to predict an event that plunges the character into major conflict. Practice making foreshadowing quite short, a phrase or two, and practice enlarging it as it becomes part of the story's action.

Page one. Foreshadow your theme. For the sake of this writing exercise, assume that you will start with foreshadowing that implies your story's basic message.

For example, imagine that Shakespeare is using this exercise, trying to start a play with a thematic speech that will guide him as he writes the rest of the work. He knows vaguely he wants to write about a man's greed for power. He scribbles idle notes — "Absolute power corrupts absolutely" — then revises the notes into a more poetic, less concrete statement: "Fair is foul, and foul is fair."

With that single speech he's written himself an IOU that tells him he is to write about a world turned topsy-turvy. Because he wants the speech to predict forthcoming developments, he decides to assign the line to a soothsayer. And so he starts *Macbeth* with the witches in a bleak and mysterious scene that sets the tone for all that will follow. Thus, the foreshadowing clarifies for Shakespeare what he must do with the rest of the tragedy to bring the theme to life, to show that fair is foul and foul is fair.

With foreshadowing on your first page, you can take advantage of the same clarity Shakespeare enjoyed: because he has the witches say in the first scene,

"Fair is foul, and foul is fair," he forces himself to write the rest of the play about reversals of morality. That short speech clarifies for Shakespeare what his play's subsequent actions will mean; a comparable short speech in the beginning of your novel can be equally valuable to guide you through the development of your theme.

Page two. Use a plant. Assign yourself to use a "plant," a kind of foreshadowing. For example, you might have your heroine search in the desk drawer for a stamp, saying "If I don't get this bill in the mail . . . " She uncovers a pistol, pulls it out, looks at it in surprise: "Oh, lord, Mike said he was going to put it in a safe place this morning. I wish that man'd do what he says he'll do." And she puts the pistol back in the drawer and continues searching for the stamp. That plant means you now are ready to use — must use, because this is an IOU to yourself — the pistol later in the story.

A "plant" also can guide you to an arrival of a person who can be expected to change the course of action: *Sally looked impatiently at her watch, then said, "Damn! The cop said he'd be here twenty minutes ago."*

Page three. Foreshadow a major event. Prepare for the arrival of a major character hostile to the protagonist's goals, or carefully deny that another character will arrive at all (and of course he will). That's the method Peter Shaffer used to open his play *Black Comedy*. Onstage are Brindsley Miller, a young sculptor who is uncertain of himself, and Carol Melkett, his fiancée, a debutante.

BRINDSLEY: Suppose Harold comes back?

CAROL: He is not coming back till tomorrow morning.

BRINDSLEY: I know. But suppose he comes tonight? He's made about his antiques. What do you think he'll say if he goes into his room and finds out we've stolen them?

Carol reminds Brindsley that her father's due to arrive.

BRINDSLEY: As if I could forget. Why you had to invite your monster father tonight, I can't think.

They continue talking about her father.

BRINDSLEY: The more I hear about your Daddy, the more I hate him. I loathe military men anyway . . . and in any case he's bound to hate me.

CAROL: Why?

BRINDSLEY: Because I'm a complete physical coward. He'll smell it on my breath.

CAROL: Look, darling, all you've got to do is stand up to him. Daddy's only a bully when he thinks people are afraid of him. What can he do? To you?

BRINDSLEY: For one thing, he can refuse to let me marry you.

Note also the bantering lilt of those lines. In addition to foreshadowing a character arrival, Shaffer issues himself an IOU, saying in effect, "Dear Peter: Remember you must keep the comic tone when Harold returns to find his antiques ill-appropriated, and when Daddy arrives to deal with Brindsley's attitute toward the man's daughter."

Page five. Enlarge the foreshadowing. Foreshadowing can be a single short speech or a paragraph. Assign yourself to write at least one paragraph of foreshadowing, as novelist Dick Francis writes in the beginning pages of *Proof:* "There was no tremble in the air. No shudder. No premonition at all of the horror soon to happen there. All was quiet and peaceful; expectant certainly, but benign. I remembered it particularly, after." The foreshadowing passage is a mandate to Francis, Telling him he must write a horrible event.

Using action, you can extend foreshadowing. For example, during the first act of Marsha Norman's *'night, Mother*, the daughter's obsessive packing, list-making and housecleaning is foreshadowing action that forces the playwright to make something grim happen in the second act. As you work with foreshadowing, experiment with using significant action to enlarge it for at least one page, preferably more.

Later pages. Continue inserting foreshadowing. Foreshadowing isn't limited to introductory pages. Shakespeare uses foreshadowing in the opening scene of Act Four of *Macbeth* when a witch says, "By the pricking of my thumbs,/ Something wicked this way comes."

Ross Thomas uses foreshadowing at the halfway point in his novel, *Briar-patch:*

Later, some were to claim that if Senator Ramirez had been where he said he would be, at any one of the three numbers, he might have prevented it from happening — or prevented at least some of it . . . Tim Dolan always argued that it didn't really matter who Dill called that morning because nobody could have stopped what eventually happened from happening.

Foreshadowing in the latter portions of the piece functions as it does in the beginning: It reminds the writer to develop more story and characterization. In your story, use foreshadowing at approximately the thirdway points to guide you through the rest of the piece.

The X Factors

Of course, it sounds horribly formulaic to say, "Put XX units of foreshadowing in the first XX percent of your short story, novel or play," but this writing device forces you to consider more carefully where your story must go, what the characters must do, the characters' needs, and the mood you wish to maintain. We know that a writer may craft in foreshadowing retroactively after writing the "fulfillment," but here we are looking at foreshadowing's function as a provocateur, an IOU from the writer to the writer.

Granted, there is something of a chicken-egg conundrum here. One can argue that when Shakespeare wrote *Macbeth* he knew in advance he intended to dramatize good turned into evil and a world forced upside down by reversal of morality, so he did not need to tell himself that fair is foul. Therefore, you can argue that the famous line isn't author-directed.

Perhaps. Perhaps not. But either way, such a neatly succinct line helps the writer think precisely of the desired total effect. Any writer, whether blessed with Shakespeare's genius or not, would benefit from having a definite line such as "Fair is foul" to guide the development of the rest of the work.

In your next story, use foreshadowing to make promises to yourself and thereby help develop plot and character. If this new use of an old tool makes writing easier as well as more dynamic, and if it forces you to serve a magnificent main course, this experimental process will be worth the effort.

Creating Immediate, Urgent Stories

by David Madden

The experience readers crave when they turn to fiction is an illusion of reality—a reality heightened by extremes of action and emotion our everyday lives seldom match. To provide that experience, your story must be written with an urgency that pulls the attention of readers into your fictional world and makes them forget they are reading words on a page. You must create instantly accessible fiction that remains more tangible, real and compelling than the surrounding real-life stimulations that constantly threaten to distract readers. Instilling such immediacy in your fiction is mostly accomplished in three areas: in the story's structure, through description, and in writing style. Here are some tips for creating immediacy in each area.

Get Off to a Running Start

Many stories flounder about, never giving the reader a chance to become involved; this happens when the writer does not begin the story by concentrating on captivating the reader, but instead looks for the easiest way into the story. If your openings stumble, review these elements:

• *Point of view.* If the point of view is clear and consistent from the story's beginning, readers won't be forced to guess whose perception they are seeing through.

• *Conflict.* Action proceeds from characters in conflict—and pulls readers into your story. If you have the conflict clearly in mind, and pose it clearly for the reader, you will reach for the more active phrases and situations that create immediacy.

• *Exposition and background.* Long, mundane descriptions of character or setting background exude artificiality and intrude on illusion. Many writers feel obligated to begin their stories with such passages because they assume that readers need the entire background of the fictional world to appreciate the story's movement. The opposite is true. A single sentence, if well-imagined and worded, can do that far more immediately. Consider F. Scott Fitzgerald's opening sentence of "The Adjuster":

> At five o'clock the somber egg-shaped room at the Ritz ripens to subtle melody—the light *clat-clat* of one lump, two lumps, into the cup, and the *ding* of the shining teapots and cream-pots as they kiss elegantly in transit upon a silver tray.

Fitzgerald doesn't diagram the room, detail its poshness, or explain exactly where in the world we are. He sets the story in motion.

In real life, we learn details bit by bit, respond intensely to a single observation before we absorb more information. You can emulate that in your stories by distributing exposition or background in small chunks. Fitzgerald's room at the Ritz has a horseshoe-shaped balcony and tables covered with white cloths—but he tells us that later in the story.

Instead of opening with irrelevant weather reports, exhaustive descriptions of houses, or minute-by-minute accounts of characters waking up, you might try allowing dialogue to carry the information. Instead of writing, "Mary dropped out of Holyoke to go to New York to find herself," have another character ask Mary, "You dropped out of Holyoke for this?" Be careful, however, not to create "talking head" dialogue, every bit as boring and windy as the exposition it replaces ("Mary," he asked, "you dropped out of Holyoke and came to New York to find yourself?").

Create Compelling Description

Fitzgerald's scene at the Ritz swirls around the reader: time passes, sounds are heard, objects move. His description is not just lying on the page; it involves the reader through action. Similarly, try to animate objects in your stories. Instead of writing, "John wore a gold ring in his ear," write "As John played his fiddle, his gold earring swung rhythmically."

Animating objects is just one technique for creating immediacy through description. Here are others to consider:

• *Create charged images.* A charged image evokes all the other elements of your story—theme, character, conflict, setting, style and so on. As the reader moves through the story, the charged image discharges its potency gradually, keeping the reader involved and intrigued.

Fitzgerald first uses the image of a green light in this passage of *The Great Gatsby*:

> . . . it was Mr. Gatsby himself, come out to determine what share was his of our local heavens.
>
> I decided to call to him. . . . But I didn't call to him, for he gave a sudden intimation that he was content to be alone—he stretched out his arms toward the dark water in a curious way, and, far as I was from him, I could have sworn he was trembling. Involuntarily I glanced seaward— and distinguished nothing except a single green light, minute and far away, that might have been the end of a dock. When I looked once more for Gatsby he had vanished, and I was alone again in the unquiet darkness.

The green light symbolizes, of course, Daisy and all she means to Gatsby. After enhancing the image throughout the novel, Fitzgerald uses the green light as the powerful final image of the story.

• *Make descriptive sentences rhythmic, as opposed to mechanical.* Fitzgerald did not write: "Gatsby stretched his arms out toward the water. He was trembling. I glanced seaward."

• *Activate all the reader's senses.* Most writers concentrate on visual description. Think about how your fictional world smells, sounds, feels and tastes. In his novel *The Big Sleep*, Raymond Chandler describes a greenhouse:

> The glass walls and roof were heavily misted and big drops of moisture splashed down on the plants. The light had an unreal greenish color, like light filtered through an aquarium tank. The plants filled the place, a forest of them, with nasty meaty leaves and stalks like the newly washed fingers of dead men. They smelled as overpowering as boiling alcohol under a blanket.

• *Filter all description through point of view.* Watch how the same scene changes with each point of view:

First person:

> What excited me more than his fervent fiddling was the way John's golden earring danced above his shoulder.

The earring is described only because it affects Mary, the narrator.

Third person, through Mary:

> John's fervent fiddling excited her, but it was the way his gold earring swung rhythmically above his shoulder that made her shiver with delight.

We are interested in the earring only because it stimulates an emotion in Mary.

Omniscient:

> In the crowd gathered around John Wynn, the only person more excited by his dancing earring than his fervent fiddle playing was Mary Walden.

The narrator tells us directly how everybody responded to the gold earring, with a focus on Mary.

• *Be brief.* As always.

Guiding the Reader

How you arrange your words, phrases and sentences also contributes to the sense of immediacy that keeps readers engrossed in your story. You can employ certain styles and techniques to create a forward flow from moment to moment:

• *State things in chronological sequence.* Instead of, "Mary went to school, having had her breakfast," write "Having had her breakfast, Mary went to school."

• *Use active phrasing.* Change "Mary enjoyed listening to the fiddle played by John," to "Mary enjoyed listening to John play the fiddle."

• *Keep transitions crisp.* Transitions enable you to move readers from one time and place to another. Do it quickly, instead of sending readers trudging over a long, elaborately constructed transitional bridge. In my short story, "The Day the Flowers Came," a man wakes up alone in his house and begins receiving condolence flowers for a wife and children he did not know were dead. I used door chimes and telephone calls to rapidly mark off scenes.

• *Impinge phrases.* Construct sentences that compress phrases or words against each other. The butting of elements will propel the reader from the first element into the second. Notice how the sentence pulls you along when "Mary decided to leave Holyoke and look for a job in New York" is changed to "Mary decided to leave Holyoke, look for a job in New York."

• *Juxtapose elements.* Select two words, images or events that have no special impact separately, and place them side by side so that they evoke a third element for the reader. My first version of this section from "The Day the Flowers Came" overtly states all three elements:

Lifting the white cloth from the tray made J.D. imagine his wife and children on a morgue slab. He felt an eerie sensation in his stomach, but the sight of the smoking food dispelled the image.

In the published version, I dropped the mention of J.D.'s family. Notice how you're forced to supply the third element—you're caught up in the immediacy of the moment:

Lifting the white cloth from the tray, J.D. felt an eerie sensation in his stomach that the sight of the smoking food dispelled.

You must make sure, however, that the connection will be clear to the readers. Otherwise, they will become confused.

• *Use reversal and surprise to sustain the reader's immediate attention.*

John lifted his fiddle to his chin, took a deep breath, sank to his knees on the sidewalk in a faint.

• *Use repetition to emphasize certain elements.* Repeating words, phrases and cadences—in moderation—provides readers with that swirling, immediate sense of being part of the scene. D.H. Lawrence uses repetition for a key scene in *The Rainbow*:

And again they were kissing together . . . He wanted her. He wanted her exceedingly. She was something new. They stood there folded, suspended in the night. And his whole being quivered with surprise, as from a blow. He wanted her, and he wanted to tell her so.

• *Avoid distractions and deadeners.* Words, phrases and other material that call attention to themselves — or don't add to the story — destroy immediacy by putting distance between the reader and your fictional world.

The Ironic Immediacy of the Past Tense

It is a paradox that we use, more often than not, past tense to tell a story, while using every technique possible to generate immediacy, the illusion of here and now. Use of the past tense would seem counterproductive. One response recently has been to resort to present tense throughout. Yet, present tense constantly calls attention to itself, and seems artificial, while readers are almost never conscious of the fact that what seems so immediate is being presented in the past tense. There is something about the paradoxical nature of fiction whereby the reader experiences as immediate what is really being presented as *past*.

Dialogue is one element of fiction that by its nature lends immediacy to your story. Readers feel that dialogue is always in the present tense, being spoken now, even though language that is couched in the past tense surrounds it. All the more reason to avoid such past tense phrases as "she said," "he said," whenever possible; they convey to the reader a sense of the dialogue's having been spoken in the past.

Immediate Help

Making fiction immediate is an awesome task. The problem is exacerbated because when we write, our own emotions, imagination and intellect are already aroused; the words and techniques I've described aren't necessary to our own primary stimulation. We often delude ourselves that what is going down on the page in first draft will be as intensely immediate for readers as it is for us.

You can, I am convinced, overcome much of this occupational hazard by imagining, as you begin to write, an audience of strangers. Try to feel their living, breathing presence, and respond to their craving for an immediately intense experience.

How to Write Believable
Love Scenes

by David Groff

During the first hundred pages of your novel, Dirk and Amber have been eying each other, wooing, feeling their mutual attraction grow as each gets to know the other. Now you, the novelist, have brought them together—and if your novel is to succeed they must in some way consummate their love. How in the name of Eros do you manage it?

Love is what most novels are about. From bodice-ripping romances to tea-in-the-parlor mysteries to passionate tales set among the well-to-do—nearly every piece of fiction contains a love story or a motivating romantic charge. Love, or the urge to love, is the explicit or implicit topic of just about every writer around, past and present, from Homer to Henry Miller. Why? Because love, in its myriad forms, is a major topic of our lives.

There are as many ways to write about love as there are styles of writing. There are also many ways a writer can go wrong. Bringing Dirk and Amber together in a way that satisfies your reader is one of the biggest challenges you face as a fiction writer. If you manage it well, then your story advances surely and authoritatively. If your approach is somehow inappropriate or inadequate, your novel can grind to a halt.

As an editor of both literary and popular fiction, I've experienced more sex on manuscript pages than I ever could in real life. I've read scenes of great power, where lovers come together with passion, originality and purpose. Such scenes have been integral to the success of the novels that contain them. But I've also plowed through fiction where the sex is a flop—gratuitous, overblown, boring, beside the point, vicious, clinical, obstructive or out of character.

What are the challenges you face when you write a love scene? For a scene to work for me as an editor—or for most readers—I think a writer must meet these criteria:

- You should write the scene, and place it, so that it is central to the story and advances the plot;

- You should shape the scene to maintain the novel's conflict and tension;

- You should write a scene that is fair to the story's characters, that is consistent with their personalities, and increases the reader's understanding of what makes them work as human beings;

- You must find a language of relating that is fresh, original, appropriately rich and evocative, consistent with the novel, and that is neither pornographic nor overmodest, neither clinical nor clichéd.

Let's explore these challenges individually.

The Necessity of Love

When do you need a love scene? That depends, of course, on how integral a physical relationship is to the story you're telling. Many popular novels are more or less required to contain at least one sexual encounter of some explicitness. The beautiful model and the celebrity doctor, the weary CIA agent and the lovely Romanian who may be a spy, the Anglo-Irish countess and the Cavalier—all must come together in a kiss, or more. In so-called literary novels—novels where the language and theme are as primary as the plot—love scenes are more often optional, or optional in their graphic content, since they are not necessarily part of what attracts readers to those books.

But for both literary and popular fiction, the rule is the same: Don't ever write a love scene just for the sake of sex. Don't do it to thrill the reader or provide a break in the action. A good physical encounter in a novel has a greater *raison d'etre*; it propels the story and reveals the characters. In this sense, a love scene is like a song in a good, contemporary Broadway musical: It tells a story all by itself and is an opportunity to demonstrate motivations, intentions, dreams, beliefs, tensions. A good love scene is not static but kinetic. If you're writing a physical scene just to turn readers on, they'll feel cheated in the long run. As a serious writer of fiction, your job is to enlighten your readers—not to turn them on but to make them feel.

Consider the scene between Rupert and Ursula in *Women in Love*, by D.H. Lawrence. These two headstrong people avoid each other, argue furiously, and even combat each other physically throughout the novel. And yet when they come together, their romantic encounter is a revelation for each. Through their lovemaking, we learn along with the lovers that these two were meant for each other. Their sex is a point of both physical and metaphysical unity for them:

> She seemed to faint beneath, and he seemed to faint, stooping over her. It was a perfect passing away for both of them, and at the same time the most intolerable accession into being, the marvelous fullness of immediate gratification, overwhelming, outflooding the deepest life-force, the darkest, deepest strongest life-source of the human body, at the base and the back of the loins.

Likewise, in a contemporary novel of Hollywood, *The Sister*, by Pat Booth, our heroine is about to have her movie career snuffed out by blackmail. But, in a steamy scene in the exercise room of a fitness club—and in language far more graphic than D.H. Lawrence's—Jane Bennett has a violently passionate workout with an instructor. That encounter may seem like random sex for Jane, but it has its purpose. As a result of this scene, Jane develops a sense of her own power and is strengthened enough to confront blackmailers and face them down.

The arrow shuddered in the middle of the target. In sleepy concentric rings the waves of shock rumbled outward, growing as they went, touching and caressing every millimeter of her body with their urgent strength, as if a hot stone had been dropped into the middle of a bubbling pool. Her legs rigid, she locked onto him, her hands buried deep in the wet hair at the back of his neck, as the life flowed out of him and into her. She could feel its magical surrender as, out of control, it spent its energy within her, and the thought of it rushed to greet the memory of the taste of him, and all against the majestic background music of the nerve-racking orgasm. Here on the hard plain of ecstasy she called to him, oblivious of who would hear, or who would care—the groaning despair of her shout mocking the bliss that had mothered it.

Sex scenes do not stand alone. When they work well in a novel, they are the natural culmination of what has gone before—a release of tension that has been building between two characters, a complication or expression of emotions, a unification of two demanding elements of the story. Imagine how different *Women in Love* would read if Rupert and Ursula had had sex on page ten instead of page 354.

One way to find out if a love scene is necessary is simply to delete it. Do Dirk and Amber really *need* to come together at this point in the story? You must ask yourself how a love scene fits into the overall scheme of your novel and how it contributes to the plot. Does sex between Amber and Dirk pull them together or push them apart? Does evil Detective Bluenose come between them? There is nothing frivolous in your decision, because a well-placed, well-paced love scene can be one of the most effective ways to raise the emotional stakes of your novel and bring it to vivid life.

The Shape of Love

Any scene in a novel, whether it be sex or conversation over morning coffee, is usually a miniature version of the novel itself: it has a rising action, a complication, a climax and a denouement—just like love. This kind of plotting is particularly important in a love scene because the action is so touchy, so personal.

What gives a love scene its shape? To some degree it can be the love-making itself that dictates the scene's natural flow. But even where there is love there is *conflict*. Conflict and tension—the collision of opposing forces, ideas, personalities or circumstances—is what makes a novel work dramatically. The same is true for love scenes; no matter how enamored of each other Dirk and Amber may be, something must be at stake for them. As a result of their encounter, the novel's balance alters.

Prior to the passage quoted from *Women in Love*, Ursula has an extremely violent argument with Rupert—railing at his cleverness, his sensibility and his lingering affection for Hermione, the local society lady. She hurls the rings

Rupert gave her into the dust. This is the first part of the love scene and, boy, is there conflict. The rising action is the gift of the rings, the complications are Ursula's and Rupert's silliness, and the climax is when they argue their way into love. In one beautifully composed sequence of some fourteen pages, Lawrence takes us from affection to anger to genuine love rendered with sensuality and smarts. Throughout the scene, we are engaged with Rupert and Ursula's fates; we are witnessing not sex but plot, not bodies but characters.

In the novels I read daily as an editor, too often the conflict in a love scene is obscured by false casualness, too much physical description, or the author's obvious discomfort. Too often it seems that the writer has not figured out what the scene is supposed to accomplish.

Consider outlining the action in a love scene before you begin to write it — making sure that the scene has the point of view, tone and pacing it needs. After all, a love scene is really an action scene. Let's say Dirk has slipped through Customs carrying a kilo of cocaine — and Amber doesn't know it. Those facts will give their love scene conflict and tension. You can choose to write the scene with the breathlessness of Dirk's encounter with Customs, or as a change of pace from that scene. If before, during or after their love scene, Amber finds the kilo under the bed, her discovery will give the scene its reason for being, its shape, its emotional force — and propel your novel along.

Editors are as keenly aware of the shape of a love scene as they are of the shape of the novel itself. And especially for an editor who may read dozens of love scenes every week, in novels, even the sexiest encounter becomes dull if it feels superfluous or slow. In this way, love scenes in novels resemble love scenes in life.

The People of Love

Just as the shape of a love scene should reflect the novel that surrounds it, your characters in a love scene must act in ways consistent with the attitudes and emotions you've given them prior to this scene.

Sometimes, when I read love scenes in manuscripts submitted to me, I find myself growing uncomfortable with the way a writer treats his or her characters. It seems as if the writer possesses something like contempt for the novel's characters. The writer may come across as sexist or wantonly violent, even if that is not the intention.

The portrayal of women in many love scenes, even in popular novels intended primarily for women readers, quite often manifests chauvinist values. Certainly, in real life, sex can be a kind of power play, with one partner overcoming the other, and certainly that is a legitimate way of consciously creating dramatic tension in fiction. But such a power play shouldn't be a reflexive act whereby a woman is taken by her male partner with unjustifiable force. This is an outdated social and sexual attitude that good fiction writers should avoid.

Similarly, male sexuality isn't all force. Far too often—particularly in "women's novels"—male characters seem only the sum of their private parts. There will be times you create such characters, certainly, but such attitudes come across in other situations beyond lovemaking. A male character who is lively and interesting when he has his clothes on shouldn't automatically become cruel and unbelievable in bed.

I'm also amazed at how many writers seem to punish their characters for liking sex. Again and again in novels I find heroines who must be persuaded to show any physical affection and where secondary characters suffer ill fates for relishing sex—or for being gay or for generally not conforming to society's strictest sexual laws. As with sexism and violence, this can be an unconscious impulse on the part of a writer, but one that should be checked.

Also, there's no ignoring that this is the age of AIDS—and of "safe sex," a reality that authors of contemporary novels should consider facing.

As an editor, I find myself consumed with worry when two strangers fall into bed with each other in a novel, with no regard for safety or for birth control. I'd like to read a novel where safe sex is eroticized and the characters are routinely—and sensually—conscious of their own and their partners' health.

There's no need to diminish our pleasure in romance, but our awareness of the risks of sex—and how to minimize them—should be evident.

The Language of Love

Here's the biggest challenge a fiction writer faces when creating a love scene: how to make the language fresh and appropriate. Love scenes have a knack of making even the most carefully chosen words sound like brand new clichés. More than in any other sort of scene, the writer must be extremely careful to create strong, precise and vivid phrases while writing about love. But the language of romance can wilt with one false move.

Bad sex scenes divide more or less equally between the clichéd and the clinical. Consider Dirk and Amber in this clinch:

Dirk clasped Amber's silky hair in one broad fist and felt her bosom heave beneath him, his manhood readying itself for the awesome challenge. Her lips parted, dewily, and she whispered breathlessly to him, "I love you, come to me." Her arms locked across his slick back, she squirmed beneath him, gasping.

Later, once the stars had exploded and the sky had gone black and then all-bright, she lay exhausted against his torso, wishing this moment could last forever, feeling his chest hair tickle her nostrils.

This scene—with the possible exception of the nostril-tickle—has nothing to do with the way real people make real love. It is, rather, a literary derivation of a literary derivation, hearkening back to the first pulp romance novel ever written: bosoms heave, lips part, people breathlessly announce their love for each other, men have *manhoods*, the world disappears, and the sky performs pyrotechnical feats not available in nature. Dirk and Amber are participants in a love scene that heats them up but leaves readers cold—and giggling a little.

Clinical scenes, where the reader is privy to all the body parts the characters are privy to, fail when they violate the overall tone of the novel, as if the writer had chosen to give readers a little thrill for no real dramatic purpose. Clinical sex scenes diminish the characters and the strength of the author's style and point of view.

The opposite of the clinical love scene is what I call the kiss-to-cigarette approach: Two characters come together and after the first kiss there's a line of white space and suddenly both are smoking cigarettes. This is a favored approach of many literary novelists, and I find it as dishonest and diminishing as the clinical style. Making love, in real life or in fiction, is an expression of character. People have different styles that reveal their personalities, and just about always they have important and significant feelings about what they do. The kiss-to-cigarette tactic is an easy way out of a challenging writing situation. For decorum's sake, the writer has declined to reveal to us any inkling of an important human experience, one that could be pivotal to the outcome of a novel. Before you let your camera pan away from the two lovers, pause and decide, consciously, if this is the tactic that best serves your work.

No matter what approach a writer chooses—clinical, kiss-and-cigarette, or somewhere in between—the same problem crops up: how to make the language of the scene work as well as it can. The author of Dirk and Amber's encounter fails on this score: we feel as if we've heard it all before. Even the most original language has a way of flattening out during a love scene, becoming pretentious, hackneyed or silly. No one really believes that the stars explode for Amber; language like that is a reflex, like gagging. You may feel trapped, as if anything you write will metamorphose into pornography or cliché, but there are ways to create fresh and engaging language for a love scene.

I take the first precept directly from William Strunk and E.B. White's *The Elements of Style*, which remains a crucial handbook for every kind of writer. That precept is: "If you've ever heard a turn of phrase before, don't use it." If you want a character to feel a shiver down her spine, don't write, "She felt a shiver down her spine." Instead, write something like, "He ran a thumb down the nape of her neck, and she felt a feathery touch at the base of her spine, as if he had stoked her there, too." It's more words, but it gets the idea across with more richness. Whenever you've drafted a love scene, go over it—as you would any other scene—for phrases that don't pull their weight, that sound like words you've heard in this combination before, and that call attention to themselves as phrases, not as description or sensation.

The second precept is to use metaphor carefully and judiciously. This also serves for all elements of a novel, but nothing brings out a writer's penchant for metaphor and simile the way love does. As with more descriptive phrases, metaphors can go stale the moment they hit the page. Even if they're not phrases we've heard before, they can sound like phrases we've heard before. Avoid whole areas of metaphor that encourage clichés. When you write about love, stay away from Amber's exploding stars, along with comparisons to crashing waves, lightning, dynamite, railroad trains, and everything you remember from 1940s' movies. A woman poet came up with one of the lovelier and more enlightening comparisons I've ever heard for a woman's experience during love: It's like going into a cavern, she said; your lover strikes a match, suddenly revealing for an instant the walls and their distant mysteries.

Surprise your reader with metaphors, just as that poet did. The smell of a man's hair, for example, might be likened to the sweet but musty smell of a garden, in early spring, after a rain. Two lovers moving slowly into a kiss might summon up images of the way snow begins collecting on the ground, disappearing at first, but growing abundant enough to color the soil gray and then white, until snow has visibly fallen and the earth has changed. There *are* many ways to write metaphorically about love; they just demand ingenuity on your part. Be careful, though; even the most elegant metaphors and similes can grow sentimental. Use them sparingly.

My third precept for creating fresh language is to remember that when it comes to sex and love, readers' imaginations do a great deal of the work; all readers need is a nudge. If you mention how Dirk nuzzles Amber's throat and moves up to breathe swiftly into her ear, your readers will feel the shiver. You need to give readers only the signals to create the ambiance of a love scene. Of course, you must make sure your signals are the most effective ones possible. Gypsy Rose Lee once said that a glimpse of black net stocking was sexier than a bare leg could ever be. Keep that in mind. When it comes to sex, less is usually more—at least on the page.

The same is true for using four-letter words or words that may not be nasty or slangy but are nonetheless explicitly clinical, unless you're working with a first-person narrator or using dialogue. Let your readers do the visualizing. Like a hot pepper in a Szechuan dish, an occasional "no-no" word or a precise anatomical reference to genitalia can startle your reader into greater sensation—but use those words only when the tone of your story allows it.

When detailing a sexual coupling, you're better off referring to the entire body rather than to specific parts in use. No writer (except maybe for those writing historical romance) can get away with using words like *his manhood* or *her love canal* without inducing giggles. If you say "she opened herself and he entered her," your readers will know exactly how.

The final precept is much more straightforward, relying on a hoary truism: Write what you know. Most of us have experienced great physical attraction and love, often with the accompanying complicated emotions that occur with such frequency in fiction. The final test of love scenes in fiction is whether they correspond with life and tell us what we didn't know we knew. Comparing fiction with real life will help keep any writer both honest and original.

"Staging" Your Fiction

by Stanley Schmidt

T
he first time I met Kelly Freas, the renowned science fiction artist, he had just published a series of posters to promote interest in and support for the space program. The entire series was displayed on walls throughout the house, and Kelly was asking the guests at a party which posters they thought most effective. He found a fascinating pattern in the results. "Verbally oriented" people always picked the one showing a Moon rocket, three ghostly sailing ships, and the phrase, "Suppose Isabella had said *no....*" "Visually oriented" people always picked the one with no words, but just a picture of a rocket hatching from an Earthlike egg.

Writers, by the nature of their work, tend to be "verbally oriented." But they would do well to realize that many of their readers are less so. Most readers do not pick up a novel or short story to admire the author's cleverness in turning a phrase, but to experience vicariously something they cannot experience directly. Your job is to make readers *forget* that they are reading, and give them the illusion of *being* in the story, seeing and hearing and smelling and feeling what's happening to your characters. Hence the dictum: "Show, don't tell."

What, exactly, does that mean? I've found that the most important key to making a reader see a scene vividly is that the *author* must see it clearly to be able to convey the illusion to someone else. And one of the best pieces of advice I can give a writer suffering from a tendency to tell rather than show is this: *Try rewriting it as a play*.

All the World's a Stage

Telling rather than showing breaks down into several specific types of faults:
- describing character rather than showing it through dialogue and action,
- directly disclosing thoughts of nonviewpoint characters,
- summarizing dialogue as indirect discourse instead of quoting it directly,
- speaking in generalities rather than specifics.

All of these faults distance readers from the scene and reduce the readers' illusion of being a part of it.

In a play, you *can't* do those things. Except for a few special cases of unusual structure—the Stage Manager in Thornton Wilder's *Our Town* or Sakini in John Patrick's *The Teahouse of the August Moon*, for instance—nobody on a stage *tells* you what kinds of people the characters are. The only way you can find out is by watching what they do and listening to what they say to each other. And they say and do *specific* things, which the playwright must spell

out. So if you've written a scene for a story in which you have told too much
that you could have shown, force yourself to find specific ways to solve the
problem by recasting the scene as a play—and then translating the result back
into story form.

Let's see how it works in a hypothetical snippet of a badly written story:

Ralph stepped nervously into Commissioner Reed's office. It was
clearly the office of a career bureaucrat, and Ralph could see at a glance
that Reed was the kind of bureaucrat who did everything by the book
and disliked anything that threatened to deviate from it. But the fate of
California depended on Ralph's convincing him in the next few minutes
that he *had* to deviate from the book.

Reed already had Ralph's dossier in front of him and seemed to be
reading the crucial article. He looked up and greeted Ralph with a few
words of perfunctory small talk. Then he said, "So what you're saying
in your paper is that you're sure the Big One is coming in six months,
but you know a way to make it less destructive?"

"That's right," Ralph replied nervously, trying to collect his thoughts
and brace his confidence for the confrontation to come.

"But your cure," Reed grated, "is going to cost the taxpayers a lot of
money. Right?"

"I'm afraid so," Ralph admitted as apologetically as if it were his fault.
He drew himself up and said firmly, "But if we let the earthquake go its
own way, it will cost a lot more."

"How much money?" the bureaucrat demanded.

How does this go wrong? We are told that Ralph is nervous, but we are left
on our own to picture how this affects his behavior. It would be better to do
it the other way around: show us how he acts and let us conclude for ourselves
that he is nervous. We are told that Reed is marked by his office and his
personal appearance as a career bureaucrat who can't stand things that don't
fit standard procedure, but we're not shown a single piece of evidence to
justify Ralph's sizing him up that way. Their conversation begins with "a few
words of perfunctory small talk," but again we're left to guess what they
are—whereas if they were *quoted* they themselves could provide some of the
character clues that we haven't been given in any other way. Once Ralph and
Reed get down to business, every speech is described by an adverb or worse,
and the author seems to be determined to find a new synonym for *said* every
time anybody opens his mouth.

Now try it as a scene of a play.

*(We see an office lined with glass-fronted bookcases, filled with leather-
bound volumes. A single desk sits in the middle of the room, its top empty
except for a telephone and a folder containing several papers. REED, a
slightly built, tight-lipped man of fifty or so, with a few strands of greasy
black hair combed haphazardly across his pate, is frowning through thick
rimless glasses at the top paper in the folder. RALPH enters through the*

door and walks to the desk, checking his belt buckle and smoothing his hair down with quick little motions as he goes. When he reaches the desk he stops, shifting his weight back and forth from one foot to the other. Reed looks up at him, not lifting his head, but simply peering over the tops of his lenses. Ralph avoids meeting his eyes directly.)

REED: Hmph. So you're Tambori.

RALPH: Yes, sir.

REED: And what you're saying here *(he taps the paper)* is that you're sure the Big One is coming in six months, but you know a way to make it less destructive?

RALPH: That's right.

REED: But your cure is going to cost the taxpayers a lot of money. Right?

RALPH: I'm afraid so. *(He straightens up and looks Reed in the eye).* But if we let the earthquake go its own way, it will cost a lot more.

REED: How much money?

A few things still must be described, of course. Furniture and other fixed features of the physical setting can't speak for themselves; human beings can and should. The theater audience will see what the scene looks like by looking at it, but the set designer must be told how to set it up for them. The actors need some suggestions (such as Ralph's avoiding Reed's eyes and Reed's peering over the tops of his glasses while keeping the rest of himself aimed at his desk) of how to convey their personalities and states of mind. But the way people talk is conveyed simply by what they say and how they say it. The adverbs and *said* synonyms are gone. There is no place for them on the stage—and there's seldom a need to put them back in when you translate it back to a story:

Nothing was in the room except some cases of musty books and a single wooden desk, and the desk was bare except for a telephone and a folder containing a few papers. Reed, a slightly built, tight-lipped man of fifty or so, with a few strands of greasy black hair combed haphazardly across his pate, seemed to be studying the top paper intently through thick rimless glasses. He was frowning, and Ralph shifted his weight back and forth from one foot to the other as he waited for the Commissioner to speak.

When Reed finally looked up, he didn't lift his head, but simply peered at Ralph over the tops of his lenses. "Hmph. So you're Tambori."

"Yes, sir."

"And what you're saying here"—he tapped the paper—"is that you're sure the Big One is coming in six months, but you know a way to make it less destructive?"

"That's right."

"But your cure is going to cost the taxpayers a lot of money. Right?"

"I'm afraid so." Ralph drew himself up and looked Reed in the eye. "But if we let the earthquake go its own way, it will cost a lot more."

Reed scowled. "How much money?"

Notice that not only are the adverbs and strained synonyms for *said* gone, but even the word *said* itself is seldom necessary. As on the stage, once the audience or readers have been given a *picture* of the characters and setting, they can fill in for themselves such details as who's speaking and in what tone of voice. On the printed page, where they can't see and hear who's speaking, they may need an occasional reminder—but with only two characters "on-stage," this can be provided easily and unobtrusively by an occasional reference to something else one of the speakers is doing, such as, "Reed scowled."

There is still room on the printed page for an occasional direct reference to the viewpoint character's thoughts, but even those can often be avoided. The original reference to how important this meeting is seemed unnecessary in the revision because that already would have been hinted at in earlier scenes, and the reason for its importance quickly becomes apparent in the dialogue of this one. The very existence of a viewpoint character is perhaps the most essential difference between a story and a play, but it's not as big a difference as it first seems. In a play, *everybody* is revealed only through his words and deeds. In a story, *one* character is known more directly—but even he, and through him the readers, remains an audience for everyone else.

As the writer, you too, see much of the action from an audience's viewpoint. But this can work to your advantage: If you visualize your characters and their doings clearly enough, all you have to do is watch what they do and write it down.

Setting the Stage

There are a number of important differences between a play and a story. One is that readers don't actually see the stage, so you as storyteller must create it in their minds—and you want them to feel as if they are *in* the scene, not looking from section 6, row 5, seat 2. I've been talking about "seeing" and "watching" and "visualizing," but those words are really metaphorical shorthand for "perceiving and experiencing." Seeing is perhaps our most vivid and detailed sense, but much of the fullness of the world comes from the fact that it is only one of several senses. Poul Anderson, probably best known as a science fiction writer but highly regarded in several other genres as well, has said that in setting a scene he consciously tries to appeal to at least three of the reader's senses. Consider the following, for example, the fourth paragraph of a scene in Anderson's novel *The People of the Wind:*

> By then they were strolling in the garden. Rosebushes and cherry trees might almost have been growing on Terra; Esperance, was a prize among colony planets. The sun Pax was still above the horizon, now at midsummer, but leveled mellow beams across an old brick wall. The air was warm, blithe with birdsong, sweet, with green odors that drifted in from the countryside. A car or two caught the light, high above; but Fleurville was not big enough for its traffic noise to be heard this far from the centrum.

This brief paragraph plants not only visual images, but also sounds, smells, the feeling of warmth, and even tactile sensations in the mind of the reader, with just a few words each. When your story is set in a place similar to ones the reader has experienced, a word or two like *rosebushes* can trigger a great deal of imagery. If the setting is not likely to be familiar to the reader, as often happens in science fiction, fantasy and historical novels, the writer can take less for granted and may have to work harder, and even use more words, to give the scene enough depth to draw the reader in. Even then, though, careful *choice* of the words is often preferable to using vast numbers of them. Anderson has a knack for bringing alien worlds to life by giving things found there instantly evocative names that human colonists might coin:

> Further down a slope lay sheds, barns and mews. The whole could not be seen at once from the ground, because Ythrian trees grew among the buildings: braidbark, copperwood, gaunt lightning-rod, jewelleaf which sheened beneath the moon and by day would shimmer iridescent.

No reader of *The People of the Wind* has ever seen braidbark, copperwood or jewelleaf—but every reader gets an instant *picture* from each one-word name, complete with overtones like suggestions of texture. No reader gets exactly the same picture that the author had, but that's not important. What is important is that each gets *a* picture, suitable as a setting for the action and substantial enough for verisimilitude.

Epilogue

When I first mentioned this idea (of rewriting as a play) to an actor and playwright friend, he said: "Good idea—but I'd take it a little further. Tell them to write it not only as a play, but as a play *without parenthetical instructions to the actors on how to say their lines*." That may sound extreme to a fiction writer used to relying heavily on adjectives and adverbs—but if you think about it, that's how Shakespeare did it.

And look where it got him.

Introducing the "Slap-Dash" Outline

by Raymond Obstfeld

Some writers prepare detailed outlines of their novels before they start. They know everything that will happen from the moment the hero pulls his gun on the first page until he kisses the heroine 358 pages later. For example, when Edgar nominee Robert Irvine spoke to my writing class about outlining, he brought with him a typical outline that he uses when writing a novel. It was seventy pages long. It included dialogue, character sketches, chapter by chapter breakdowns, just about everything. On the other hand, when Ross Thomas spoke to my class, he claimed he never started with an outline, that it took away the thrill of discovery. When his protagonist walked into a room, he wanted to be looking over his shoulder, just as surprised as his character.

I fall somewhere between. I use what I call a "slap-dash" outline, one that illuminates not the entire book, but the chapters immediately ahead of me.

When I write my first chapter, I often have no idea what the novel is about. And for the next couple chapters, I avoid thinking too much about what will happen in the novel. Technically, the beginning of a novel should establish tone, character and plot. But let's face it, the beginning's *real* purpose is to grab the readers by their throats and not let go until they are committed to finding out what happens next. So when I start a novel, I'm thinking only about writing an opening that does just that to me. It must interest me so much that I'll want to *write* the rest of the novel to find out what happens. If it works, I know the reader will be satisfied. But if I know too much about the story, I might try to get fancy with the opening, do things that are cute but not grabbing, because I already know what's coming up. Remember, if the readers don't like the first chapter, they will never reach those other gems you've been waiting to spring on them.

However, once you've written that wonderful, riveting chapter, you do need some kind of an outline. Most writers know the ending of their book when they start. They may not know exactly how they're going to get there, but they know their general destination. Will the protagonist survive? Will the couple get together? Will the ending be happy? Sad? Outlines are just road maps to that destination. For me, the "slap-dash" outline is road map enough. Such an outline lists the next three or four chapters and what will happen in each. The outline doesn't have to be neat or too detailed, because you just want to keep far enough ahead of your daily writing that you're never stuck wondering where to go next.

Take a look at the example below of one of my "slap-dash" outlines. Granted, those notes may look like the drug-induced scribblings of someone who claims frequent sightings of UFOs, but they make sense to me. The names bracketed under each chapter are the characters from whose point of view that chapter is written. The scrawled "action" beside one of the chapters helps me with pacing. The rest of it will seem like gibberish and, in fact, the actual chapters are quite different from what this outline reveals. Yet, this "slap-dash" outline allowed me to get an overview of the chapters. This review showed me that chapter ten needed to come before chapter nine, because it had been too long since the reader had been in the protagonist's point of view. With this outline propped up next to my word processor, I was able to see the shape of the book's next few chapters as I wrote, building and adding texture because I knew what was coming up.

When I jotted this outline, I had only a vague idea of what would happen after these chapters. While I was halfway through these chapters, I figured out the next five chapters and prepared a similar outline.

Once you've prepared such short-term outlines, you might want to transfer them to a more complex outlining system involving note cards and such. I do. But for now, this quick jotting will help keep that novel from drying up.

The complexity of your outline, your road map, will depend on what kind of "traveler" you are. Perhaps you like to plan your trips in careful detail, make hotel reservations in advance, pick the sights you'll visit each day. Or maybe you just like to climb in the car and drive, see where the road takes you. Wing it. Either way has proven successful for many authors. You might want to try both methods during your writing career to see which fits your temperament best. In the meantime, this "slap-dash" technique can be adopted for either philosophy. The result will be the same: a completed novel.

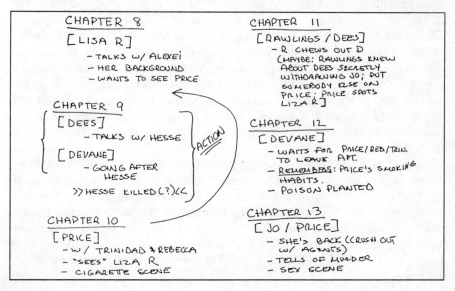

Where's Your Story?

by Lawrence Block

In *Only in America*, the late Harry Golden wrote of a sign he'd seen in the offices of a company that traded in flour. A milling firm, I suppose they were. *"Does It Sell Flour?"* the sign demanded. If it didn't, one was given to understand, then the hell with it.

I probably ought to hang a sign like that over my desk. I'd have to change the wording, since I'm not in the flour-selling business. I am, on the contrary, in the storytelling business. That's my primary purpose as a fictioneer, and when my doodling on the typewriter keys fails to advance the story I'm telling, I'm not keeping my eye on the ball, my shoulder to the wheel, and my nose to the grindstone. I'm not selling flour, and it's gonna cost me.

"Where's the Story?" That, I submit, would be a useful sign to hang over almost any writer's desk. And such a sign would need regular dusting and cleaning, because it seems to me that the longer one practices this trade, the easier it is to lose sight of one's chief objective. It is often the veteran writer with considerable technical facility who is most likely to wander off on a tangent—and leave his story somewhere in the lurch. (The lurch is situated right between left field and the boondocks.)

Here are some of the tangential byways off on which you might find yourself wandering:

1. Anecdotage. Ever since *The Friends of Eddie Coyle*, I've greatly admired the writing of George V. Higgins. His prose is lean and crisp, his dialogue crackles with authenticity, and his stories are tough-minded and affecting. Sometimes, though, I find his books harder to get through, although any individual page of writing is as appealing as ever. The problem I have with the books is that the story line gets completely lost in a web of anecdotal material.

Kennedy for the Defense is a good example. Every time any two characters are talking, one of them is reminded of a story and tells it at length. The titular narrator is similarly anecdotal. Now the anecdotes are all good material and Higgins's characters tell them well, but a third of the way through the book I found myself gasping for breath. I wanted to grab the author by the throat and insist that he get on with it.

2. Small talk. The eighty-seventh Precinct police procedurals which Evan Hunter writes as Ed McBain have maintained a consistently high level of quality. The plots are involving and the cop characters well drawn and appealing. At least once in almost every book, however, two homicide cops named Monaghan and Monroe make their appearance, and they banter. They toss the old repartee back and forth, and then they go away and leave the case to the boys of the old eighty-seventh, and I'm always relieved when they get off the stage.

Monaghan and Monroe have a mercifully brief turn at bat, but their particular sin is one that some authors commit in every chapter. Cute exchanges between characters, flip remarks tossed back and forth, are hard to resist. If you have the knack for that sort of thing, they're easy to write; one line feeds right into the next and the pages pile up like crazy. And they're easy to read, but reading whole books full of this stuff is like making a meal of popcorn. Your dinner is mostly air, and you wind up tired of chewing and still oddly hungry.

3. Character tags. "I have a great idea for a mystery novel," people write me. "The detective is an Albanian dwarf who hybridizes gladioli, and he lives in a packing case in an abandoned subway station, and his girlfriend is a Korean giantess with three breasts, and he always wears one blue sock and one black sock, and he drinks stingers before dinner and Orange Crush after dinner, and he insists on being paid exclusively in silver bullion, and—"

Now there's nothing inevitably wrong with all of this, although I don't think I could possibly enjoy reading about anyone who would drink stingers before dinner, but my point is that it's all too easy to let the external trappings of character get in the way of your story. It's especially apt to happen in series novels, in which you've created a whole trunkful of props for your lead character in the course of several books. Every time you open the trunk, you're tempted to trot out everything it holds.

In my first Bernie Rhodenbarr novel, my hero hadn't yet defined himself. By the third book, he had a bookstore and a best friend. In the fourth book a character introduced in book two emerged as his girlfriend. And by the fifth book I was in a little trouble. I had too much stuff in Bernie's trunk, and I had to remember not to dump it all out on the floor whenever I reached in for a wig or a pair of gloves.

I wound up starting that book over after writing 175 pages of it. One problem was that it needed replotting, but that wasn't all that was wrong with what I wrote. It was pumped airily full of repartee—Bernie and Carolyn and Ray Kirschmann and friends all found too many witty things to say to each other—and it was top-heavy with bookstore bits and poodle salon bits and, oh, assorted junk from Bernie's trunk.

There may be too much of that kind of stuff in the final version, and only those of you who go out and read *The Burglar Who Painted Like Mondrian* can say for sure. But it was a lot easier to avoid excesses in that direction in the final draft because by then I knew where I was going with the plot, and I didn't have to mark time.

4. Marking time. I just gave that a separate heading, and not only because it's about time for another numbered entry. I wanted to stress it because I think it explains why some of us find it easy to wander away from the story on one or more of the above-described tangents. In the first draft of *Mondrian*, such tangents were a welcome alternative to the horrible chore of figuring out what would happen next. When I didn't know what turn the plot ought to take, I could kill time by having one character tell a story to another, or by having Bernie exchange mal mots with Ray or Carolyn, or by letting something cute happen in the bookstore, or whatever.

This provided me with the illusion that I was working, that the pages were piling up beside the typewriter, and that the book was getting written. It wasn't. I was getting further from the beginning without getting closer to the end because I was not getting the story told. I was running in place. I was shuffling my feet. I was marking time.

5. *Library paste*. I do a fair amount of research, and spend plenty of time and money on it. But when people tell me they can see that I did a whole lot of research for a piece of writing, I know I've done something wrong.

Research is best when it doesn't show. It underscores the work, supplying an authentic grace note here and there, a detail that reinforces the impression of reality. If you write a book set in Florence in the fifteenth century, you're going to have to do considerable research and some of it's going to have to show. But if the reader's constantly dazzled by how much you know about the time and place, if he's getting a lesson in art history even as he's reading your story of love and betrayal, your research may very well be getting in the way of your story. It's like watching a dancer and being constantly aware of the performer's virtuosity. If the performance were truly first-rate, you wouldn't be aware of the skill involved; it would all seem altogether natural, and you'd be caught up entirely in your response to its artistry.

Local color's much the same. Whether you're publishing your research or showing off your own first-hand familiarity with a locale, you can put so much work into the background that the story pales against it.

Some years ago I wrote a series of novels about an adventurer named Evan Tanner. The books danced all over the globe, which was more than could be said for their author. I found to my surprise that I was most at ease writing scenes in settings where I hadn't been, and which I had researched minimally. Otherwise my research, on the spot or from books, tended to get in my way. I could get bogged down trying to provide a realistic description of rural Ireland, say, or the Montreal Expo, both of which I'd visited. But I could make up areas of Eastern Europe out of whole cloth and cut them to fit the plot at hand.

The Story Isn't Everything

Early on, I mentioned that the problems we're examining here are apt to be the faults of experienced and accomplished writers. One reason, of course, is that they can get away with it; a bestselling novelist can throw the cat and the kitchen sink into a book, and who's to tell him to take them out?

Another reason is that these faults are often skillful faults, faults to a purpose. Because, paradoxically, the story isn't everything.

We read fiction for more than its story line. We read some writers—James Michener comes quickly to mind, and Leon Uris and Irving Wallace—at least as much for the factual material they provide as for the fictional framework into which their data is arranged. We read others for the glimpse they give us into areas of our world that we are unable to experience firsthand. We read books for the dialogue, and because we enjoy spending time with the characters. We read them, too, to appreciate an author's masterful use of the language, yet this too can be tangential in that it leads us away from the story.

In a sense, every novel is a balancing act, and every writer is forever faced with the task of keeping its various elements in proportion. Every component that enriches the reading experience must be allowed full expression — as long as it doesn't get in the story's way.

Sometimes you get to feel like a juggler. I had that feeling writing *Eight Million Ways to Die*, a book which was very specifically concerned with two major elements beside its story. One was the decay of New York City and the perils of life therein; the other was the lead character's alcoholism and his struggle to get sober and stay sober. These were central themes and they deserved a lot of ink, but I had to keep them from eclipsing the primary story, which dealt with the detective's efforts to solve a murder. If other concerns slowed down that story, the whole book would suffer.

It's hard, in that sort of situation, to know to what extent you're successful. A few readers thought there was too much emphasis placed upon alcoholism. Other's felt the booze theme was the book's greatest strength, and that it was realized without cost to the story.

I hope they're right, because the story has to come first. It's not everything, but without it nothing else really has a chance to work. If it doesn't sell flour, they'll have to shut down the mill.

Writing Is Rewriting

by Dorothy Bryant

Writing is rewriting." I don't know who first said that. Everyone, I guess. Everyone who's ever seriously tried to write says it sooner or later.

Writers are fond of comparing the writing of a novel to the gestation and birth of a child. The only thing wrong with the metaphor is that it is not carried far enough. The planning stages are rather like a pregnancy, and the writing of the first draft is like the labor of childbirth: intense, joyful, exciting, painful and exhausting.

But finishing the book, bringing it through rewriting to completion, is more like raising the born child to adulthood: a long, time-consuming, often tedious and exasperating job that requires more patience and devotion than we thought we were capable of. Conceiving and giving birth does not make a woman a mother. A mother is the person who, after birth, puts in those long, caring years. Finishing a first draft doesn't make you a novelist. Anyone can do the rough draft of a novel, and it probably won't look much worse than the first draft of any great novel you care to name. The difference between "anyone" and a serious writer is rewriting, rewriting and more rewriting, sometimes over a period of years.

This may discourage most beginners. But the serious novelist reads these words with cautious yet growing elation. "Do you mean the first draft of (fill in the title of your favorite great novel) looked as bad as mine does?" Probably. "Does that mean that if I rewrite and rethink and rewrite, I can write a novel as good as that?" Possibly. Not likely. But possibly. We serious writers remember Einstein's "Genius is the infinite capacity for taking pains" and, grinning over our gritted teeth, decide we can work as hard as anyone.

The Rest of the Novel

It used to be the almost worldwide custom that after the birth of a baby the mother was exempted from all duties, except nursing, for six weeks. She was waited on, pampered, indulged and encouraged to be irresponsible and lazy.

The same period of time seems to be the minimum rest period for manuscript: six weeks or more in which you don't write in it, read it, or if possible even think about it. One reason for this layoff is that you need to get distance from it. You should aim to get so far away from it that when you look at it again, it will seem almost as if you are reading the work of someone else.

The second reason for a layoff is that physically and spiritually you are empty, exhausted. Before you can get back to work rewriting your infant book, you need a period of recovery.

182

Ideally you'd spend a couple of days sitting in the sun talking with warm, intelligent friends, followed by a few weeks of comfortable travel. Then ... but *you* can go on filling in this dream. Lacking the money or the time for such an idyll, most of us have to make do with other changes. Probably you've let so many things go that catching up with the rest of your life will provide plenty of change: getting reacquainted with your family and friends, catching up on domestic chores, reading. (Some writers find it hard to read while working on a novel.)

Adventures are even more conducive to recovery, so try to do something different: a walk you've never taken before, a trip to the zoo, an art exhibit, or anyplace that's off your usual rounds. During one period of my life, when I was broke and busy with job and kids, I could take only an hour or so at a time for "adventures" that would speed recovery. So I answered want ads: "Antiques for sale," or "Apartment for rent," (in a part of town I hardly knew) or "Moving, selling record collection." (That one turned out to be a Persian trapeze artist who was going to Africa on tour. He served me a cup of tea while we listened to some records, and we had a long talk about the decline of the circus in America.) Answering ads took me, at no cost, into unfamiliar settings and occasionally into situations almost as foreign as those I might encounter on a long trip.

If you are a compulsive writer like me, you may find that two weeks of no writing is the absolute maximum before a case of high anxiety threatens to wipe out the rest and change benefits. The answer is to write something else, a short story, a review (Virginia Woolf rested by doing some of the best critical writing we have), long journal entries, letters to neglected friends, a few notes on books you plan for the future—anything, as long as you don't touch The Novel until you are, as an editor once put it, "well rinsed."

If you have a family and a job, you will find that writing is impossible during certain periods like Christmas holidays or inventory days at work. There is no escape from these enforced layoffs, which are all the more exasperating because they're nobody's fault. But one way of living with them is to schedule rewriting stints around them, using them as rest and change periods.

Am I seriously suggesting that artistic inspiration can be put on a schedule? Well ... uh ... yes, sometimes it can, especially if the only alternative is letting it wither away.

Policing the Manuscript

I always read the whole manuscript through fairly quickly before I choose what to work on. This is no time to get bogged down in correcting the spelling. What I want is a general sense of how it moves and where it doesn't. As I read I pencil notes in the margin to remind me of my initial reaction as reader-critic. Often these notes are in the form of questions: *Would she have said it that way? Cut this? Credible? Introduce sooner?*

Gradually or suddenly I become aware of parts that don't fit together, of huge gaps where something is needed to connect things. I may put in an extra sheet of paper on which I outline these bigger problems. In the second part of the book, I will find things not prepared for in the first part, or I may find that something I started in the first part was allowed to fade away later. I make notes on everything, surveying the manuscript like a policeman at the site of a collision. I try to list the damages coolly, in the cop's mood of alert but routine investigation, though part of me feels like the driver who caused the accident, standing there in the midst of broken glass, partly in shock, partly furious at my wrong turning.

Too often we think of criticism as purely negative, telling us only what's wrong. Or we think of the critic as passing down a sweeping verdict on the whole book: good or bad. That's because we read "good" or "bad" reviews that hand down a verdict based on careless reading or ignorant bias. These reviews are not written by *critics*.

The rare, real critic is generous. She will unerringly spot a weakness, but she delights in finding strength, celebrating good writing and praying for its increase. You must be that rare, complete critic, identifying all the weak spots but paying special attention to the strong ones.

As you read through your first draft, you will come to places where you forget you are reading and you enter the world of the book. These are the parts that work! Maybe for a couple of pages. Maybe for only a couple of lines. But they take you in, they live, and you know that these parts can stand as they are. What you have to do is to make the rest of the book come up to them. You examine these good parts and wonder how you did them; you can't remember! Sometimes, you can't even remember having written them.

Examining the "good parts" may give you mixed feelings of elation and despair, because you wonder how you can consciously *make* good writing happen. But you should pay some attention, show respect, because these good parts are the keys to what you do well. They are the signposts that point you in the right direction toward developing your voice, your style. I don't often use the word style because most beginning writers think of style as some kind of elegance or grace they must impose on their material. Your style is just you. You cannot learn it, copy it, or invent it out of nothing. You can only discover it, first recognizing it in these occasional "good parts," then nourishing it and helping it grow.

I don't mean that when you do something well, you should keep doing it over and over, never trying a new challenge. Your style is deeper than that; it is your special strength that supports your attempts to do many things.

Making Change

What do you do first? Overhaul the third chapter? Change that word? Redo that character in the beginning to match what she became in the middle? Give the central character two children instead of three? Cut out that whole scene?

When I think of the process of working over a manuscript, I think of my father, who has been a natural mechanic from the time he was big enough to hold a wrench. He made our living fixing cars, but he could fix anything. Long after I left home, I was always bringing him my can and every small appliance that broke down, with total faith that, "Pop will fix it."

He would take a strange machine apart and silently contemplate it for a while. Then would come a series of grunts and mumbles, to himself and to the machine, as he began to tinker with it. He tried this and that, never in a hurry, rearranging parts, improvising new parts from the wires, washers and other bits and pieces stored in the garage. Then, after minutes, hours or days, he would bring it to me and say, "Now try it." And, of course, it worked perfectly, even better than before, because he had probably oiled and cleaned it as well.

Good rewriting demands this kind of easy, unhurried tinkering with words. Each unsuccessful try eliminates another wrong solution and leads you to the right one. I can't emphasize too strongly how important this is, the fact that writing leads to writing, that failed attempts lead to eventual success, that the solution to a rewriting problem is made up of all the attempts that led nowhere.

The trouble is that when you're just beginning to write, you may believe that words committed to paper are sacred, fixed, immutable. But you're not dealing with a finished, printed, copyrighted book, only with an idea, a pile of words that will change many times before they take shape as a book.

RE: Rewriting

All you need are patience, a pair of scissors, and a roll of scotch tape. Yes, at last I can give you one definite, universal rule for writing: Don't make additions and changes in the margin or on the back of the page. Cutting and splicing, rather than scribbling and squeezing in your changes, postpones having to type a clean copy just to be able to see what you are doing.

Start wherever you can, fixing a little problem first, perhaps, to give you courage to tackle a big one. Then fix up whatever you disturbed by fixing, because rewriting leads to more rewriting.

Rewriting is tedious, especially if you do it well. You will miss the excitement of writing the first draft. The exhilaration and spontaneity are gone. But so is the tension, the fear that you'll lose it, abort the novel before you're halfway into it. This means less energy is drained in rewriting, and you may find you can work for longer periods without anxiety, without feeling your nerves stretched like rubber bands at the snapping point. Interruptions won't bother you as much, nor will working for short periods more than once a day (if necessary because of other demands on you) rather than the longer sessions of first draft writing. Often, in rewriting, you'll find the solution to a problem while you're doing something else, not even thinking about the book, and you can make a note of it and do the change whenever it's convenient, with no danger of losing impetus.

Rewriting involves a lot of time during which you may seem to be getting nothing done. Not true. You are rethinking. Robert Frost said his famous "Stopping by Woods on a Snowy Evening" came to him spontaneously, as if dictated, fully formed, written out in a few minutes and never revised. I have heard similar accounts of the creation of some short stories and even, occasionally, a novel. It is possible. Even remembering that the inspired, perfect work usually comes "spontaneously" after years of daily uninspired work, like the basketball player's perfect toss that came after thousands of tries, I do believe a novel could be written that would require almost no revision. But not often.

Written and Rewritten

A working example of how writing leads to more, and better, writing.

I wish I could give you an authentic sample of my own rewriting, step by step, but I doubt that I could ever salvage the real thing. Those facsimiles you sometimes see of a famous writer's manuscript, with scribbled corrections, don't begin to show the think-scribble-retype-patch-up process as it really takes place. Out of curiosity I once tried to keep every version of one short story, to keep track of its formation. But I gave up when I found myself getting lost in a mass of tattered scraps. I'm puzzled when I hear writers say they keep working manuscripts for collectors' archives; if I did, I'd soon be buried under a mountain of paper.

However, I did keep the rough first draft manuscript of my novel, *Miss Giardino*, so I can offer you a sample from that. And, while I can't show the stages it passed through, I'll try to recall some of them and explain how it became the final version.

"Then let me ask you one more question," said Maria. "Does it help if I tell you that you were the best teacher I ever had? If I say, in spite of what happened between us, I learned more from you than from anyone, that I found myself using methods I learned in your class, and that they're still good. Does it help, in your feeling about Camino and all those years, when I tell you that?"

Anna smiled, then took a deep breath. "A little, but . . . " She shook her head slowly. "No, it doesn't really touch anything deep, it doesn't change anything, if that's what you mean."

"That's what I was afraid you'd say," said Maria. "That's why I . . . tell me, why didn't you leave teaching?"

"Leave teaching?" Anna looked at Maria without comprehension. "I can't imagine doing anything else. Teaching was what I did well. It was my work. From the first moment I walked into a classroom when I was a child, I knew that was where I belonged."

"You can say that, and at the same time think about what it did, what teaching does to your life?"

Now Anna felt very impatient. "It is quite possible to hold in the mind two ideas which cannot be reconciled. One: I have hated teaching more than I loved it. It has hurt me and taken much from me and given back little. Two: It is my work. It is what I do. If I were to live my life again, I would have to be a teacher again." She said it as though pronouncing sentence on herself. She could see the slight shake of Maria's head that showed her retreat from this. She pointed her finger at Maria, in the same way she had often pressed an important point in the classroom, drilling it into them whether they liked it or not. "Take care how you reject an idea that doesn't please you. That's how you stop thinking, and once you stop thinking, you stop being human."

Maria surprised her by laughing. "Oh, I used to love when you stood in front of the class that way. It was frightening but thrilling too."

Anna dropped her hand into her lap. She felt ridiculous.

"I guess I've tired you," said Maria.

Anna shook her head. "You've just reminded me of many things, many more things. You see, I keep trying to remember what happened to me the other night. It is blacked out, blocked. But I keep remembering things from years ago. Things I'd rather not remember. Those are the things that tire me."

"Sorry," said Maria. "We were going to talk about your . . . injury, and we went all around again and back to teaching."

Anna laughed. "That's what Arno . . . an old friend of mine . . . used to complain of. He said you couldn't have two teachers in a crowded room without the conversation turning to teaching . . . that teachers could talk about nothing else."

Maria stood up. "I've got to go . . . pick up my son at nursery school."

"I'm glad to have seen you again, Maria." Anna stood, took her hand and shook it. "No matter what I said . . . it meant a good deal to me, this visit. I'm only sorry that I wasn't able to be of more help in talking to you about your problems."

Their eyes were on a level now and Maria looked into hers steadily as she said, "Miss Giardino, I've never spoken to you without learning something."

Clearly, a lot of fat must be trimmed from this. The first thing I eliminated, as I remember, was Anna's speech about her hate-love relation to teaching. That was implied everywhere in the book and could be adequately summed up by a simple, "Teaching was my work." I threw out the reference to Arno's statement, which also was intrinsic to the book. Then I eliminated Anna's reference to the mysterious incident she was trying to remember. I had already sprinkled enough references to it throughout the book.

It was a harder decision to get rid of Anna's fingerpointing gesture. I loved that part. I could just see her doing it, and I loved defusing it with Maria's delighted laugh. But I finally concluded that there were too many statements of Anna's austerity. If the reader were to be able to sympathize with her, and if Anna were not to sink into stereotype, some of these gestures would have to go.

After redoing this scene a few times, and after working on the end of the book, I began to feel that Miss Giardino's final decision about her life carried her austerity too far. I had left her too much alone at the end. It was in character for her to choose the hard, independent, austere way, but it was not in keeping with her change that she should drop back into the isolation she had suffered for several years. So I went back into other scenes, adding a few letters received from former students. In the final scene I spread these letters out on a table where Anna was seated, answering them, a hint of renewed contacts with people. Then I added her mention of a dinner date with Maria, hinting that the young former student might become her friend. To support this, I had to go back to the earlier scene between them, adding a hint of future contact between them, with Maria's statement that she wants to see Anna again. This statement also added some warmth to Anna, indicating Maria not only respected her but also liked her. Anna's surprise at this possibility made her, I hoped, even more likeable. So here's the final version:

"Then let me ask you one more question," said Maria. "Does it help if I tell you that you were the best teacher I ever had? If I say, in spite of what happened between us, I learned more from you than from anyone else, that I use methods I learned in your class, and they're still good. Does it help, in your feeling about Camino and all those years, when I tell you that?"

Anna smiled and took a deep breath while she thought. "I'd like to say that makes it all worthwhile. But . . . " She shrugged. Did knowing you were in the right help after the car had run over you?

"Then I just can't understand why you didn't leave teaching."

Anna hesitated, almost stammering at such a strange question. "Teaching was my work."

Maria waited as if Anna must have more to say. But what else was there to say? Finally Maria stood. "I have to pick up my son at nursery school."

"I'm glad you came, Maria." Anna stood and extended her hand. Their handshake was firm, as if sealing an agreement. "No matter what I said it meant a great deal to me, your visit. I'm only sorry that I wasn't able to be of more help, to tell you something useful."

Maria looked steadily into Anna's eyes as she said, "Miss Giardino, I've never spoken to you without learning something. May I come again?"

Anna was surprised. "Why, yes. If you really want to."

"I really want to."

And now as I look at that scene, I see a place where . . . but no, I'm done with it.

Finish That Novel Before It Finishes You

by Raymond Obstfeld

Everyone is writing a novel. The post-person drops off my mail and describes her mystery, *Dead Letter Delivery*. The garbage man is four chapters into his occult novel, *Refuse From Hell*. My neighbors' fourteen-year-old carries his science fiction manuscript wherever he goes, hoping to read chapters to the unwary. He calls it, *Humanoids That Look Like Parents*. And so it goes. That doesn't even count the one hundred fifty students I get in my novel workshops every year, each waving three can't-miss chapters of a soon-to-be-a-major-motion-picture novel.

Whatever happens to all those novels? Are they all just so bad that no publisher will buy them?

Nope. Last year four of my students sold novels, received money, had parties thrown on their behalf, and got a chance to stand around bookstores fondling their covers. Why them and not the one-hundred-forty-six other students? Simple. *They finished their books.*

Okay, finishing your novel doesn't guarantee publication. But not finishing it guarantees no publication. The true test of whether you're a real novelist isn't that you're working on a book. It's that you finished one.

In the eight years I've been teaching how to write novels, I've heard every excuse for why an author can't possibly finish this book. In the twelve years I've been writing novels, I've made plenty of excuses as to why I can't possibly finish this novel. Yet, somehow I've finished each one I started. Nineteen so far. How? Read on, Macduff.

Tip One: The Unbendable Schedule

First, you must design yourself a schedule. You can make one by drawing eight columns on a sheet of paper. Label the first column "Time," and the remainder for each of the seven days of the week. In the first column, list each hour of the day from the time you wake up to the time you go to sleep. Draw lines across the page to create a box for each hour under each day of the week.

Now, fill in every block of time that *absolutely, positively is taken with some activity*. Eating, sleeping, working, tennis. Whatever cannot be changed. Be honest and complete. If you must watch that favorite TV show, pencil it in.

Once you finish the grid, study the blanks carefully. Try to find at least three days a week with two-hour blocks, preferably at the same time each day. This is probably the most important factor in finishing your novel. Lots

190

of aspiring writers think that writing eight hours on a Saturday is the same as writing two hours a day four times a week. It isn't. A writer needs the consistency of constantly working on the novel, knowing that within a day or two he or she will be back at the typewriter. This keeps the novel fresh in the mind, forcing the writer to think about the pages between writing sessions.

Writing in long stretches on weekends doesn't take into account the time necessary to reread all your pages to refamiliarize yourself with the tone and characters. Nor does it allow for those times when you're having trouble getting started. If you write only once or twice a week, a small writer's block can wipe out a whole week's writing. And that usually leads to NA: Novel Abandonment. However, if you are writing three or four days a week, there's no need to panic about an occasional block. There's always tomorrow.

Don't violate whatever time you finally fill in as writing time with errands, chores, or anything but a real emergency. Take the phone off the hook and kick out your kids, pets, friends and spouse. Let everyone know that *Do Not Disturb!* means just that. It's too easy to pretend that trivial things are more important than your writing, especially if you haven't earned any money from it yet. Don't measure the worth of what you do by money. That's an attitude imposed by others. The novel, especially the first novel, is a work of love and a challenge of your spirit. Don't treat it as anything less.

Tip Two: The Projection Calendar

A writer usually has a good idea how long the novel will be. Two hundred pages. Three hundred. More. Knowing this helps decide how to pace the novel, how many subplots to include, when the climax should occur. A four-hundred-page thriller is far different from a two-hundred-page thriller; the former often will have "false" climaxes, more characters with broader characterizations, more elaborate plotting.

So, just how long will your book be? Make a rough estimate—within fifty pages or so—then haul out your calendar. Using a red pen, outline the boxes of the days each week that you write. At the bottom left of those boxes, starting with the nearest writing day, write the number of the page you aim to complete that day. For example, you write Mondays, Wednesdays and Fridays. You are on page twenty-five of your novel. You write three pages a day. Tomorrow is Monday, so jot "28" at the bottom of that box. That's the page number you should be on when Monday's writing is done. Wednesday's number is "31." Keep going throughout your calendar until you've projected the day you will be done, based on your estimate of how long your novel will be. Of course, the schedule won't be exact, but if you stick to it, you should come fairly close, give or take a couple weeks.

Don't overestimate how many pages you can comfortably write in a session. I used to write three pages a day. Ten years later, I'm up to five pages a day. Sometimes it's more, sometimes less, but it averages out so that I usually finish my novels within a week of projection.

Tip Three: The Cure for the Fifty-Page Syndrome

"Mr. Obstfeld, I want to quit my old novel and start a new one."

"Why?"

"It's just not happening for me anymore. I've lost touch with the characters. I've outgrown them since I started. I'm not sure what to do with them anymore."

"How many pages have you written?"

"Fifty."

Right. Fifty glorious pages. I can't tell you how many fifty-page novels are buried in musty drawers around this country, abandoned so the writer can start yet a new novel which, in all probability, will also be abandoned around page fifty.

What's so magical about fifty?

Anybody can write a pretty good fifty pages. What with character introduction, plot hooks, suspense elements, you're practically guaranteed to be a fifty-page writer. But once you've gotten that far, the inevitable question bites into you like your neighbor's dachshund: What do I do now?

Page fifty is the seven-year itch of novel writing. You've already done the really fun stuff—the getting-to-know-you part—but now you're expected to do more. You aren't sure what to do or how. That wonderful idea you had when you started doesn't sound so wonderful anymore. If you follow your original outline, the book will be done by page sixty-five. How could this happen? When you started, you thought this would be the best damn novel ever written. Now you just want it over.

Stick with it. I have felt that same dread with every one of my nineteen novels. And I've spoken to many other professional writers who suffer the same affliction. If you keep writing, pushing yourself past the "seven-year itch," you'll get over it. You'll see your novel more for what it is, strengths and weaknesses alike, which will help you shape those pages into a better novel.

Oh, and don't be alarmed when the feeling returns almost every fifty or one hundred pages, depending on how long your novel is. That too is natural, and it will pass. If you keep writing.

Yeah, yeah, I know. "Easy for him to say, 'Keep writing.' When's the last time he had to bring in an exorcist for his typewriter?" Answer: every book. And I've learned some practical steps you can take to propel you through those spooky shutdown periods.

Polish. Reread every word of what you've written so far as if it were a death threat, and make sure every word is the best possible choice. Of course, I'm assuming you've been polishing all along, as any writer would do. This is different. This is a microscopic search for Areas of Opportunity. An AO may be a character sketch where adding a line about the way a character peels an orange suddenly makes him more fully realized, gives him some extra depth.

Or one more detail might make a setting clearer, more vibrant. Or adding a simile or metaphor might vitalize an otherwise flat paragraph. Don't overwrite at this stage; just add those touches that rekindle your interest in the manuscript. Sometimes something as simple as changing the name of your protagonist or of the city where the story is set will allow you to look at the book with fresh vision.

Read. If you don't read constantly while you're writing, you won't be a writer. Period.

Now you're expecting me to tell you to read only the best books in your genre or masterpieces of world literature. Wrong! Sure, you should read the best; they demonstrate what the novel can achieve. If you're writing suspense, for instance, read Ross Thomas, Elmore Leonard, William Goldman. Read them slowly, underlining passages. If, say, a characterization is particularly effective, stop and figure out how the writer did it.

But don't underestimate the lessons to be learned from reading a bad novel. The good novel is an example of how something ought to be. It's like watching a master magician perform flawlessly. You're amazed, but no closer to duplicating the trick. However, you can see what a bad magician does wrong. And learning what to avoid in writing is as important as learning what to do.

Sometimes when I'm hunched over my own fifty-page novel, whistling "Alexander's Ragtime Band" into my empty Seven-Up bottle, wondering if it's too late to become a professional basketball player, I jump up, pull a stack of thirty or forty books from my shelves — good and bad, some I've already read, some I haven't — and start reading. Usually, I don't read the whole books, just the first few chapters. If it's a good book, I get excited — and jealous. Being excited reminds me why I started writing — to create powerful prose, to tell a memorable story. And being jealous makes me challenge myself to do as well as this author. It's like being an athlete; a superior opponent will force you to bring out your best performance. Use your excitement — and your jealousy. As soon as you feel either start bubbling up, run to your typewriter and start writing. You'll surprise yourself.

But if the book I'm reading is bad, I use that too. I convince myself how much better than that I can write, and that too inspires me. It's all just a form of self-hypnosis, writer's voodoo. A few years ago I read about a high school football coach who inspired his athletes by biting off the head of a live toad before each game. My method is less messy — and you won't get warts.

Think. Sounds simple enough. Too simple. Like maybe I needed to make this article longer by a couple paragraphs so I threw something real obvious in. Boy, don't you ever get tired of being wrong? Thinking is one of the most neglected aspects of writing, maybe because it's the hardest to control.

Patricia Geary, who wrote the excellent *Living in Ether*, once spoke to my novel-writing class and explained how she had been working on her novel for three years. One day while driving along Pacific Coast Highway, she had a vision of how to revise the entire novel. Many students hearing this mistakenly assumed that writers must wait for these mystical revelations to hit them before they can continue. But what Geary described wasn't mystical; it was the Writer's Sixth Sense. Athletes have a similar sense: they've practiced their sport so often that their bodies move without the athletes consciously telling them to.

It's the same with a writer. You've been working on your book so long (remember, Geary had been writing hers for three years), that your mind is sorting and shuffling without your conscious effort. Now all you must do is give the information, the solutions an opportunity to seep through to your conscious mind. Which brings us back to *Think!* Situate yourself in a relaxed atmosphere where you do nothing but contemplate your novel. Often, I will go for a drive, without radio or tapes playing, and just think about my characters, the plot, the dialogue. Or I'll soak in the bathtub for an hour, all the time thinking. And shriveling.

Sometimes you can't go on in your novel because this sixth sense nudges you, telling you that something is wrong, that you must think things through. When I started writing, I tried to ignore this sense, convince myself I was just being lazy. But now I respect it as an important writer's tool. If I'm stuck, there's usually a reason. Something is wrong, either with the pages I've already written, or with what I'm about to write. All I must do is identify the problem. And that means silence-all-around-staring-into-space thinking.

Dream. I wrote my first novel while attending graduate school. My studies demanded eighteen hours a day of reading, paper writing, library research. And I had a part-time job. Every night about midnight, exhausted and bleary-eyed, I worked on my novel, a comedy-mystery story about a million miles away from the kind of literature I was studying. I wrote for two or three hours every night.

I now wonder what kept me going. Not only *why* I did it, but *how*. No, there's not going to be any swelling music, no theme song from *Rocky*. But every night when I finished writing and went to bed, my head whirling with the day's overexposure to words, I pictured myself in a bookstore watching people buy my book. I saw myself checking into a hotel, the clerk looking at the register, asking me: "Are you *that* Raymond Obstfeld? The writer?" I imagined myself going back to my high school, addressing an assembly of students and teachers.

Okay, maybe all this is corny, but never underestimate the power of a person's dreams. I assume you have similar dreams about yourself: Autographing books at B. Dalton, your friends and neighbors staring jealously. Well, enjoy those dreams, but also *use them*. Prod them, elaborate on them. Last year I had five books in the bookstore, and every time I went in and saw one of them, I still got that giddy feeling I'd dreamed about.

I still use my dreams to help me finish my books. ("Keep writing, jerk, or Meryl Streep will never star in the film version.") Oh yeah. Last year I spoke to an assembly of students at my old high school. Dream on.

Tip Four: The Mingling Factor

Join a writers group. Maybe a local writing club or a community college offers classes. Or start a group yourself. It's important for beginners to mingle with other writers, not just to share the agonies and ecstasies, but also to benefit from the healthy competition.

Writing and publishing is competitive. There's only so much time readers have for reading. Why should they read your book? And only so many titles are published a year. Why should yours be one of them?

Competition has gotten bad press in the last couple of laid-back decades. When one of my writer friends sells a novel, I want to jump for joy, but I want to land on his or her face. Still, there's nothing like having somebody you know sell a novel to inspire you to quit making excuses and finish your own book. You can still be happy for that person and transform your envy into energy for your own writing.

Tip Final: Enjoy Your Success

Talent and genius are wonderful qualities. I've had students with an abundance of both, yet they still haven't been able to finish a manuscript. So no one will ever enjoy their abilities. I've also had students of average talent and ability who have written wonderful tales and sold their novels. I can't help but respect them more than the geniuses. Novel-writing is not for the flashy sprinter who burns out in the first mile. It's a marathon of endurance and discipline. And heart. Yet, crossing that finish line that says THE END is like no other feeling in the world.

How to Chart Your Path to the Bestseller List

by Russell Galen

There's a fellow named Lou Aronica at Bantam who, among other things, runs its science fiction and fantasy imprint, Spectra. I knew him at the beginning of his career when he was the assistant to another editor with whom I did a lot of business, so when Lou was promoted into the Spectra job, I made a submission to him immediately. It was a first novel by someone who'd gotten a bit of attention in the magazines.

Lou called me up quickly and started firing questions about the author. How old was he? Did he have a job? If so, was it a lifelong career or merely something to keep bread on the table over the short run? What were his next four or five books going to be about? How long did it take him to write a completed manuscript? Where did he want to be ten years from now as an author?

I answered all the questions and then said, "Excuse me, Lou. Did you like the manuscript or not?"

"Of course I like it," he said. "The guy is brilliant—you know that."

"So, are you making an offer for it or what?"

"I'll make an offer when and if I'm convinced that this is an author for whom we can build a master plan for the future."

And I said to myself: This guy is going to go far. (He did; by his early thirties, he'd gone from being an editor to publishing director of a vastly expanded Spectra program, to publisher of the entire mass market program at Bantam.) Most editors think only of the book that's being offered: Will it or won't it sell? But the smartest are interested in finding authors, not just books. They know that the biggest successes come from long-term master publishing programs that stretch over many books. (Incidentally, Lou liked the author's ideas for future books and was impressed by his intention to quit his job one day and write full time. I wound up selling him that novel plus the author's next three books.)

If you're an author who is not already highly successful, whether you're on your first or your twentieth book, understand something right now: you're a risk. Probably a big risk. These days a book must sell a *lot* of copies to earn even a small profit, and the odds are that unless you have a guaranteed blockbuster, your book will lose money.

So why should a publisher even give you the time of day? Because, unless your cover letter begins by saying, "By the time you read this I will have thrown myself off the Brooklyn Bridge," *you have potential*. Who's to say, no matter how modest your achievements, that your next book, or ninth, won't be the one that will be so successful that it will put all three of your publisher's kids through college? Just as the bomb squad must view every paper bag as a potential bomb, the publisher must view every author — and I mean *every* — as a potential star.

This point of view has been rising dramatically in recent years, as midlist, modest-selling books drop in sales and the industry becomes more obsessed with blockbusters. Blockbusters are hard to find. An editor might get lucky and have Stephen King decide he wants to leave his regular publisher and come with him; more often, he must grow his own stars, find beginning authors with potential and groom and develop them. More and more editors are starting to understand that if they want to be successful in the year 2000, they'd better start looking now for authors who'll be successful in the year 2000, not just the ones who are successful now.

Which brings us to you. Where will you be in the year 2000? If you don't know the answer to that question, you need a master plan — a sense of where you want your writing career to go, so you can make decisions based on whether your actions bring you closer to or farther from that goal. A complete guide to forming a master plan for your career follows, but it should be easy to understand the basic idea: You should start thinking not just in terms of "How do I get this current project sold?" but "What steps should I be taking now that eventually will get my work on the bestseller list?"

You don't really need to know about all this if you just want to get a sale. But you do if you want to be very successful one day, partly because having a master plan is your best bet at being successful, and partly because the editors with long-term vision are the ones who can take you to the top and thus the ones to whom you most want to sell. You won't get them interested unless you learn to speak their language, and learn what they're looking for and how to convince them you're it.

Before you start building your plan, let's go over the ground rules these editors follow in Long-Term Land.

Galen's Guide to Long-Term Land

• *The words* young *and* inexperienced *aren't the pejoratives in this land that they usually are.* Remember that in Long-Term Land, there are only three states of being: on the rise, successful and washed up. If you're not already successful, it's far better to paint yourself as on the way up, rather than as having had your shot and done nothing with it. While you might ordinarily be tempted to bloat a résumé and make yourself out to have been around a while, that will backfire here. The writer with twenty unspectacular book credits looks not like a solid pro, but like someone who has already peaked.

If you *have* been around a while, all is far from lost: there are other ways around this problem. Even the most cynical editor realizes that it can take writers a long time to hit their stride. Authors like Martin Cruz Smith and

Marion Zimmer Bradley published scores of paperbacks and were around for decades before finally producing the hardcover bestsellers (*Gorky Park* and *The Mists of Avalon* respectively) that made them famous. The point is that Smith's and Bradley's track records were obstacles to be overcome as much as they were strengths.

A writer just beginning a writing career at the age of fifty or older faces a similar disadvantage. If you've been, say, an insurance salesman for twenty-five years, and you walk into Exxon and say you'd like to become a petroleum engineer, you'll have less chance at the job than a kid just out of school who doesn't know half what you do about life and business. Questions will be raised: are you really serious about becoming a *great* petroleum engineer if you're just getting to it now? How big is your talent if you managed to suppress it for so long? Midlife career changers face these obstacles in every profession and it's no different in Long-Term Writing Land where your future, not just your current manuscript, is the issue. The only way to overcome this prejudice is to know it exists and to have your answers ready when these inevitable questions are raised.

• *These editors are buying you, not just your manuscript*. They want to be convinced you're dedicated to becoming successful; that you have more than one book in you; that your current work is better than your past work, and that your future work will be even better; that you're looking for a publishing relationship, a long-term home for your work, and not just a deal. Learn which of your qualities are assets in Long-Term Land and emphasize them; learn which are negatives and de-emphasize them.

Don't boast that you can write a novel in eleven days—as one writer did to me recently—when editors are looking for evidence that you take pains to make each book as good as it can possibly be. Don't boast that you always meet your deadlines, when that is far less important to editors than evidence that you strive to make each book better than the one before, at whatever cost. Don't mention that you're sure the book you're working on is going to be a hit, when what we really want to hear is that you're aiming so high and thinking so grandly that, far from being cocky about your success, you're scared to death you might fail. Don't tell the editor you're not devoted to, but are merely dabbling in, the genre of your present submission. (What romance editor, for example, looking for writers who can be built into stars, is going to respond to a letter from a mystery writer saying, "I thought I'd give this genre a whirl, just to get a break from my regular stuff"?)

• *Don't be afraid to reveal that inside you is a seething, fiery core of ambition and lust for success that would appall Napoleon.*

Drawing Up Your Battle Plan

Michael D. McQuay isn't out to rule France, but he is an ambitious writer. After writing and selling—without an agent— his first five science fiction novels, Mike sensed that something was wrong with his career. He knew he was good, but his sales didn't really show it. There was no growth, no sense that things would improve if he'd just hang in and keep writing.

So he came to me and we hammered out a master plan. That was five years ago, and while his story is still far from its ending, it's far enough along to illustrate these basic points about your own master plan:

• *It isn't any easier or quicker to become a successful writer than it is to become a brain surgeon.* Kids in their first year of medical school don't whine to their professors, "When do we start making real money, sir?" They know they have ten years of schooling ahead of them first. Writing a successful book isn't any easier than slicing away at people's cerebrums, and it takes just as long to learn how to do it right.

I'll give you the same warning I gave Mike: it will be five years before you see any results from the plan at all, and ten before you achieve your goal.

• *Andrew Carnegie's advice for becoming wealthy is important: "Put all your eggs into one basket and then watch the basket."* I studied McQuay's writing and determined that his strength was in his savagely powerful characters and strong story lines. Therefore, mainstream suspense fiction, which showcases these elements, was going to be the field in which he would one day make his stand. From that moment on, every choice we made, every new story he created, was designed to further his reputation in this single field. He still wrote science fiction because that's where the easy sales came for him, but his science fiction became increasingly contemporary and realistic, less far-fetched and exotic. He gradually would move over to writing exclusively mainstream suspense.

There's not much overlap between groups of readers. Romance readers don't buy Westerns; thriller readers don't buy biographies; and so on. If you're bouncing around doing many different kinds of books, you're reaching different audiences with each book. Individual readers aren't staying with you from book to book, forming a loyalty to your work; they're reading only the one book you've written for them, and then abandoning you. By contrast, if you stay in the same field, readers in that field will be reading two, three, four books by you in a row, and becoming loyal fans.

By building on this core audience, you can create momentum. With each new book, you only have to find a small group of new readers in order to have sales figures that are going up steadily. Let's say a new book can, with luck, find one hundred thousand readers who had never before heard of the author. If each new book is in a new field, it must find one hundred thousand brand-new readers every time—and if you trip up even once and sell only fifty-five thousand, you're seen as someone whose sales are slipping. But you stay in the same field, your second book could be picked up pretty automatically by the one hundred thousand readers of your first, if it was any good. Thus, you only need to make fifty thousand new converts in order to have a dramatic increase in your sales. If your new audience base of one hundred fifty thousand gets you eighty thousand new converts for the third book, and your new audience base of two hundred thirty thousand gets you one hundred twenty converts after that, and so on, it's not going to be long before you're selling in the millions.

Decide in advance what kind of writer you want to be, and then bend every effort toward making it in that one field. It's no disaster if you need a little variety now and then and want to do a different kind of book, but you should have a home base.

• *You can't execute a master plan alone.* It's essential that your agent and publisher think in terms of your long-term future and share your hopes and dreams. If your editor feels he has no future with the company, or your agent is planning to quit and hike around the world while still young enough to enjoy it, or if your agent or editor simply can't think beyond tomorrow, you're with the wrong people; they will discourage you from doing what's best for you if it makes this week easier for them.

• *Now is not the time to take it easy.* A master plan involves far more than cranking out books that hew to some formula. More important than all my little points is that you do the work of your life. Mike did. Each book was better than the one before. If the plan had an editorial impact on Mike's work, it was in the tremendous level of inspiration it supplied him. He felt as if he were working not just to fulfill a contract and get the latest advance, but to achieve something of vast scope, to make a ten-year plan a reality.

It's like the difference between having sex just to have sex, and having it because you're trying to make a baby. As most parents will attest, there's something unforgettably intense about the latter, a sense that all your energy is going to create something significant. The first book Mike delivered after we began to work together, *Memories*, was a hundred million billion times better than anything he'd written before, and won some important awards and got a lot of attention. The critics started saying things like "Who *is* this guy?" and "From a completely unexpected source comes one of the best books of the year." Part of the phenomenon was McQuay's own discovery of how good he really was, but part of it, I like to think, came from my whispering "Plan . . . plan . . . plan. . ." into his ear all the time, reminding him that he was working for something Jupiter-size and that there was someone in New York who believed he could do it.

The great goal of your plan should bring great work out of you. Every book must be your absolute best to take you closer to achieving your goal, or it will take you backwards. If you're in the mood to try something goofy, something light, something uncommerical, something dangerous, it would be better to save that for after you've acheived your goals.

What all of this is really about is *building your audience*. Newer writers are cursed by one terrible plague: small readerships, rarely more than five thousand in hardcover, fifty thousand paperback. Those audiences are too small to make anything happen, to generate the kind of word of mouth you need for a book to become a bestseller. As in atomic physics, these audiences are too small to start a chain reaction—they're below critical mass. So you must build up your audience, get it to the point where it's big enough to generate the word of mouth that will get you an even bigger audience that will generate even bigger word of mouth, and so on. Avoid anything that decreases your audience even for one book, causes it merely to remain steady for one book, or causes it to have only a small rise for one book.

McQuay and I decided that he should stay with his current publisher. As luck would have it, his five previous books had all been acquired by Bantam, and his current editor was Lou Aronica (who acquires both science fiction and mainstream fiction). Since we already had precisely the kind of editor we wanted — one who would accept short-term problems and sacrifices if they served a long-term goal — there was no need to find a new home for him.

• *Momentum is everything*. The next part of the plan involved McQuay delivering a new book roughly every nine months. Fortunately, with Aronica and Bantam willing participants in the plan, I anticipated no difficulty in getting sales every nine months. In fact, the first deal I negotiated under the plan was for two books, so that McQuay could begin the second immediately after delivering the first, rather than have to wait for new negotiations, new contracts, etc. After that we made a four-book deal.

Audiences have short memories. They can enjoy a book, buy it in huge numbers, and then, eighteen months later, not even remember the author's name. Nine to twelve months is about the right interval between books; the new book catches an audience that has fond memories of the previous one. This is a problem for writers who also hold down full-time jobs, but I'm afraid that if your job prevents you from doing more than one book every two years, there's a much smaller chance you'll ever make enough from your writing to be able to quit the job.

These figures are for paperback originals. It's different with hardcover, since a paperback reprint will appear a year after the hardcover and keep the readers' memories of your work alive. I advise most of my hardcover clients to have a book out every other year.

This plan involves making each book your very best, with no lapses or detours. And it involves bending every issue to the question of whether it contributes to building your audience. A decision that in any way compromises the goal of building the audience is a mistake, even if it involves a short-term benefit (such as taking a higher advance from a weak publisher that is overpaying in order to build up its list, but that can't distribute its books effectively).

You may need to make short-term sacrifices in order to further your long-term goals. For example, you might be running low on money when along comes a publisher who needs you to do a quick novel in the Young Nurses in Love series, and he won't let you use a pseudonym. Refuse: having your name on such a book might make it harder for another publisher to take you seriously. Or you might want to postpone that uncommerical labor of love you've wanted to write until later in your career when you can better afford to have your sales figures take a sudden drop. Or you might want to spend some time on a magazine article or story that won't make much money but will get your name in front of a new audience, an audience that might then start buying your books. Make your business decisions based on how they affect your master plan.

• *When you've done all the planning you can do, and laid all the groundwork you can lay, the time has come to go for the Big One.* Mike McQuay and I bided our time. Then he came to me one day with an idea for a book that I thought could be a blockbuster. This is the key moment in the master plan: what you have been preparing for all these years in the marketing, selling, writing and publishing of a Big Book.

The problem was that Mike's idea was so much more ambitious and daring than anything he'd ever written that I was afraid no publisher, even his own, would believe he could bring it off. But I knew he was ready, and advised him to write the entire novel on spec (that is, without a contract); we would then offer publishers the proven, finished commodity. This involved a spectacular sacrifice for Mike; while working without a contract, his income dried up because he couldn't simultaneously work on his bread-and-butter science fiction projects. Our agency loaned him some money, he took some breaks now and then for short writer-for-hire projects, and he managed, over a year, to write about two hundred fifty pages of the novel plus a one-hundred-page proposal.

This seemed to be sufficient for our purposes and I showed the material to Lou Aronica with a speech about how our years of working together to bring McQuay along had finally borne fruit. I told him we were going to want $100,000 for it—ten times what McQuay had received before. While Aronica didn't say anything, there was that little sound in the throat editors sometimes make which means, "You %*$*%#%$ agent! Are you out of your *@#%$@% mind?"

Aronica took the material home and read it. He called and said, "You want $100,000 for this book?" I, getting ready for a fight, said, "That's right, and not a penny less." And he said, "Could I have two?" That's how Michael McQuay, some fifteen years after becoming a professional writer, became an overnight success with a $200,000 deal.

(Let me be fully accurate here and say that the deal is a complex one in which certain conditions must be fulfilled for the entire $200,000 to be paid. However, the deal still guarantees McQuay a minimum of $150,000.)

It's Never Too Soon

I realize that many of you would be happy just to get a sale and may be thinking it'll be years before you need to worry about any of this stuff, if ever. But even if you're still dreaming about making your first book sale, it's not too soon for you to put a plan like this into effect.

There are three reasons.

• *Editors look for writers who think this way.* Thus, when your chance at that first sale comes, you could blow it by answering the editor's questions in the wrong way. If the editor asks, "Can you do new books at the rate of one a year?" you must know that the right answer is *Yes*.

• *Even at the beginning of your career you're making decisions about what to write and where to concentrate your resources.* You need to make these decisions with your long-term goals in mind because mistakes made at the beginning of a career can take years to undo. If you decide that investigative journalism, for instance, is the basket into which you want to put all your eggs, it's important to realize that it's a mistake to begin your career with a thriller just because you have a shot at a sale. You'll be typecast as a thriller writer and editors of investigative journalism books may never take you seriously.

• *As I'm sure you've already learned, nothing is more discouraging than the early years of a writing career.* Having a master plan reminds you that, tough as those first steps might be, they are steps nevertheless — the beginnings of a journey toward a specific destination. The knowledge that you're working toward something, no matter how distant it may seem, is a hell of a lot more inspiring and exciting than feeling that you're flailing around, collecting random rejection slips. It keeps your eyes on the prize, as the saying goes.

Choosing Your Category

by Michael Seidman

Here's an easy one: What do Sue Grafton, Elmore Leonard, Stephen King, Dean Koontz, Stephen Donaldson, Arthur Clarke, Piers Anthony, Rosemary Rogers, V.C. Andrews, and Danielle Steel have in common? Right! They're all bestselling authors who began their careers writing what John Gardner, in *The Art of Fiction*, called "drugstore fiction." We know it as *category* or *genre* or *popular fiction*. And as *formula fiction*, too.

Each of the novel categories—romance, mystery, suspense/thriller, science fiction, fantasy, horror, action/adventure, and western—does indeed have a formula, a basic guideline or philosophy, that drives it. The writers who have transcended genre, the ones whose mysteries, for instance, are now called simply fiction, are those who have taken the formula and played with the mix a little, who have stretched the boundaries of the fiction and their imaginations, and who have become accepted in the mainstream of American letters.

This sort of transcendence does happen, and it could happen to you. Even if it doesn't, though, you can have a very successful, rewarding, and profitable career. In either event, however, you must master the basics first, must learn the formulae that make a category "work" for the reader . . . and the editor. In some instances, the publisher will have tip sheets describing exactly what it is that is needed for the list; in many cases, the best guideline is the publisher's backlist (its catalog of previously published titles), the books that reflect a particular editor's tastes and philosophy.

No matter how specific a publisher is, the general rules for the category remain pretty much the same from house to house (although arguments sometimes occur as the definitions become refined). What follows are descriptions of the genres that are at the heart of a publishing list, the categories that help a list to grow and prosper. Keep in mind that if you want to write for a particular publisher, it makes sense to read its books closely and to request tip sheets or writer's guidelines; after all, it isn't always easy to go from the general to the specific, and that is what you'll be doing.

In the meantime, the guide that follows will be more than enough to get you started.

Mystery

At its simplest, mystery fiction is a puzzle story: the classic whodunit, with all the clues present for the reader. The game, and that's what it is, is to see if the author can fool the reader while "playing fair"; the fan and the detective both receive the same information at the same time. But nothing is simple.

In the broadest definition, the mystery category is about crime, and the solution to the puzzle or the prevention of the criminal action. Thus, the Mystery Writers of America can comfortably present their annual award, the Edgar, to such disparate books as a cozy or a spy novel. The packaging and presentation of the novel is often a marketing decision: "If we call this suspense, will we get wider distribution?" Every publisher comes up with its own answer to the question.

The basic forms of the mystery are the *cozy*, the *private detective*, and the *police procedural* novels. Each offers the reader a protagonist (the detective, even if he or she isn't officially an investigator in a legal sense), a crime worth solving, and a series of clues, information, and background (and some red herrings . . . false leads). The differences lie in the way in which the story is told and the degree of real-life information necessary.

The cozy is the least realistic form. And the most popular. The detective is an amateur, a local citizen with an interest in everything (otherwise known as a gossip). He or she may be expert in some area: Jessica Fletcher is a mystery novelist, Father Dowling enjoys mystery fiction; other recurring characters are antiques experts, wine mavens, jockeys—your own imagination as a writer is the only real limit on your choice.

Violence is generally minimal and offstage; the detective uses powers of deduction (one of the hallmarks of the fiction), his or her expertise in a particular area coupled with knowledge of human nature, and some solid questions to come up with the murderer (usually; it is, after all, a crime worth solving), and in a final scene explains how the solution was found.

The settings tend to be less urban than p.i. and police procedurals present, but a cozy novel can be set anywhere; it is a matter of attitude and voice. Characters are often eccentric, the police at a loss for answers, and the storytelling gentle.

The flip side is the hard-boiled novel, most often in the form of a p.i. novel. The private investigator is almost always licensed by the state, probably carries a weapon, and is involved in the kinds of cases that give meaning to the phrase mean streets. Tough, cynical, and jaded, the p.i. deals with street people, petty criminals, and the down-and-out on a regular basis. They are, after all, the best sources of information about missing people. These detectives also get involved in cases dealing with industrial espionage and security matters, the ugly side of family relationships (cheating spouses, missing heirs, and runaway kids), and stumble onto murder enroute to solving the case.

The traditional detective is always cracking wise, especially to a police officer. While they all have sources on the job, there's always a ranking officer who resents and dislikes the investigator. The resentment is rooted in the real world; in the fiction it serves to allow for a presentation of the facts to that point, giving the reader a chance to catch up.

Until very recently, the p.i. was male, and the storytelling was based on the works of Raymond Chandler, Dashiell Hammett, and Ross Macdonald. Now, however, thanks to the work of Sue Grafton, Sara Paretsky, and Marcia

Muller, we're seeing more and more women as lead characters. Their characters are not men with women's names; the sensibilities reflect liberated women as they really are (and I don't think it's sexist to say that there is a difference).

The police procedural is the most realistic form of mystery, and while deduction and investigation plays the same key role as in the other forms, the nature of police work means that the snitch coming forward at the right time is also an element. Procedurals tend to have more than one "hero," because cops — on the job — are rarely loners. The supporting cast is also larger: police departments have access to a wide range of investigatory help, are bound by law to act in a certain way, have district attorneys and politicians breathing down their necks, and come face to face with the general public — civilians — on a regular basis.

Because we see the police daily, either on the streets or on the news, procedurals must be the most carefully researched novels in the category. Because regulations are always changing, you may want to lift a page from Ed McBain, who turned New York City on its side to create the city of Isola and his 87th Precinct.

Espionage novels are a form of procedural, of course, and *romantic suspense* might fall (with a little push) into the cozy vein. Many writers mix and match within the category: *Silence of the Lambs* is a procedural, Al Guthrie's *Grave Murders* is a private eye novel that reads like a cozy. Your own strengths as a storyteller, coupled with an understanding of what makes each category work with its audience, will allow you to experiment and move the genre forward.

Suspense/Thriller

The novel of suspense is an offshoot of the mystery, and in the minds of mystery editors the "suspense" tag is more a marketing ploy than anything else. Since most bookstores (especially the chains like B. Dalton and Waldenbooks) budget for just a certain number of mysteries a season, putting the suspense or thriller label on the novel helps the publisher get around the quota problem.

But there are intrinsic differences: the mystery is first and foremost a puzzle based on whodunit (or how); the thriller is better seen as a howcatchum. Another way of looking at the difference is in recognizing that in the mystery we don't know any more than the detective; in the thriller we usually don't know less than the bad guy.

One of the reasons for that is in the fact that suspense novels offer multiple points of view. They are longer books, with more involved story lines; we see the action from the varied perspective of more characters. The stories have a wider scope and present a greater threat; in the mystery we're in a one-on-one situation, the crime has been committed and the criminal must be caught.

In the suspense novel the fate of the world—or the entire citizenry of a city—
is the prize.

That's why most *espionage* fiction is considered part of the suspense category, rather than mystery, and so are three of today's most popular forms: the
technothriller, the *medical thriller*, and the *woman in jeopardy*.

Technothrillers, because of glasnost, have replaced the straightforward spy
story in the hearts of readers. As the label implies, the current and projected
technology is as much of a character in the novel as any of the humans.
Popularized by the work of Tom Clancy, Dale Brown, Stephen Coonts and
others, the high-tech thriller takes the reader soaring in tomorrow's jets or
diving beneath the seas in sleek submarines. The equipment itself is often
the prize, and its capabilities provide the twists and action.

Another kind of technology is at work in the medical thriller, and a crime (or
threat of one) is present. Now, though, that threat takes the form of unleashed
plagues, illegal—and deadly—experiments, or any other harmful action that
might be begun in a hospital or medical setting. Robin Cook, who exploded
onto the scene with his first novel, *Coma*, is still the author to whom newcom-
ers are compared. The hero is usually a doctor who stumbles onto the plot or
realizes that for one reason or another, bubonic plague has returned to the
world in an even more virulent form.

Mary Higgins Clark is the hallmark author in what may be the most popular
suspense form today (if not in sales at least in the number of editors looking
for new materials)—the woman in peril novel. A descendent of the gothic,
these contemporary tales focus on a woman who suddenly finds herself the
target of some frightening criminal action. The problem is not always a rapist
or serial murderer; the stories are much more convoluted than that. She may
have been the witness to a crime (completely innocently and still unaware of
the fact), she may remind the "attacker" of someone, there may be something
in her apartment or home . . . the variations on the theme are endless. What
seems to be most important to the readers is a pervading sense of menace, of
real danger. While a male character may appear to help the heroine, she is
able to deal with most of the situations she faces, once she gets a handle on
what is going on.

In the "womjep," most storytellers are following the ground rules of the
mystery: we often don't know why or who; we just know that a puzzle must
be solved in order to save the woman's (or child's) life. Because the woman
has to function as a detective, a case could be made for these books to be
classified with mysteries. However, the suspense element is more crucial
than the puzzle—and because it is easier to market as suspense, that's where
it is generally found. (Of course, when you go into a bookstore, they're probably all together . . . but no one ever said this business makes sense.)

The espionage novel has fallen into disrepute as world politics changed.
Because it is believed that certain countries do not appeal to the American
reader—Latin American nations, South Africa, most of the Middle East—and
because most of the best of the category has, in our time, been tied to the

cold war, publishers (who are informed by the booksellers) shy away from the international confrontation. However, with technology and industry becoming more and more important, industrial espionage seems a rich vein in which to dig for publishing gold.

As in the mystery, play fair with the reader. If clues are necessary, present them; if deduction is a weapon, use it; and plant the story firmly in a real world that the reader can identify. After all, it is the threat of losing that world that lies at the heart of most suspense novels.

Romance Fiction

The romance market, publishers and readers alike, are hungry for product, making the field extremely lucrative. Being lucrative, it is also highly competitive. Each of the houses that publishes the category (and virtually all of the paperback houses do at least some) has its own tip sheet (perhaps several) explaining exactly what it is the house is looking for, covering everything from word length to the degree of acceptable sensuality. So, aside from a taste for — and belief in — the category, requesting the writer's guidelines is mandatory. That said, let's consider the genre in general terms.

As with any good fiction, conflict is at the beating heart of the romance. They are not simply love stories; today's reader demands involving action with strong heroines. (The hero is neither a politically correct male of the 1990s nor a raging chauvinist.) While the story must deal with the romance between these two characters, it is made up of equal parts tortured love, business or social conflict, and local color in terms of place and time.

The female lead is independent of mind, alone (either orphaned, kidnapped, or somehow separated from family), attractive, passionate, and involved in an exciting love/hate relationship with the hero. He is older, wealthy, strong, a man of few words (except where she is concerned), and given to action.

With that as a blueprint for the foundation, almost any kind of building may be constructed. The pure *historical* uses America from just before the Revolution through the late 1800s, and a Boston-Washington-Richmond-Charleston axis is popular. Another rich period is the era of westward expansion. That has given birth to the *Indian romance* in which either character may be a full or halfbreed member of one of the Indian nations, but nonetheless fluent in English and, as often as not, very well educated. The historical demands a knowledge of the time and people you are describing (but, then, so does all fiction).

Historical by definition, but not considered as such, are the *Regency romances*. Set in England (usually; there are always attempts to try something new) during the Regency period [1811-1820], these novels are noted for their wit, charm, and humor. Mistaken identity is a favorite plot device, but whatever element you choose, research is crucial. The readers *know* the period, the mores, the language, and they will expect you to recreate a gaslit drawing room for them.

The *gothic romance* is easily recognized on the book racks: dark cover; fleeing maiden; a house on a hill with a tower light; a storm whipping the waves, the heroine's hair, her cloak. Gothics are very much part of the "had-I-but-known" school of writing, and bring a strong element of suspense to the tale and, often, a feeling of supernatural events. A young woman arrives at the kind of house she shouldn't enter (as a visiting relative, a governess, a housekeeper) and immediately discovers that there are very strange goings-on going on . . . and the handsome relative/employer/owner seems to be at the root of it all. And she is the target of whatever evil is afoot. Of course, nothing supernatural is occurring (though a minor haunting as a subplot can still work), and the danger—which is real—is coming from a different quarter, some enemy of the family, for instance.

The *contemporary romance* is often called a "glitz" novel: the setting is someplace exotic, the characters generally wealthy, the conflict often one centering around control of a business. The male—as he does throughout the genre—represents thrills and danger; he is the contemporary equivalent of the pirate, the gambler, the noble savage.

Those four subgroups (the historical, the contemporary, the gothic, and the Regency) represent the basics of the category. However, in the unending search for something new and different, other themes are beginning to gain favor.

Romantic suspense is a mystery novel (either straightforward or one of international intrigue) in which the relationship between the woman—a civilian—and the man—a police officer, detective, strong neighbor—is at least as important as the puzzle. Elizabeth Peters has turned that tradition on its head with her Amelia Peabody novels, in which the heroine is the detective (in the generic sense of that word), and much of her other fiction. Which may be why they're published as mysteries rather than romance.

Time travel romances have their contemporary roots in novels like Jack Finney's *Time and Again*: one of the characters is literally out of his or her own time and finds love, usually, in the past. The conflict is self-evident.

Carole Nelson Douglas has been experimenting with yet another crossover, the *science fiction romance*, which uses the conventions of that genre as background for romantic involvements. The *fantasy romance* (and aren't they all?) uses magical beings and situations along with mere mortals to offer the reader something different. Both the sf and fantasy romances are still very new and so not well established. They are not suggested places to begin.

While each subcategory has its own conventions, the unalterable rules are the relationship between the lovers, which goes from a seeming disaffection (if not downright hatred) to happily ever after, and the development of vivid settings into which the reader can escape.

Action/Adventure

The action novel is not held in very high regard by anyone except the people who write them and their hundreds of thousands of fans. The reason is simple:

they are the male equivalent of the romance novels. The detractors say they are unrealistic, cartoonish, banal. Maybe.

But they are also pure escape, making no demands on the reader. They are fantasy-fulfilling entertainment—one of the reasons we turn to a storyteller, after all. They prove that careful planning and a strong right arm can do wonders to save the world from itself. And they are a way of letting us get back at the bad guys, the ones who slip through the nets of law and order. They provide a way for us to get hostages out of Iran and Lebanon, to get the streets back from the Crips and the Bloods, to make the world safe for democracy.

And to some extent, they tend to be conservative in outlook. The hero may be an individual (The Executioner) or a group (Delta Force); he may be a private citizen committed to a cause or part of an organized, legal (or paralegal) military force, but the old Superman tagline about truth, justice, and the American way can be run under any display of action/adventure fiction.

The story lines are simple: white hat vs. black hat, good guy vs. bad guy. Characterization is at a minimum; we know what the motivations are. The story deals with the discovery of a problem, choosing the personnel and/or weapons to correct it, getting to the scene, engaging in battle, losing some ground, regaining it, gaining more, and getting home to await the next call. If you think about it carefully, the story often follows the traditional form of our myths and legends, and that's how it should be in this category.

While many editors cringe when a novel "as fresh as today's headlines" comes in, those headlines do serve as viable springboards when you're dealing with action. Some of the better writers will, I think, look past those news stories and project events into tomorrow, whether it is in choosing the locale for a new brushfire war or in developing a situation based on current experiments; at that point some of the elements of the techno-thriller creep in and we've seen outlines for series based on an orbiting space station or undersea community. (These aren't fully qualified as science fiction because the science and technology is limited; the reader is asked to accept that something is in place, and the story goes on from there.)

Wherever the story is going, make certain that you can keep it moving for a few years. In acquiring action/adventure titles, publishers are looking for series, for characters who are going to survive the action and go on to do it again. When submitting a proposal, think in terms of not only presenting the outline and chapters for the first book, but a couple of paragraphs of action from the next three or four books.

Many of the team-oriented action titles include female characters in strong supporting roles, and there have been attempts to develop some in which the woman is the central figure. While they haven't met with success yet—Modesty Blaise is as close as anyone has come—the day can't be too far away when that approach will work.

As in all categories, crossover and a fudging of the lines of definition always occurs. Adventures dealing with future wars might be termed science fiction,

a character fighting crime might be considered a detective, and some action/
adventure fiction appears under the general rubric of *war*. What will serve to
define the work, at least in the initial stages, is the focus. If what your novel
is really about is the action, the fighting—the adventure rather than the
growth of characters and carefully thought out puzzles—and if there is some
credibility and plausibility to the situation, you will have succeeded in creating
a marketable action/adventure novel.

Remember, too, the problems espionage writers are having now that the
cold war has been won: stories dealing with battles between US and Soviet
forces are no longer in vogue. But the action doesn't have to tie into that
aspect of international relations: Barry Sadler created the immensely successful Casca series, which followed the adventures of the eternal mercenary, a
man cursed to live always in his role of warrior. Properly handled, any fantasy
may do as well. And as we said at the beginning, action/adventure is a fantasy
form, a chance for men to again be the kind of men they think they should be,
living life as it should be lived: full-tilt, flat-out, pedal to the metal . . . and safe.

Western

The western is one of the simplest categories to discuss because it isn't
cluttered by a herd of subgenres. But that doesn't make it any easier to write.

The traditional western—once the most popular of categories but now
fallen on hard times—is a straightforward adventure novel, a story of conflict
with good guys and bad clearly defined. The setting is usually west of the
Mississippi, the time between 1860 and 1880, and the characters cowboys,
Indians, ex-soldiers, Mexicans, and the occasional city slicker passing through.

The conflicts are about land (sheepherders vs. ranchers; whites vs. Indians), wealth (a mine; land that the railroad is going to want), and revenge for
past wrongs.

The traditional western novel is about a myth, about a West that never
was. The characters are larger than life, single-minded, focused on what the
problem is and rarely looking to either side. The most popular of the contemporary authors in the area is, of course, the late Louis L'Amour, and moseying
through a couple of his novels is one of the best ways to learn the basics of
the genre. At the same time, it doesn't hurt to read Jack Schaefer's *Shane*,
the works of Will Henry, Ernie Haycox, or even Zane Grey to get a complete
picture of what most publishers mean when they say they are looking for
westerns.

In an attempt to recreate a once insatiable market, a couple of publishing
houses are trying to move into other areas that are still rightly called westerns.
One of the most popular of these new-fangled tales are the stories of the
mountainmen, the early trappers who walked the mountains in seven-league
boots, searching for beaver and other fur, meeting and treating with the tribes
they encountered and beginning the taming of a rugged land.

The time frame is much earlier than the traditional western's, matching the period of the trappers' days of glory. Historically, these novels could be set as early as the beginning of the eighteenth century, and would run through the mid-1800s. Conflicts here are as much man against nature as they are man against man.

As with every category, keeping your facts straight is important. While the reader is going to want the myth and legend, he (usually) is also aware of the fact that the Henry Repeating Rifle came on the scene at a particular time, that the movements to the reservations began when they began, and that certain battles—crucial to the history of the period—were fought in a given time and place, whether we're discussing Wounded Knee or the O.K. Corral. A good reference library, therefore, is important.

Even within these general guidelines, there's lots of room for a clever writer to manuever: pick some aspect of the West and exploit it. Can you discover a new approach to tales of the Pony Express? Wells Fargo? The Pinkertons? What about a series of novels dealing with life in particular mining camps or towns? As in any form of mass-market fiction, what you want to do is find a hook, bait it, and begin trolling for readers. The problem in the western is that you'll have to pull readers from other categories because the base in this genre has eroded.

There was some talk at the time that *Lonesome Dove* was published of it serving to revivify the genre; after that it was *Dances With Wolves*. Neither has done the job fully, but there are a couple of western series on television these days, and the occasional made-for-TV movie. While the plots on the television shows are pretty much standard, there is a clear understanding that the audience has matured; therefore, bringing a degree of sophistication to the storytelling, an understanding of psychology and the other factors that serve as motivators—rather than going after the slam-bang—will, in the long run, make new work salable. It just may take time.

Science Fiction

There's a famous story that circulates through science fiction fandom about the sf writers who, at the beginning of World War II, were called in by the FBI because it was thought that they were giving away national security secrets in writing about atomic energy. The story is told defensively: it proves that these tales of imagination are not silly and childish, that they are, to the contrary, right on the cutting edge and a telescope into tomorrow.

And how can you argue the point? Men have walked on the moon. Soviet cosmonauts live on the Mir space station, orbiting earth. Flash Gordon's ray gun is today's laser. That's why, in many circles, science fiction is more often referred to as "speculative fiction."

Traditional sf is hardware oriented. Projecting tomorrow's technology from today's science articles, the stories are about space travel, first contact (often adversarial), military operations. Science fiction is action/adventure tales that parallel the traditional western—which is why the stories were called space operas as opposed to horse operas.

The ideas behind the stories became increasingly more sophisticated: time travel is more fascinating than space travel, because the latter is no longer fiction . . . unless you get into faster than light, warp speed engines. Contact stories are no longer about conflict; rather they have taken on a political correctness that reflects in the anthropological and sociological aspects of the adventures. To a very great degree, contemporary sf is parable, an opportunity to explore not only the stars but ourselves.

Hardware still has a function, of course, not only in getting there, but in the development of robots, androids and other helpers, communications, weapons (they're still necessary, even if most of the cultures we come into contact with are superior to us), and power sources.

Aspiring sf writers have the advantage over most other category writers: there's still a broad, active, hungry market for short stories, magazines devoted to the form, and a rabid fandom that sponsors conventions on almost every weekend of the year. This offers the writer a strong network for support, and most important, a place in which to practice and hone his—or her—craft. (Science fiction is no longer a private club for male writers or fans.) Each magazine has a particular spin, an outlook and philosophy, that defines what it is looking for, and reading them not only serves as a market guide, but keeps you in touch with the many directions and choices you'll face in the area.

Very few writers are successful in the sf field if they have not grown up reading it. Whether it is still necessary to follow Asimov's Laws of Robotics is moot; knowing what has happened in the genre, knowing how to create the world necessary to support your story, and understanding the mix of physical and social sciences, comes from intimate familiarity with the past. Then you add reading not only in the contemporary fiction, but in the science magazines and other journals that touch on the forces that will be at play in our society tomorrow. Then you hope for the best.

Science fiction is a crowded field, and editors are deluged with manuscripts; there seems to be a feeling that anyone can write this stuff because we can just make it up as we go along. You can't.

Most of the major mass-market houses have sf publishing programs; there is some hardcover publication, but not much relative to the total volume.

As in the other major "fantasy fiction" categories, you are only limited by your imagination and your ability to create worlds. Most sf is not character oriented; it is the situation that drives the story. That situation must be brought to life, and you do that by knowing everything about the world you are creating before you sit down to write the tale.

What's going to separate your sf novel from a technothriller or an action/adventure story? As often as not, it might be a marketing decision—at least for those stories set in or near our own time. (And don't forget that sf works in both directions.) Don't limit your options by restricting your thinking. If your novel about a plan to disrupt a space flight can be more easily handled by publishing it in another category (perhaps resulting in more sales), that's fine. And it will work because you have kept a crucial thing in mind: the story, the action, is all plausible given the rules that have been dictated when you sat down to begin.

Fantasy

A case could be made for fantasy as the oldest category. After all, the stories are filled with strange creatures—some good, some bad—wishes that come true, and magic as a way of life. Call it myth or call it fairy tale, it is all fantasy.

The current vogue was born out of the success of J.R.R. Tolkien's Ring trilogy, but the genre has always been with us: horror was once considered *dark fantasy*, the stories of Conan the Barbarian fall into the general area of *heroic fantasy*, and the worlds of elves and magic was *light fantasy*. And most of it appeared in the magazines devoted to science fiction. As storytellers, as publishers, and as marketing people, we've become a lot more sophisticated.

And we've complicated matters, blending the definitions in some cases and trying to broaden them in others: the still popular stories of King Arthur are a category unto themselves—*Arthurian fantasy*. There are, of course, horror elements present in some of the stories, certainly the fairies—good and evil— of light fantasy, and characters who fulfill the definition of a Conan-like hero. (And there is, as always, revisionism: Marion Zimmer Bradley's *The Mists of Avalon* is Arthurian fantasy with a feminist twist.)

Because magic and "unnatural" beings are pretty much a necessity in the genre, your first task is to decide what kind of world you are going to create and what rules of nature govern it.

Then, what kind of creatures are you going to create? Over the years, certain traditions have developed and an awareness of these is important because readers are going to expect your characters to behave in a particular fashion. You *can* change these elements, of course, but you'll have to go carefully.

Finally, which voice are you going to use: the gentle, the violent, or somewhere in between? Will your characters have wit and charm or will they bull their way through the action, resorting to arms before magic? Or will magic be one of the weapons?

Fantasy is also a questing category: there is a prize to be won. It might be the hand of a princess (real or fairy), or a shield, or gold; whatever it is, something is at stake. (If you're beginning to see parallels here to *Dungeons and Dragons*, give yourself a few power points.)

Finally, keep in mind that with the exception of one or two writers, this is not a hardcover market, although it is a good one for short story writers.

An interesting development, and one that is moving into the world of science fiction as well, is the creation of *shared world* anthologies. These are collections of stories set in the fictional worlds of other writers whose works have become very popular. There are Thieves' World collections, Pern collections, and others. You cannot simply write a story or novel set in one of these worlds and then sell it; the works have become part of marketing strategies and are protected by copyright. Market reports in magazines related to the genre will make you aware of publishers who might be looking for submissions for such a project; most often, though, they are by invitation only.

The best fantasy novels are blendings. Black-and-white magic, unspeakable evil, great heroes (male and female) all meet on the field of battle, and that battle can go on for two, three or more books. Sustaining the pitch, the action, the interweaving of lives for that long is no easy task; sustaining reader interest for that long is even more difficult.

Conan (and his female counterpart, Red Sonja) serves as a model for heroic fantasy. The worlds they inhabit are more barbaric and rough than sylvan, the magic tinged with darkness. While there is a readership for the form, it does not represent the area with the greatest growth potential for a writer.

The fantasy can be set in the real world or, at least, impinge on it. One approach (which also appears in science fiction) is the *alternate universe*. What if we didn't kill all the fairies long ago and they are still in the world is the question being answered. The other most popular way of bringing the worlds together is to have a perfectly "normal" human be taken into the magical world, either for nefarious purposes or as the specially chosen hero or heroine for the forces of good. Those books tend toward parable, and also allow you to make interesting comparisons. What would happen, do you think, if you suddenly were given the power to do something extraordinary? With that as a premise and a jumping-off point, creating a fantasy is easy.

Telling it, however, is where the challenge lies.

Horror

One of the easiest ways to consider this genre, and attempt to define it, is to think of horror as being about the elemental battle between good and evil. At another level, one that Stephen King uses, horror is about the things that scare us, the things we check for under the bed before we go to sleep . . . the things that go bump in the night.

As with many categories, horror is subject to vogues. For a brief period in the 1980s, something called *splatterpunk* was popular: violent, gory, driven by murderous rages, the fiction had a shock value that the writers felt was important. They were trying to make us aware of the horror around us, the real horror. Others, however, continued to write and publish stories that used the supernatural to provide the *frisson*. Ghosts, vampires, and werewolves have always had their place in the pantheon, and always will. Finally, writers like Clive Barker, especially in his novel *Weaveworld*, attempted to recreate the wheel bringing together everything from splatterpunk to the world of H.P. Lovecraft. And it all works. It's all valid. It all has a place. What you must do is study each publisher's list and see how a particular house is defining the category.

Publishers and fans seem to be quite accepting these days of "revisionist" writings in the category: the traditions of a particular character—the vampire, for example—are still used, but the reasons for those traditions are being examined, as are the roles of the creature. We've seen the vampire-as-hero in the works of Anne Rice, Lee Killough, and Nancy Collins, and others are continuing to explore and experiment.

Certainly feel free to try that. But remember that in horror, as in its collateral relatives science fiction and fantasy, your first and most important job is to develop the reality, the day-to-day logic, of the world you are creating. The literature has set the basic guidelines for the behavior of a werewolf; you must either continue that way, or make clear the ways in which your world is different. You cannot cavalierly have your werewolf immune to a silver bullet without explaining why. That "why" has impact on other aspects of your story and you must keep all those facts in mind and clear.

Horror is a way of defining not only the things that scare us, but a way of putting a face on the more amorphous fears in our lives. When we see it in contrast to the more banal realities, the contrast and shock is all the more striking. The best writers in the category begin there, begin rooted in "real" life, sucker the reader in with the commonplace, and then let loose the demons. It is in the slide from the mundane, in the disruptions from the commonplace, that the manipulation of our emotions is the most successful.

So, figure out what it is that you're most afraid of, give it a face and a name, and put it down in Central City. Make it sneak up on your characters and your readers, make it shock and disturb, and make it real by maintaining the internal logic of your world.

Each generation of horror writers seems to bring a new—or, really, rediscovered—myth to challenge our security and sense of well-being. Voodoo had its time in the sun but doesn't seem to be a very popular subject right now. The vampire was thought to be safely in his coffin, firmly staked, but now he's risen. Hollywood has popularized the splatterpunks' efforts through the *Friday the 13th*, and *Halloween* movies, but there seems to be a growing away from that style.

Cursed ground (old Indian burial areas), possessed children, and hauntings still have their place, generally in paperback originals (which is probably the best marketplace; new writers are finding it extremely difficult to break into hardcover), while witchcraft, satanic cults, and stories that don't have a solution, that end with people not knowing what has happened to them but fearing it will happen again, are in disrepute.

Horror is, in the end, one of the categories that most welcomes the "what if" approach and the only real limits you have are those of your own imagination.

When Should You Put Yourself in an Agent's Hands?

by Dean R. Koontz

The incomparable Frank Sinatra once said, "Hell hath no fury like a hustler with a literary agent." Elitist intellectuals may grimace and inquire why I would quote a saloon crooner in matters literary. Well, in addition to being the greatest singer of pop songs this country has ever produced, Francis Albert Sinatra is street-smart, profoundly so, and street-smart is something every writer must be if he is to survive on publishers' turf. As regards literary agents, I could offer a quote from Alfred A. Knopf, the famous and prestigious publisher, in place of that crooner's wisecrack. "Trust your publishers," Knopf said, "and he can't fail to treat you generously." Now, if you have any street smarts whatsoever, you will have no difficulty determining which of those two quotations contains the most truth and wisdom.

Marvin Josephson, the agent, said, "The relationship of an agent to a publisher is that of a knife to a throat." Josephson might have overstated the case a bit, but if Sinatra had to choose a companion to accompany him on a long walk through a bad neighborhood at night, I have no doubt that he would prefer Josephson to Knopf.

I have had several knives protecting my interests during my career. I have been with my current knife for nine years, and I expect the association to last much longer, in part because this blade is sharper than the others that were previously brandished in my behalf.

I did not, however, begin my career with a knife. Unassisted, I sold three novels. Although an agent is eventually of great value if one is going to have a well-managed career, I recommend that every writer start by marketing himself, for he will learn invaluable lessons about the depth of the publishing river, the coldness of the water, and the treachery of the currents, by wading in alone.

When I have spoken at writers conferences, I have been dismayed by how many new writers are *obsessed* with getting an agent. Often, they are frantic to line up representation even though they have not yet finished a book. From their point of view, a literary agent is a sorcerer, someone who has the magic, the proper spells, and who never fails to place what he markets, regardless of its quality. This is, of course, not true. An agent can only sell what is publishable, and if the agent can sell it, so can the writer. Agents perform many invaluable functions and can be the writer's shield against the world, making it possible for him to produce more and better books. But agents cannot work magic, and it is a serious mistake for new writers to expend as much energy searching for representation as they expend creating their books.

Knife Guys

New writers frequently operate under the misapprehension that putting a Dudley Moore suit on Orson Welles is easier than an unagented writer selling a book. On the contrary: Though some houses do not accept unsolicited manuscripts, most do, even though the economics of reading over-the-transom material is crazy. If one in five hundred unsolicited books is publishable, bleary-eyed first readers are jubilant, and their employers continue to consider them worth their paychecks. No self-respecting efficiency expert would argue in favor of the slush-pile system, but most publishers continue to read everything—or at least a few pages of everything sent to them. Why? Because they are hungry for product, *starving*, and the competition for good writers is so fierce that no source of potential bestsellers can be overlooked.

Some writers function well for years without an agent, and some never acquire one. Isaac Asimov, author of more than three hundred books, has never used an agent. Although he did not begin to reach the bestseller lists until he had written at least two hundred eighty of those volumes, he was not starving in the meantime. For years, Irving Wallace had no book agent, relying upon a knowledgeable attorney to vet his contracts. Joseph Wambaugh, the Los Angeles police detective who first wrote novels as a sideline and now is a fulltime freelancer, has no agent. Perhaps skill with a .357 magnum is even more persuasive than a knife.

If you are writing only short stories or articles, you virtually have to represent yourself—in the beginning, anyway—for you will not be of interest to most agents; handling lots of short manuscripts that are sold for small fees is not cost-effective. Until you have a book in print from a major publisher—or a letter in hand from an editor expressing the desire to acquire one of your books—the chances are very small that you will be able to get a first- or even second-rate agent. About the only other way an unpublished writer can acquire a *good* agent is through the persuasive intervention of a writer-friend who is a successful client of the firm; thereafter, until you actually *do* sell something, you will always be "the *schlemazl* who's a friend of Joe's," a pity case. Otherwise, those who would take you on as a client when you are unpublished are very often crooked or incompetent or both.

(Perhaps I should not be quite so declarative. Good and honest agents are always looking for new clients, and most of them will read a businesslike query letter and the first fifty pages of a manuscript, but in this article I am dealing with the *best* way to get the *best* agent.)

Nameless and Aimless

To the new writer struggling to break in, even a third-rate agent can seem attractive. Better a bent, dull-bladed knife than no knife at all. Right? Wrong.

There are people out there, claiming the ability to make new writers rich and famous, who can do far more harm than good.

Consider "Mr. Nameless," a guy who constantly acquires new writers for his list and who might be a big-league agent if he spent as much time and energy representing his authors as he devotes to bilking them. He once had—and may still have—a neat scam that worked like this:

1. Upon signing up a new client with a finished project, Mr. Nameless eventually finds a home for the book at a legitimate paperback house, which we will call Humongous Books, where he tentatively accepts an offer for, say, $5,000.

2. He does not pass this good news along to the author.

3. Instead, he phones his client and says, "I love your book, but it just isn't publishable in its current state. I've shown it to several editors and got turndowns. However, there is this company, Dreck Salvaging, Incorporated, that specializes in taking almost-publishable books and transforming them into salable properties. They cut, paste, polish, do a general all-around editing job, and then try to sell the revised version. They take a big risk with a marginal script like yours because they might never sell it, so of course their advances are small. And they don't pay royalties. Now, if there were *any* hope of selling this book as it stands, I'd hammer on doors and talk my head off for ten years until I found a home for it. But I'm convinced the only deal we'll obtain is the one from Dreck Salvaging. The price is $1,000 for all rights, not a lot of money but *real* money, and at least it's a start for you."

4. Sometimes the client says, "Well, gee, why don't you tell me what's wrong with the script, and I'll do the rewriting myself rather than give away all rights to Dreck Salvaging." In which case, Mr. Nameless says, "You're too close to the book, too fond of it to be able to chop it apart and reassemble it with the necessary objectivity. Besides, before you can learn how to revise a book properly, you've got to know how to write one pretty solidly in the first place, and you're still learning *that*. Listen, you have such tremendous raw potential that I don't want you wasting more time on this minor book. No matter how much you improve it, we can't get much dough for it. Better to start another project than waste energy on this dog."

5. The client, admittedly tantalized by getting even just $1,000 for his work, starry-eyed at the prospect of seeing his name on a book, usually agrees to the Dreck deal.

6. Mr. Nameless then sells the novel to Dreck for $1,000, takes a $100 commission, and forwards a check to the client for $900.

7. An employee of Dreck spends one day on the script, changing descriptions, cutting some, adding a little, but doing nothing to improve upon or particularly detract from the original story. The only reason for making any changes at all is to allay the suspicions of the author, who will eventually read the finished book to see how his prose was "cleaned up."

8. Mr. Nameless takes the altered but unimproved script back to the paperback house that made the original offer and, as agent for Dreck Salvaging,

sells it for the $5,000 offer. The key to the scam is that Dreck Salvaging is a paper company, totally owned by Mr. Nameless, who pockets $4,100, plus all rights and future royalties, while the hapless author takes home $900.

Nameless fleeces some authors once or twice, others more often, before telling them that they are at last good enough to sell straight to a publisher without Dreck's assistance. Most never learn they have been taken, and even if they discover the truth, it is difficult to prove the "editorial assistance" provided by Dreck Salvaging was not, in fact, essential to the sale of the book. Nameless's deception of the client is conducted on the phone, never in letters, so the content and tone of those conversations cannot be independently verified.

Over the years I have heard about this scam from three editors in different publishing houses. Each thought the practice was scandalous, and each felt sorry for the victimized writers, *but none ever hinted about these improprieties to the authors being cheated*. Startling? Shocking? Wait—there's worse. Of the three, two dealt with Nameless and Dreck Salvaging on a regular basis! Why? For one thing, they lived in the same city as Nameless, worked in the same industry, went to the same restaurants and parties; therefore, keeping peace with him took priority over defending the rights of authors who lived else-where and who moved in different social circles. More important, editors dealt with Nameless and Dreck because they needed product, lots of it, to fill their monthly lists, and Nameless was a reliable source of bottom-of-the-list books that could be bought cheaply. Understandably, even the best editors put writers third on any list of priorities: 1) they look out for themselves, primarily (and rightfully) concerned first about their own careers; 2) they protect the interests of the publishers who employ them; 3) they do what they can for their authors. Mr. Sinatra would be embarrassed for you if you expected more than that.

Some new writers will feel that paying Mr. Nameless's price might be worthwhile if that made it possible to get books in print, establish a track record, and then use that record to obtain a better agent, but they are mis-taken. What I said earlier is dismayingly true: A couple of years with a lousy agent can do more harm than good. Mr. Nameless's authors are tainted by association with him. Because he is a third-rate agent, the good agents in the industry consider his writers third-rate, as well. Some *are* bad writers, but some are not, yet, regardless of their abilities, they might find it a bit difficult to get a reputable agent to consider them seriously when they are ready to leave the Nameless stable. Furthermore, because Nameless deals almost exclusively with the least powerful editors at the bottom of the ladder, his clients' books are usually released as "fillers," to plug gaps in the lower half of the publisher's list, and they receive no advertising budgets or publicity. Therefore, if you *do* get a better agent after a few years with Nameless, your credits will work *against* you; influential editors will look at your published titles, will see a string of unheard-of books that sold modestly at best, and will probably decide that you do not have what it takes to reach a wide audience. Then you will have to spend years trying to prove that you are better than they think you are.

The lesson is clear: Do not worry about getting an agent until you have first written a publishable book *that an editor wants to buy*. After all, creating the product must come before selling it. Obsessive concern about getting an agent can lead you to make rash judgments that you will later regret. The best way to find a *good* agent is to have one recommended to you by an editor who likes your work and wants to pay for it; that editor might not be able to place you with the top literary rep in the best agency in town, but he will surely steer you away from the crooks and the incompetents.

Rights and Wrongs

Once you have a good agent, your worries are not necessarily over. Even a good agent may not be the *right* one for you. For example:

I was once represented by an intelligent and amusing and honest and altogether charming person I will call Mr. Formidable. I liked him immensely, and I always had a good time in his company. He had a well-deserved reputation as a shrewd and aggressive bargainer, and he had done very well by several clients. For a time we worked together without friction, and Mr. Formidable wrangled higher advances for me than I had gotten before. Then, one day while my wife and I were lunching with him in an extremely expensive restaurant that served overrated food, I wondered aloud why my most recent novel, which had seemed perfectly suited for the movies, had received no offers whatsoever for film rights — and I got a shock that almost made me faint face-first into my unpalatable spring-vegetable soup.

"Oh," he said, "we had an offer for an outright sale at $100,000, but we turned it down."

For a moment I was speechless while I watched him consume scallops in a curdled sauce. Finally I said, "We turned it down?"

And my wife, in an uncharacteristically squeaky voice that sounded like a Mickey Mouse impression, said, "Why did we turn it down?"

Formidable explained that the man who made the offer was a fine producer but a poor director, and unfortunately he wanted to buy my novel with the intention of both producing and directing a film based on it. "He'd screw it up," Mr. Formidable said. "It'd be a bad film. We'll sell the rights to someone else, with a better chance of getting a good picture made, and that'll be more helpful to your career."

I had such respect and affection for Mr. Formidable that I took a deep breath, calmed myself, and managed to make myself believe that he knew best.

Weeks dragged by without another film offer turning up, and in fact none ever did, but it was not Mr. Formidable's autocratic rejection of 100K that finally drove me to seek new representation. I was able to forgive him that transgression because I convinced myself that he knew best in the long run. Oh, I was *young* then! However, subsequent to that never-to-be-forgotten luncheon conversation, I sent Formidable an outline for a more ambitious book than any I had yet attempted—and he refused to handle it. He told me that it was not the kind of thing that I could do, and he said that even if I *could* do it, the market would not be receptive to a novel of that sort. Unmarketable, he said. He wanted me to stick with the shorter, less-complex books that I had been doing and that he had been able to place with ease. *That* was what made me go elsewhere. An agent can offer guidance and market suggestions, but he must not be the absolute determiner of what stories his client will tell. He must encourage his client to grow, to try new ideas that challenge the client's talents. If an agent will not trust a client's artistic instincts, if he will not sell what the *client* wants to write, he is the wrong representative for that particular author.

Firing Mr. Formidable was one of the most painful things I have ever had to do, for I felt a special bond of friendship with him that I had reason to believe he felt as well. I know he was hurt by my departure, and his unconcealed pain made me feel even worse. But I found new representation, and that supposedly unmarketable outline was sold for the largest advance I had yet received. When the book was published, it went through seven printings and one million copies, appearing on several bestseller lists, with royalties mounting well into six figures. That novel was a turning point in my career, and it taught me a vital lesson that freed me from a lot of hampering illusions: In essence—even a *good* agent is not always the right agent.

Rights and Wrongs, Part II

You will know that you have found both a good representative *and* the right one when: 1) he always answers or returns your phone calls promptly (assuming that you do not call every day); 2) he appreciates the strengths of your writing but forthrightly notes your weaknesses; 3) he will explain his marketing intentions for a project in detail and will give real weight to your objections if you have any; 4) he urges you to be artistically ambitious, to write better and more complex books every time out of the gate; 5) he will risk antagonizing and even alienating a publisher to obtain something that is rightfully yours, such as long-overdue royalties or a revised accounting of what appears to be grossly under-reported sales; 6) he talks with you about long-term goals specifically rather than generally and does not try to load you up with too much quick-buck work to grab nice commissions in the short run; 7) he never turns down *or accepts* a deal without discussing everything with you; 8) you can have harsh words with him, forcefully express your dissatisfactions, and not damage your relationship with him; 9) he laughs at the same things you do.

Number nine is more important than it may seem. Publishers can be encouraging and honorable, but some of them can also be demanding, obstinate, inconstant, imperious, and sometimes even crooked and spiteful and consciously cruel. More writers fail than succeed; some go a little loony from the pressure and disappointment and uncertainty of a freelancer's existence, many become horribly bitter, and most have difficulty keeping body and soul together. If you care passionately about your writing, the freelancer's life can be a heartbreaker. Even if you are a survivor, even if your hard work ultimately pays off big, there are many times when sanity is saved and perspective restored by having an agent who is also a friend and who shares your world view, so the two of you can make jokes about the insanity of the publishing madhouse and try to lighten the dark moments with comradely laughter of the sort that helps soldiers survive battlefields and trenches.

You will know that you have the *wrong* agent if, among other things I have already discussed: 1) you do *not* laugh at the same things; 2) he does not promptly return your calls; 3) he does not read and report on your manuscripts within two weeks of receipt; 4) he is not open with you when you ask him about his marketing intentions for a project; 5) he professes to love everything you write; 6) he dislikes most everything you write; 7) he tries to steer you into writing in whatever genre is currently hot, without regard for your interests and style; 8) he is unwilling to show you a client list. (If he is any good at all, there should be several authors on his list whose names you recognize. In fact, there should be at least one client on the list who has made the major bestseller lists, preferably more than one.); 9) he wants to charge you a whole series of reading fees.

(It may be valuable to pay a reading fee for editorial and market suggestions, *but only once or twice*. The best agencies do not charge those fees. Agents who charge for reading scripts are often readers first, agents only secondarily, generating most of their income from fees rather than actually making sales and earning commissions. In those cases where the fee-reading income *is* the minor part of the business, the agent will seldom review your manuscript himself; he will be busy selling the work of successful clients, so he will hire people to read your stuff and write reports, to which he will sign his name. You are not his *client* if you are paying him to read your work; in a genuine agent-*client* relationship, the agent receives no compensation other than commissions from work that he sells.)

Finally, he is the wrong agent if the majority of deals he makes for you and for his other clients are with book packagers rather than directly with publishers. An agent who works almost exclusively in that fashion is more likely to be on the lookout for finder's fees and subpackaging fees. Those bites of the pie, taken in addition to his standard commission, come out of the author's piece.

Take heart: There are at least as many good agents as bad, and the vast majority of them, both the good ones and the bad ones, are honest. Incompetent representation is usually the worst problem a writer will have with an agent, and when you have finally found Mr. — or Mrs. or Miss or Ms. — Right, your life will be made infinitely easier. That perfect representative will relieve you of many business worries, will act as buffer between you and your publisher in order to preserve both your dignity and sanity, and will be a diplomat when antagonism develops between you and your editor. He will know which editors and houses will best suit a particular writer's talent and temperament. He will know what your work is worth and will be able to get the top dollar for it. He will do battle to see that your books are advertised, that they receive publicity, and that they are placed as close to the top of the publisher's monthly list as possible, rather than in the middle or at the bottom where the salespeople will not pay attention to them. Such exemplary agents deserve more attention than they receive from literary historians, for they give their authors the peace of mind, confidence, financial security and encouragement that make it possible for good books to be written.

The Good Fight

With the ideal agent, a writer gets more pleasure from each success than he might otherwise have felt, more joy from each triumph, for he has a fellow soldier in the trenches with whom to share the shining moments. Shared joy is always more satisfying than that experienced in solitude. If the new writer is patient, if he realizes that all new writers begin without agents and that most place their first books on their own, if he lets go of his many illusions about the magical power of an agent, if he relies solely on his hard work to gain him a publisher and *then* an agent, if he fully understands that writing is a craft—and an art—but not a racket, if he accepts that there are no shortcuts to the top, he will one day find first-rate representation. He will experience the intense pleasure of winning against all odds, with a business associate at his side who is also a friend, a reliable ally, and a paladin who fights the good fight to clear the barbarians and deadfalls out of the artist's path.

Sell Your Novel

by Darrell Schweitzer and John Gregory Betancourt

When should you write a query letter? Or should you just send in your manuscript?

If you're submitting a short story to a magazine, just mail it in. No query is necessary in most cases, particularly in such fields as mystery and science fiction, where large, active markets for short fiction exist. A short story is short enough that an editor can evaluate it almost as quickly as he can read and reply to your letter. So a letter to, say, the editor of *Ellery Queen's Mystery Magazine*, saying, "I have written a story about such and such" is largely a waste of everyone's time. If it's any good, *of course* the editor wants to see it.

With novels, it's quite another matter. Most editors do indeed want to see your novel. (Just how do you think all novelists started? It's not a secret handshake, we assure you.) But a novel manuscript is big—at least two hundred double-spaced typewritten pages, which will take someone several hours to read all the way through.

Often an editor will want to see the whole manuscript, but (more frequently in recent years) sometimes a query letter is needed, sometimes an outline, and sometimes both.

Dear Editor — The Query

A query letter is something you send an editor to arouse his interest in a specific work. Writing a good query letter is often the first step in getting a novel published.

Assuming you choose to approach a particular publishing company yourself (remember, most writers handle their first novels themselves—you can always get an agent *after* you have sold your novel), it becomes your job to find out the appropriate editor's name and how he or she works. Does he prefer to see a complete manuscript? Sample chapters and an outline? Just a query letter?

This sort of information can be found in *Writer's Market* and *Novel and Short Story Writer's Market*, or in various specialist journals. (In science fiction, *Locus* or *Science Fiction Chronicle* or the publications of the Science Fiction Writers of America; in other genres, publications from the Mystery Writers of America, Western Writers of America, and so forth are helpful.)

If you do your research and still aren't sure how your chosen editor works, a preliminary letter never hurts. A brief note—with a self-addressed, stamped envelope (SASE)—will almost always get a quick response. Just ask how he or she prefers submissions.

When you have that information, it's time to get to work. Let's say you've discovered that your editor (we'll call him Editor X) prefers a query letter. A query must tell its reader (Editor X) at a glance whether your book is worth looking at. *Be careful*. It's quite possible to tell Editor X that a book *isn't* worth his time. Suppose you wrote a letter like this:

Dear Whoever Reads These Things,

I have always wanted to be a writer, and now, finally, I have succeeded. I have braved the ridicule of my family and spent the last twenty years slaving away at my novel, in between raising eighty-seven children; divorcing twelve husbands, three wives and a dog; wrestling alligators in my spare time; and a long retreat in a Trappist monastery.

My novel is about Love, Truth, Beauty and the Meaning of Life. It defies commercial categorization, since I am not a hack writer who panders to idiotic popular taste. My novel comes from the <u>heart</u>. You will find it wonderful and gripping. You'll just <u>have</u> to give me a million dollars for it.

I await your offer. Meanwhile, I am simultaneously inquiring of every other publisher in the business.

Yours humbly,

Aside from the fact that such a letter makes the writer sound more than a little deranged (not to mention lazy, since our author didn't bother to find out to whom to write), it is *useless* to the editor. It tells him nothing he needs to know. Now a letter from a professional:

Dear Editor X:

My recently completed novel, <u>The Hound of the Baskervilles</u>, is a sixty-thousand-word mystery set in England. The hero, Sherlock Holmes, is a private consulting detective summoned to an English country estate to unravel the puzzling case of the Baskerville Curse.

Sir Henry Baskerville is the last of a line of unlucky noblemen, whose father, like his father and grandfather before him, was mauled to death by an enormous and apparently supernatural hound. Holmes and his colleague Dr. Watson (who narrates the story in the first person, in the form of a memoir) travel to the rural Baskerville Hall, and encounter mysterious servants with dubious motives, neighbors who may not be what they seem, an escaped lunatic, and, ultimately, the dread Hound itself. Tension is sustained between possible natural and supernatural explanations for the mysterious happenings, and much atmosphere derives from the moorlands themselves — treacherous bogs where a good deal of the action takes place and where, as Holmes puts it, "The powers of evil are exalted."

Would you be interested in reading this manuscript? I have been previously published in <u>The Strand</u>, <u>Beeton's Christmas Annual</u>, and other British and American periodicals.

Yours,

A. Conan Doyle, M.D.

See the difference? Dr. Doyle may get somewhere. His letter tells the editor the essential facts quickly: what sort of book it is, where it is set, who (and what sort of people) the main characters are, and how the story proceeds.

So Editor X thinks: *Mystery. Male detective. English setting. Mix of supernatural/folkloristic and medical background. Sounds interesting. Even the title has a nice ring to it, and this Doyle chap sounds like a sensible professional I can work with.*

Outlines and Sample Chapters

Let's assume that in response to your query, Editor X requests "chapters and outline." What then?

Send the editor between forty and sixty manuscript pages. Always send the *first* forty to sixty pages of the novel, whether it's three chapters or sixteen chapters, or even one chapter. The idea is not to send a specific number of chapters (though some people recommend sending three chapters); the idea is to provide Editor X with a sample of your writing. The sample must be large enough to show your skill, and shorter, obviously, than the whole manuscript. If Editor X wants to see more, he'll say so. The trick is making him want to see more.

To that end, you must choose *the right stopping point* for your sample chapters. Always end with a cliffhanger of some kind. You must make Editor X *want* to find out how the characters escape, who did it and how, or what the Hound really is. If he must start reading the outline to find out what happens next, you have him hooked.

Outlines, just as important as sample chapters, must convince Editor X not only that you're writing at a professional level, but also that you're *plotting* at a professional level. All editors read outlines with attention to detail. They must make sure the story develops properly. (Nobody would want to read more of *The Hound of the Baskervilles* if they knew Doyle killed all the characters in a train wreck in chapter six, after which the Hound — who was actually a Martian — delivered a lecture on Love, Truth and Beauty for the next hundred pages.)

Editors have other uses for outlines, too. Often in modern publishing the editor can't just say, "Okay, I will buy this book." He must persuade his superiors, often a board of senior editors. He may also have to persuade the company sales force. A really effective outline can be passed around to others, and help persuade people *who may never read the book* that it's the next best thing to sliced bread. A good outline might make the difference between acceptance and rejection.

An outline is not a graph with a bunch of boxes and charts. It is a synopsis written in plain language, which tells your story in miniature all the way to the end (quite unlike the query letter, which — like the sample chapters — may deliberately build up to a cliffhanger). A good outline tells the whole story, touching on all the important scenes. It is to a complete novel what a treatment is to a movie script.

The language is, indeed, synoptic:

> Watson remains at Baskerville Hall, while Holmes is apparently busy with other work in London. The doctor writes to Holmes daily, but unbeknownst to him, a mysterious stranger is intercepting the letters. He wonders why Holmes does not show himself, as events become progressively beyond the doctor's own meager deductive abilities.
>
> The butler at the Hall is clearly up to something. Then one night Watson and Sir Henry observe him signaling with a lantern at a window. From out over the moor, an answer flashes back.

Notice that there is no dialogue here, and no description. But an outline still requires a kind of storytelling, as it takes the reader from salient point to salient point. It must be well paced, with the important parts brought to the fore. And it should be in the present tense to give a sense of immediacy.

But most of all, an outline must be exciting. Nobody likes a dull story; who wants to read a book whose outline makes it *sound* dry and uninteresting? Consider the difference between "They go out and look for the dog" and "Watson and Sir Henry creep onto the moor, searching for any sign of the phantom Hound." The usual rules for good writing apply. Avoid the passive voice; focus on action, characters and interesting plot twists; don't be flowery or overly adjectival; etc.

Remember the famous *Dragnet* slogan: "Just the facts." For nearly a decade *Dragnet* kept viewers' attention with "just the facts" by telling those facts in an interesting way.

In the outline of *The Hound of the Baskervilles*, for instance, it would not be very helpful to tell the editor about each minor scene with Holmes and Watson chattering, how the characters are introduced, what they say to each other over dinner, and how each step of the deduction proceeds. These things belong in the book; they definitely add to the story. They just don't belong in the outline.

An outline is a sales pitch, a commercial for your novel. But it can't look like a sales pitch. It must grab its readers—Editor X and everyone else at the publishing company—and make them come away saying: "This sounds really exciting! I can't wait to see the complete book!" You can't just say in the outline "This is the most exciting mystery of the year." Editors are trained to ignore hype. You must make them come to that conclusion themselves. In other words, *show, don't tell*.

After that, when Editor X asks to see your novel, you prepare your cover letter and send the complete manuscript.

The Cover Letter

When you submit a short story, you don't need a cover letter in most instances; the manuscript speaks for itself. With a novel, though, cover letters are vital. Every cover letter for a novel needs four things:

- *The editor's name and address.*

In most publishing houses, mailrooms sort mail and deliver packages to editors; sometimes they open the packages first. You need the editor's name and address on the cover letter to make sure it actually reaches him.

- *Your name, address and telephone number.*

You want the editor to be able to find you!

- *A short description of the book.*

The editor must be able to tell at a glance which genre your novel falls into. Example: "Enclosed is *The Hound of the Baskervilles*, a mystery novel involving consulting detective Sherlock Holmes, set in England." (If the editor asked to see the complete manuscript based on either a query or sample chapters and outline, say so here.)

- *Professional credits, if any.*

If you're a regularly selling writer, make sure the editor knows you're a professional. Example: "I have sold fifty short stories to professional mystery magazines; *Hound* is my first novel." (If you don't have any professional credits, don't list anything. Let the editor assume — based on your sterling prose — that you sell short stories regularly.)

Remember, cover letters must be as concise and businesslike as possible. Don't waste the editor's time with your opinions of the book; the editor doesn't *care* what you think about it. His opinion is the only one that counts at this point.

And it's the quality of the book that will make it sell.

Negotiating Your Book Contract

by Michael Seidman

I t is the best of times; it is the worst of times. The manuscript you mailed off into the void has been accepted. An editor calls. Sweet-voiced and excited, she makes an offer: So much in advance, so much in royalties. Little else is said. You respond, "Yes, yes." The contract is in the mail, you are told. If you have any questions, feel free to call, you are told. Perhaps.

The contract arrives. You have questions. You are also nervous: If you start making waves now, will the manuscript arrive by return mail? Will you alienate this kind editor, creating a negative force around the publication of your book? Just what *can* you do, how far can you push? Have you made a serious mistake in agreeing to the offer you received over the phone?

Having an agent, of course, relieves you of the pressure; but we know how difficult it is to find an agent these days. Forewarned, however, being forearmed, and knowing that editors usually have some room to negotiate— and are willing to do so—you are no longer alone.

I've taken several standard contracts, amalgamated them, played with them, and now offer you a look at the contract, at your options, and where and how hard you can push to protect yourself. Having an agent is still better, but with this information you will be able to speak intelligently and knowledgeably to the editor who calls. Thus being more comfortable, you will be able to negotiate the best possible contract for yourself.

Contracts begin simply enough: The Publisher is named, the Author is named (and perhaps a pseudonym, if you have chosen to use one). Then the contract begins:

The Parties Agree as Follows:

1 Grant of Rights. The grant of rights is what the Publisher is acquiring, and it lists everything you are selling. It generally begins with the words *The Author hereby grants and assigns exclusively to the Publisher and its successors, representatives and assigns the rights in and to an unpublished work of fiction (or nonfiction) tentatively entitled:*

That "tentatively entitled" is sacrosanct. You may think that your title is brilliant; as with so much in publishing, however, the marketing department may have some very different ideas. For instance, certain words are thought to have a negative impact on buyers, and publishers want to avoid them. The editor may know of another book with the same title that has just been released (it happened to me recently; fortunately my novel is still in outline). Whatever the reasons, good editors will work with you to select a title. This is also the last time the title of the book appears in the contract; hereafter it is called the "Work."

The Publisher acquires rights for the full term of copyright and all renewals and extensions thereof

in all languages throughout the World, including all US military installations, the right to print, publish and/or license and sell the Work, in a hardcover and/or paperback edition or any part or abridgment thereof. And the rights of digest, condensation, anthology, quotation, book club, first serialization, second serialization, TV and performance rights, with exclusive authority to dispose of such rights.

That's the *boilerplate*, the wording that's part of the printed contract before changes are made. The Publisher has acquired *all rights to your work* in every form imaginable. (Some contracts also mention "or forms yet to be devised or developed," which takes care of CD-ROM disks and whatever may come along tomorrow.)

An agent would begin by striking out the translation rights, world rights, performance rights and, as often as not, first serialization rights. Your agent is in a position to sell those rights for you, and it thus makes sense for him to retain them. The Publisher also has representatives attempting to place rights throughout the world. If your Publisher places the rights, you'll receive a percentage of the monies earned, usually 50 percent. If your agent places them, you receive 100 percent of the monies, less the agent's commission. (And, in both instances, the representatives in foreign countries or in Hollywood also take a percentage, which is deducted from the top.)

The problem you face, *right now*, is that you don't have an agent and it is virtually impossible for you to place most of those rights yourself—you don't have the contacts. The editor you're dealing with knows this and will make a good case for being allowed to retain the rights. You, on the other hand, are thinking of getting an agent now that you have a track record . . . but you can't count on it. What to do?

Ask the editor to amend the clause so that the rights in question revert to you if the Publisher hasn't placed them within eighteen months of publication. This allows the Publisher to try to do that part of the job (which it will—selling such rights represents additional income, after all), and still protects you. If the Publisher hasn't sold the rights, and you have now acquired representation, your agent will be able to go to bat for you.

In agented acquisitions, the rights sold are usually for publication in the United States, its territories, the Philippines and Canada, and are for English language publication only. The Publisher generally receives book club, second serialization, anthology, condensation and abridgment rights, as well. (It is also standard for the Publisher to retain the right to allow Braille or other editions for use by the physically handicapped to be produced at no fee and with no royalty.)

The next clause is generally the copyright clause, which authorizes the Publisher to copyright the work in your name and guarantees that the copyright notice will appear according to U.S. Copyright Law and the Universal Copyright Convention. You agree to protect the copyright, and that if you dispose of any rights you've retained, you will see to it that the proper notice appears. There's nothing here for you to worry about.

2 Delivery of Manuscript. You've sold a completed manuscript. At least, that's what you thought. But changes may be requested. (Or you may have gotten lucky beyond all expectations and sold your book from an outline.) The first lines of this clause read:

> The Author agrees to deliver to the Publisher a manuscript of _____ words on or before _____. Such manuscript shall be a complete and legible copy of the Work, properly prepared for the press and in form and content acceptable to the Publisher.

So far, it's easy. You know how to do a word count; you know how to prepare a manuscript. But "form and content acceptable to the Publisher"?

That's where the editing comes in. If in your editor's opinion the book isn't ready to go to press, the Publisher has the right to demand changes:

> Publisher shall notify Author within _____ days of its receipt of the manuscript as to its acceptability or nonacceptability. If, in the sole opinion of the Publisher, the Work is unacceptable to the Publisher, the Publisher shall provide the Author with a detailed list of reasonably required changes, and the Author shall have _____ days from the receipt of said list to make changes. If, in the sole opinion of the Publisher, the revised Work is unacceptable to the Publisher, the Publisher may reject it by written notice within _____ days of delivery of the revised manuscript, and may thereby cancel this Agreement.
>
> Upon such cancellation, the Author will repay to the Publisher all sums of money advanced.

You have the right to expect your editor to work with you. In the wording in this delivery clause, the editor is required to tell you exactly what is wrong and to make specific suggestions as to how to correct the problems. (You're right if you're thinking that that's pretty much the definition of an editor. Unfortunately, not all editors live up to the definition.)

The sticking point might be the words *sole opinion of the Publisher*. Most publishers won't change that and trying to get it changed is undoubtedly an exercise in futility; certainly, there's no way to get two immovable forces to move. You might try, however, to amend the words *Upon such cancellation . . . money advanced* so that you have a *first proceeds* right. Simply, such wording permits you to repay the advance if and when you resell the manuscript in question.

This is a time for good faith on the part of both parties. If you're selling your first book, odds are the editor has already discussed the changes she wants with you, and you know whether you a) agree and b) accept the suggestions. If you don't agree and accept, or if you feel that you can't do the work requested (for whatever reason), you won't have reached this stage of negotiation. A good editor will also recognize your intent and integrity as a storyteller, and shouldn't be asking for things that change the point of your work.

It is certainly easier for an established author to get a first proceeds clause; publishers have every re~son to believe that the author will be in a position to repay because he or she will be in a more realistic position to resell. (And, too, the author may have an ongoing relationship with the editor or publisher. An author recently sent me a book that was not only unacceptable, but also — for him — unfixable. Because of our relationship, we were able to agree on the delivery of a different book entirely . . . one he was more comfortable with and one I knew he could do without encountering problems.)

You may have to be a judge of human character in deciding how far to push here, deciding whether you "trust" the editor with whom you are dealing. If you don't, you shouldn't have gone this far.

The amount of time to allow for the work called for (all those blanks in the quoted paragraph) is probably negotiable. It's not unreasonable to expect reactions within sixty days; by the same token, the Publisher should be able to count on you to do the necessary work in the same amount of time.

The rest of the delivery clause will often refer to rights, permissions and nontext items. If you're quoting from someone else's work, if you're using a line from a popular song, if there are maps or other supplementary matter, it's your responsibility to acquire all the rights and permissions to use those items . . . in *every* territory licensed to the Publisher. Those rights are often expensive, and you are solely responsible for the expenses.

In the contract we are using, you have sold hard- and softcover rights (a situation that pertains more and more often these days). The person selling you the rights to the quote or the song or the map will ask about the number of editions, territories, etc., and will charge accordingly. (Permission to use lyrics often comes at a price that will make you seriously reconsider whether your character should sing a song, or simply hum it.)

3 Editing of Manuscript. After you've done your rewriting, the editor and copyeditor begin work. According to your contract:

> The Publisher has the right, in its discretion, to make any editorial changes in the Work deemed necessary by it, with the Author's approval, which shall not be unreasonably withheld. The Publisher also has the right to request additional material or revision of the Work from the Author. The Publisher will make the final decision on title, cover art, format, and retail price of the Work. In the event the Author is more than one person, the Publisher shall determine the order of authorship credits.

You have the right (in fact, it may be demanded of you) to see the edited and/or copyedited manuscript, to check it, and to discuss any problems with your editor. Editors rarely work by *caveat*, and the changes in your manuscript have been made to ensure better reviews and better sales, and to prevent embarrassment to either Publisher or Author. Editors have enough to do day-to-day to guarantee they won't make changes capriciously.

We've discussed the title; don't bother arguing about cover art or format (hardcover, trade paperback, paperback). These are tied to marketing decisions that represent the Publishers informed opinion as to how to best sell the book. There are certain authors who, by dint of their position in the firmament, may be able to approve covers, but they are few and far between. If your book is in a special category, or it in some way reflects specialized knowledge (e.g., a historical book set in a period which you know backward and forward) you might suggest that you supply stock art — examples of period clothing, perhaps — and offer to look at sketches for the cover art to be certain that a character is not depicted carrying a weapon that hasn't yet been invented. (Do you get the idea that this may have happened to me?) However, it will be virtually impossible for you to change the wording in this clause, and you are well advised to trust in your editor. Again, everything is being done to help the sale, not hurt it.

If you've done your homework and research, it's safe to assume that you're already familiar with the kinds of cover packages your Publisher uses. If you've laughed every time you've seen a particular publisher's packaging, you wouldn't have submitted to that publisher. So don't worry about it.

4 **Copyedited Manuscript and Page Proofs.** Most contracts give you the right (and *obligation*) to read, correct and approve your Work in both of these production stages. If the contract you receive doesn't, demand it. You'll be given from ten to twenty days (depending on the Publisher's production schedules) to do this work. You want to catch editing problems — changes that somehow negatively affect your work — now, because you will be charged for changes you make in the page proofs. Make certain the clause states clearly that you're not responsible for "printer's errors in accurately reproducing the approved copyedited manuscript."

If that clause isn't in your contract, you may be surprised by what appears in the finished book. If you don't do your checking quickly and accurately, you have no one to blame but yourself. If your Publisher refuses to agree to a clause giving you the right to approve the manuscript and page proofs, find out why.

5 **Warranty and Indemnity.** This clause will appear in every contract. It is something no editor will change, no attorney will allow to be deleted. There are, however, some things you might wish to discuss, depending on the nature of the book.

The Author warrants and represents that he or she is the sole proprietor of said Work and has full power to make this Agreement and grants that it in no way infringes upon the copyright or proprietary right of others and that it is original and not in the public domain; and that it contains no libelous matter and does not invade the right of privacy of anyone. The Author agrees to indemnify and hold harmless the Publisher and Seller of the Work against loss or expense, including court costs and reasonable attorney's fees, incurred by it by reason of any finally sustained claim that said Work violates any rights whatsoever. All warranties and indemnification hereunder shall survive the termination of this Agreement.

You are guaranteeing that you have the right to sell the Work and that it contains no libelous material. Given the readiness of people to sue these days, it's reasonable to expect that your Publisher wants to be protected. This clause doesn't give you something you might want—the right to agree to any out-of-court settlement—but it does specify that any action must be "finally sustained." If it's a nuisance suit, then you aren't responsible for any costs; if the suit is valid, well, you blew it.

Also watch out for a warranty clause that mentions obscenity. No one has a definition of obscenity worth the paper it's printed on right now, and you may have used a dirty word or two. Most editors are aware of the general community standard and will protect you in the editing, but whether you want to *warrant* that the Work is not obscene is a matter of personal choice.

Keep in mind, though, that no editor has the authority to make any changes in this clause, and that it is rarely, if ever, changed in any way.

6 **Advance.** When your editor called, she told you she'd pay a certain amount for the rights to your book. *Then* was the time to decide whether you would accept the offer. Don't accept, wait for the contract to arrive, then ask for more . . . it's too late. If you're unsure and want to talk to friends, do it before you say yes to the deal. Just tell the editor, during your initial discussion, that you "want to think about it" and will get back to her. Indeed, if you are not satisfied with the offer, those words should represent your manuscript. Don't feel pushed or pressured. Don't let your emotions rule you. Don't say that you're checking with your writers workshop, your best friend, your spouse, or an agent you met five years ago. As in writing, the principle is K.I.S.S.

I should point out that while an editor may have some room to maneuver at this point, advances are not arbitrarily decided. Many factors go into arriving at the figure (not the least of which is the boss saying, *"That's what you're going to offer!"*). Editors work with profit-and-loss worksheets, forms that take into account sales in the category, production costs, cover costs, royalties, freight costs . . . and the list goes on. After a certain amount of grunting and groaning over a calculator, a figure is arrived at, and the offer made. The astronomical advances you read about in the papers are newsworthy only because they are so far from the norm. Whether you want to accept $3,000 or hold out for more is up to you. Don't forget, however, that the advance is *against royalties*; if the book has legs and outsells everyone's reasonable expectations, you will be making more money in the future.

Generally, the advance clause reads:

The Publisher agrees to pay the Author as an advance against all earnings hereunder the sum of _____ payable as follows:

Note first, that the advance is not only against royalties; but also against "all earnings." That takes into account all the subsidiary rights you've signed over to the Publisher. Every penny of your earnings is accounted against the advance, helping you "earn out."

What follows the words *payable as follows*? It's likely that the editor didn't mention the "split" on the phone, and you didn't think to ask—it wasn't something you were expecting.

The most common split is fifty-fifty, with half the advance money coming to you on signing, the other half on delivery of the *finally accepted* manuscript. You may also run across signing and publication splits, which give the Publisher another eighteen to twenty-four months to hold onto your money. If money doesn't mean that much to you (did I really say that?), you may be willing to accept that second split; odds are that the editor will, after some hemming and hawing, agree to an acceptance payment, especially if the advance is $7,500 or lower.

As the amount of the advance goes up, payout becomes more creative. On a $50,000 hard/soft contract, for instance (you are receiving that amount; the Publisher will do a hardcover edition followed in a year or so by a paperback edition), you may be offered $20,000 on signing, $15,000 on delivery, and $15,000 on publication of the hardcover edition.

The variations on the theme are endless; authors who receive multimillion-dollar contracts aren't receiving the money in one lump sum; few writers receive advance money all at once. It is not unheard of, when the amount is small, for an author to receive the full advance on signing. In those instances, the editor knows that the book is complete and that the writer could use the extra grand right away, and the Publisher is willing to agree as a sign of both good faith and good will. Keep in mind that the editor does not necessarily have the authority to agree on her own and might very well do the same thing you're doing: Tell you that she'll have to get back to you ... even if she already knows whether or not she's going to agree. That's what makes it fun, right?

The standard split, however, is half on signing, half on acceptance. You can ask for something different if you are offered anything else (especially at the lower end of the advance spectrum). Make certain, though, that you agree on the split before the contract is drawn up.

7 **Royalties.** Hardcover royalties are standard in the industry: 10 percent on the first five thousand copies, 12½ percent on the next five thousand, and 15 percent thereafter. Your editor will simply say "standard" or "10, 12½, 15." If she does say standard, check to make certain her standard is the same as yours.

Paperback royalties are all over the board. Certainly, you should try to get a 6 percent royalty as the minimum. A royalty offer of 2 percent or 4 percent is not unheard of.

It's possible to negotiate the point: you might ask for a split, the most common coming when one hundred fifty thousand copies are sold. If you begin at 6 percent, the royalty jumps to 8. If you begin at 8 (more usual if you are established), the jump goes to 10. If you begin at 10, take the offer and run.

Royalties, like advances, are not arbitrary; they are factored into the profit-and-loss sheet the editor prepared, and are considered, rightly, an expense by the Publisher. Keep in mind that while you're receiving your percentage based on the full cover price (at least you should—your contract should specify "retail" instead of "net" price), the Publisher is selling the book at a discount—perhaps as much as 50 percent off. Ideally, the estimated royalty payment will be equal to, or more than, the advance. Not so ideally, you have no idea of what the sales are going to be (and the editor has but a little more information), so it's difficult for you to find the balance point.

You can, for your own pleasure, do some simple math that might give you a ballpark figure. For instance, in the case of a hardcover book, estimate—for a first novel in a popular category—that you won't sell more than four thousand copies. Multiply that by an average cover price of, say, $14.95. That brings you to $59,800. Now, multiply by 10 percent: $5,980 is what might be expected as earned royalties; therefore, an advance of between $5,000 and $6,000 is reasonable. *Please* keep in mind that this is a very rough way of estimating, that it takes none of the other expenses of publishing a book into account, and is—at best—an informed guess as to what the book will earn in royalties based on a rough guess of sales. While the same paperwork may be done in order to ascertain mass-market royalties, it is impossible to offer estimated sales figures for you to use in your computations; the market is simply too volatile and a sales estimate may as easily be thirty-five thousand copies as one hundred thirty-five thousand.

The rest of the royalties clause lists other types of sales: These are special sales, remainders, premiums, sales for export or through mail-order, etc. The Publisher earns less on these sales than on normal ones; therefore your royalty will be lower. You will be told that no royalty will be paid on review copies, damaged copies, or those sold below manufacturing cost. I've yet to hear of a successful negotiation on most of those subparagraphs, and the reason, I think, is no one bothers. The lower royalties exist because of exchange rates, bulk discounts and other such factors. Given everything else you must think about, I think you can just make sure nothing seems outrageous in the contract you receive, and if you're bothered, ask the editor for an explanation.

Another subclause in this section will make it clear that "copies" refers only to copies in a particular format, and that the specific royalty breakdowns apply only to specific formats. In other words, you can't lump your paperback sales together with your hardcover sales, and expect hardcover royalties on the total. Eminently fair.

8 **Subsidiary Rights.** When you granted your Publisher all those rights in paragraph #1 you weren't giving them up for free. In most cases, you will receive a fifty-fifty split of subsidiary rights sales. Here it's important to understand the principle of "flow-through" in order to know exactly what you're getting. Here's an example:

Your Publisher has sold rights to a French publisher for an edition in that language, and received $3,000. Half of that is yours, half is your Publisher's. *However*, your half "flows through," becoming the "earnings hereunder" we looked at under point #6. If you haven't yet earned out your advance, your money is applied against the advance. (There are contracts that still call for unearned portions of the advance to be repaid. I can't recollect that clause ever being invoked; but you don't want it there anyway.)

It is only after the book has, through royalties and other sales, earned back the advance that your percentage goes into your pocket as cash. Your royalty statement should list every bit of this income, however, whether or not it is still flowing through. If your editor tells you of a sale, and your next statement doesn't reflect it, call. It's possible that the monies didn't arrive until after the statement closing date; it's also possible that someone made a mistake.

Some writers have attempted to insert into the contract a subclause stating that once the book has earned out, any monies received from subsidiary sales shall be paid immediately to the Author. The more usual procedure is for that money to be accounted for at royalty time and, as you can imagine, changing that procedure is difficult. It means setting up a separate accounting procedure and even in this day of computers and data bases, publishers are reluctant to do this. You might consider using it as a bargaining chip: Request it and then give in—in exchange for something more important to you.

It's also possible to change the percentages. You might be able to request, and receive, a seventy-five/twenty-five or even ninety/ten split on movie rights, for instance, and most editors are amenable to that change. Remember, the usual split *is* fifty-fifty, and on most of the so-called standard rights (paperback reprint, book club, second serial) there's little room to maneuver.

Make certain that all the rights being sold, and the percentages being paid, are spelled out clearly, and check back to the first page, where the grant of rights appears first, to make certain that nothing has been left out: Because both the subrights paragraph and the grant paragraph are part of the boilerplate, it's always possible for a correction made in one to be missed in the other.

You have the right, at the time the offer is tendered, to ask just what rights are being acquired and it's wiser to make changes then, rather than waiting for the completed contract to be in your hands.

9 Reports and Payments. This paragraph in the contract explains the Publisher's fiscal cycle: when the accounting procedure comes to an end, and when the royalty report will be drawn up. Each publisher uses different timing, based on its own fiscal calendar, and you're not going to change it.

There will also be a clause that states that the first statement won't be issued unless it covers a period of more than six months from the date of the Work's first publication. That means that if your book is released in the last month of an accounting period, you must wait until the next period for a statement. The reasoning is simple: In the first month the Publisher has absolutely no idea of how the book is doing and what the "returns" are going to be. Bookstores may order, say five thousand copies of your book. But that doesn't mean you have sold five thousand copies, as the stores have the right to return unsold copies. Therefore, the Publisher will report the number of bookstore orders, minus an anticipated number of books that will eventually be returned. This is called the reserve against returns. Because the Publisher has no way of estimating a reserve against returns, a statement prepared too soon after the book goes on sale could earn you a payment that far exceeds the book's real earnings. Some contracts call for the return of overpayment, either in cash or by applying the amount against future earnings; others make no mention of the problem.

You can understand why a publisher would want to protect itself in cases like this, and this statement clause is, therefore, virtually untouchable.

Some contracts specify the reserve against returns, others never mention it. In all cases, though, publishers take it. The rule of thumb is that returns are in (or at least 90 percent of them are) after a year on sale.

You can attempt to pin the Publisher down, requesting that the reserve figure be made part of the contract. (The lower the reserve figure, the better for you.) Most editors do not have the right to grant it and most publishers refuse to even discuss the matter. Professional organizations, such as the Science Fictions Writers of America, are lobbying to change this situation and at some point in the future we may see it not only get into the contract but also appear on the royalty statement. There's no way of telling how long it will take, or how successful the writers will be.

If you're going to attempt to have the reserve written in, don't push the matter and if the editor offers a 50 percent reserve, accept it, especially in mass market where the returns — as I write in September 1989 — are averaging well over 65 percent industrywide. Another approach is to request a clause that calls for the release of the reserve after four royalty periods.

A reasonably standard subclause in this section of the contract states that if the royalty figure is below a specified amount (between $25 and $50 usually), the Publisher isn't obligated to pay the amount or issue a statement, and may defer it until the next period. You can usually amend that to read that you will receive the statement and you can fight for the money, too. Publishers don't think it is worth fighting over, and it is also the kind of argument that can leave a bad taste in the editor's mouth.

You also should have the right to examine the Publisher's books and records. The boilerplate on this clause (in those contracts in which it appears) grants you the right to have your representative, during regular business hours, come to the Publisher's office and examine the books . . . not more often than once a year. You are required to bear the expense of such examination, unless it is discovered that the errors come to more than a specified percentage (usually 10 percent) of the total sum to your disadvantage. In other words, if you've been jobbed, the Publisher not only pays you, but also pays for the discovery.

Any royalty statements you receive are binding, unless you let the Publisher know, in writing and specifically, of any objections. The letter should be received within a year of the date of the statement. Cashing a check generally signifies your agreement to the amount.

10 **Free Copies.** Your contract should offer you some copies of your finished book, and allow you to acquire additional copies at a discount. Ten seems to be the usual number of free copies; you can request more. Check for any language indicating the manner in which you will pay for additional books: Can you have them charged against your royalty account, or must you pay? Some publishers hesitate to allow authors to bill against royalties, because it's possible that the book won't earn any. (Sorry about that.)

Your commitment here is to not sell the books you're receiving; they are intended for your personal use. While some contracts will have language pertaining to that, others don't. Rest assured, however, that if you suddenly order five thousand copies of your book, someone is going to notice.

11 **Reversion of Rights.** The Publisher has acquired rights for term of copyright; this doesn't mean, though, that you have lost control for that period of time. The contract should have a reversion clause:

If, after _____ years from publication the Work is out of print, and the Publisher, on receipt of a certified letter from the Author requesting that the Work be reprinted, either refuses to reprint the Work or within _____ months of said receipt has failed to do so, or commence work on a new edition, then the license herein granted shall automatically terminate, and all rights herein granted shall revert to the Author, except that any sublicensing arrangement granted pursuant to this Agreement will continue in full force and effect.

The number of years varies—anywhere from five to seven seems to be the boilerplate special; you'll never get anyone to agree to less than five, and they may push for nine. You don't have to give in; compromise works.

The final phrase in the above clause also prohibits you from getting back full rights to license arrangements. If your publisher has sold rights in England

and the book is still selling there, you will continue to share in that income until such time as the sublicense expires.

The Publisher will have the right to sell off any copies printed and in stock prior to the date of notification. And, while it may not be in the contract you receive, you should ask that a sentence be added giving you the right to acquire, at cost, any copies that will be remaindered (that is, sold off to discount marketers) at this time. (Actually, a clause to this effect may appear in the royalty section. In any event, you want the right to acquire overstock, at cost, before the book is remaindered.)

If the book is being reverted, make certain your Publisher is obligated to let you know of any licensing agreements in force. This not only lets you know the state of your business at that time, but also prevents a less-than-scrupulous publisher from making a quick deal (to sell off some rights that should belong to you). This becomes especially important in those instances where a reversion clause disallows a reversion if any licensing agreements are in effect. Wherever possible, you would prefer wording similar to that in the example.

12 **Mandated Publication.** You have the right to have your book appear within a reasonable amount of time. What's reasonable? A year is too short—most schedules are done well in advance of that kind of timing. Eighteen to twenty-four months seems reasonable to me; any longer than that is outrageous. The clock should start ticking when the manuscript is accepted; you've done all that has been asked of you; now it is up to the Publisher to perform.

Additionally, if the wording does not appear, try for something like this:

In the event the Publisher shall fail to publish and distribute the Work by said date, then upon receipt of a certified letter from the Author demanding that the Publisher do so, if the Publisher either refuses to publish or arrange publication, or within _____ months has failed to do so, then this Agreement shall terminate and all rights hereunder shall revert to the Author, and the Author shall retain any payments made under this agreement.

This gives you everything, including the money. The Publisher may want to add (if it isn't already in the contract) an "Acts of God" sentence, allowing more time to publish in the event that floods, famine, war, and other things — such as strikes — that are out of the Publisher's control, are the reason for the delay. The extra time is equal to the amount of time the Act of God has been interfering.

13 **Option.** The option clause may very well be one of the most difficult and controversial in a publishing contract. To some writers it represents an attempt by the Publisher to hold an author in unwilling servitude. From the Publisher's point of view, it's there for your protection, a sign of commitment on the part of the Publisher, a guarantee that the Publisher will support the book you've signed to do, and ensure that the investment it's making won't be lost, that the book won't be a one-shot.

The essential boilerplate of the option clause is pretty much the same from contract to contract, publisher to publisher. It is in the differences, however, that many problems lie.

> The Publisher shall be offered the Author's next work in this genre at least forty-five (45) days before another publisher. Should the Publisher offer to publish that book and should the Author thereupon refuse the terms offered by the Publisher, the Author may offer to another publisher but not contract without first notifying Publisher of terms and offering Publisher the opportunity to match that offer.

The first thing to note are the words *next work in this genre*. This means the Author is free to write something else and place it with a different publisher, without showing it to the option holder. Whether you would want to do that is something you will want to consider and undoubtedly will want to discuss with your editor. If you are, however, planning to move back and forth between historical romances and hard-boiled detection, make certain the option clause has built-in limitations. This can be in the form used in our example, or stated as "the next work in this series," "next work with the same characters," or "next work of this kind." (That last choice leaves the door open for some nasty debate, obviously.) What you definitely don't want is a clause that calls for the submission of "the next work," without any limitation or discussion of what that might be.

The next key phrase is the one referring to the amount of time the Publisher has in which to tender an offer for rights. In our example, you must receive an answer within forty-five days. Others range between thirty and ninety days. To me, forty-five to sixty days seems reasonable, from both sides of the desk.

The last two lines of the example also allow for some negotiation. We've quoted what is called a *matching option*, because it permits the Publisher to match any other offer you receive, and acquire the book for that amount. (The "amount" may also include hardcover guarantees, royalty rates, and other terms of the offer.) As always, there are variations on the theme, and you have to decide what you want, and then see what you can get.

The most common variant is the *topping clause*: In most instances, that allows the Publisher to acquire the rights by bettering your best other offer by 10 percent.

It might be possible to keep the option to a simple "first look." In those cases, the Publisher has a given amount of time in which to respond to your new manuscript; if you don't accept the offer made at that time, and are unable to reach a compromise, your obligation to the Publisher is complete. Because you aren't committed to negotiating, however, this is an approach that publishers are not eager to accept.

Looking back at our sample clause, you'll notice there are some things not mentioned. For instance, there's no indication of how much material must be submitted to fulfill the intent of the clause. Are you free to simply send an outline, or must you send an entire manuscript? Most agents will probably fight for an outline (and, perhaps, allow for a couple of chapters); your editor, however, may not be comfortable with that at this point in your career. To a great degree, the editor's decision may be based on how comfortable she is with you and your work, and how well you take direction—and at this point in your relationship most of these factors are unknowns.

Another item that doesn't appear above—and that I mention because it does appear in some contracts—also involves timing. The contract in which I saw this clause gives the Publisher ninety days to respond. So far, so good. The kicker is that the clock doesn't begin to run until ninety days after the publication of the last book on a two-book contract.

The Author who signed this particular contract was facing a no-win decision, compounded by some other nasty clauses. The original contract gave the Publisher rights in perpetuity to his pseudonym, an option on the next work in the genre, and an unbearably long time in which to make a decision. The two books originally contracted for had been delivered; the pub schedule, however, had book number two being released in 1991. By contract, then, the Author was effectively blocked from doing any further work under the name he had developed—a name that had begun to have a following in the market-place.

There are two simple lessons in that unfortunate tale: First, unless you have contracted to write an episode in a series under an already established house name, *never* give a publisher the rights to a pen name . . . unless you have no intention of using it again.

Second, the Publisher must agree to deal with the option book in a reasonable amount of time. There are understandable reasons a publisher might not want to consider an option title before the first book is released (and why you might not want to have it considered yet. After all, if there's no track record, there's nothing available to your editor on which to base an increased advance, right?).

Options are part of every contract and no editor will strike the clause, though I can't imagine why a writer would suggest it. In the final analysis, editors don't want disgruntled writers, and if things are not going well, the option won't be exercised.

14 **Laws, etc.** Most contracts contain a bankruptcy clause that will—in the event that the economy takes a downturn and the Publisher does, too—give you back all the rights in your work. If it isn't there, you want it; otherwise, the Publisher may try to sell your contract as an asset.

It has happened more often than any of us likes.

There will also be notification that the laws of a particular state will govern the contract, that any changes must be made in writing, and that the Publisher's obligations under the contract may not be assigned. After twenty-five years, I've come to the point where I don't even look at that clause.

There are some other things you may want to look for and/or request: Try to get an advertising clause, which prevents the Publisher from placing any advertising in your book, except for its other books. Once upon a time, as the story begins, publishers sold space in their books to cigarette manufacturers — and others. The writer didn't share in the income thus derived. Book club ads and the Publisher's own mail-order card help all writers; it's obvious that your book will be advertised in someone else's. Most ad clauses limit the Publisher to advertising its own product.

Look out for the contract that gives the Publisher exclusive rights to your name (or pen name), characters, situations, etc. Some houses do this and if you agree to it, the Publisher can hire someone else to write books under your name and with your characters. Publishers do this in case a writer decides to stop working on the series; after investing in the creation, publishers want to protect their position.

Finally, if you're signing a multiple-book contract, which may be offered if the editor sees the opportunity to develop a series (or if she just wants to tie you up for a while because of blazing talent), keep it to no more than three books at a time, and make certain the option clause calls for negotiation rather than subsequent titles being sold under the same terms as the original contract. Make certain that you have the opportunity to take the series and characters elsewhere if the option negotiations fall apart. Selling a series to a new publisher is not always easy (they want to know why the original house is no longer doing the books), but you want to keep your options open.

You and Your Copyeditor

by Maron L. Waxman

The editor tells the writer, "All finished," as he neatens the manuscript pages on his desk. The writer begins to relax, the labors of revision, reorganization and rewriting behind her, the manuscript at last just the way she wanted it. "Now off to copyediting," the editor says casually. Copyediting? The writer tenses. She has worked long hours with the editor on the manuscript, and they are both, she is sure, completely satisfied. What is left for anyone else to do?

In the process that takes a manuscript from typed pages to published book or article, it is understood that writers write and editors edit. It is also a fact that copyeditors copyedit, but exactly what copyediting means and what copyeditors do are not entirely understood.

There are, quite simply, two kinds of editors and each one does a different kind of editing (though these jobs are often combined on smaller magazines). The primary editor, often the person who signed the book or article for the publisher, works with the author on general issues of content, coverage, organization and structure. This editor may catch a misspelling here and there, but that is generally not his job. The copyeditor, on the other hand, reads the manuscript line for line, word for word, and is charged with preparing the manuscript for the typesetter. This means, specifically, correcting errors—in spelling, grammar, punctuation, language, usage and, occasionally, fact—and styling the text for consistency. Copyediting is, in fact, so essential to preparing a manuscript that publishing contracts often include a clause that assures the publisher the right to copyedit.

Most writers do, of course, expect a certain amount of cleanup and correction during the editorial process and are grateful for it. They are less certain about what to expect in those areas that come under the heading of "style." Told that changes are made for reasons of style, with no further explanation, writers frequently suspect that the change is arbitrary, made for no better reason than that the copyeditors liked their wording better than the writers'. For you to head off this kind of misunderstanding and to work effectively with copyeditors, you must understand what "style" means.

Style is the consistent application of rules governing capitalization, punctuation, abbreviation, spelling and usage when there is more than one correct way of presenting material. For most copyeditors who work on books, the editorial bible is the *Chicago Manual of Style* (University of Chicago Press). Newspapers and magazines, by and large, set their own house styles, the rules their copyeditors follow. In setting a house style, a newspaper or magazine not only gives the publication consistency, but also gives it a distinctive tone. *The New Yorker*, for example, achieves a slightly British or literary tone by using the spelling *theatre*; *Newsweek*, as American as apple pie, uses *theater*, as have almost all other US publications for the past forty or fifty years. The *New York Times*, which considers itself the nation's newspaper of record, carefully avoids most slang and sometimes puts quotation marks around colloquial expressions; *Time* magazine keeps its brash-young-kid-on-the-block tone by running with the latest street terms and coining imaginative phrases.

Without seeing a copyeditor in action, you may find this explanation abstract. The brief passage below, as seen through the eyes of a copyeditor, will give you a clearer idea of what to expect from the copyeditor working on your manuscript:

> During a stormy session the government announced its decision to send advisers, accountants, and analysts to assist in the election. On September 25, a team of several hundred men hit the scene.

The passage has no misspellings and no grammatical errors, but nevertheless the copyeditor must make a number of decisions.

Decision 1. Should a comma follow *session*? The placement of commas is generally governed by the rules of punctuation, but this is one of those few instances for which there is no absolute rule. The trend in contemporary American usage is to omit optional punctuation, and a comma after a brief introductory prepositional phrase — usually six words or fewer — is optional. The copyeditor will make a choice based on house style or, if he is copyediting a book, his own preference. For the sake of consistency, he will style the phrase *On September 25* in the second sentence the same way. This decision is, by editorial practice and convention, the sole province of the copyeditor or publication, and generally you should accept the copyeditor's decision.

Sometimes, however, a copyeditor might be too consistent. Look at this sentence:

> For that animal instinct was inadequate.

Without a comma after either *that* or *animal*, the sentence is unclear. The copyeditor has no way of knowing what you mean, and so, in the language of editing, he "queries" you — that is, the copyeditor calls or writes you with his question. When you explain your meaning, the copyeditor will insert the comma in the right place.

Decision 2. Should the word *government* be capitalized? House style governs this decision.

Decision 3. *Its* or *their* for government? American usage is *its*; British, *their*.

Decision 4. *Advisers* with an *e* or an *o*? Contemporary American spelling is with an *e*.

Decision 5. Should a comma follow accountants, the second word in a series of three words? The so-called serial comma (the comma before *and*) probably has touched off more copyediting discussions than any other piece of punctuation. Today its use is governed by house style. Magazines usually omit it; books usually retain it.

Decision 6. What is the right style for a date? Once again, the copyeditor makes his choice based on house style. Here's a short form of the list he will choose from:

- September 25 (conventional usage)
- 25 September (*Chicago Manual*)
- Sept. 25 (*New York Times*)
- September (or Sept.) 25th
- September (or Sept.) twenty-fifth
- the twenty-fifth of September (or Sept.)

The last three, although not generally accepted forms, are within the realm of possibility. Given a choice, the copyeditor should pick the usage least likely to attract a second glance—probably the conventional usage.

Decision 7. Men? This word should set off an alarm for every copyeditor. Do you really mean *men*, or do you mean *men and women?* Can the designation *men* be omitted? Is there an appropriate neutral word like *assistants* or *aides?* Here the copyeditor can perform a real service for you by querying what might be a careless, inaccurate and potentially embarrassing statement.

Decision 8. Is *hit the scene* acceptable usage? No, it's slang, and unless you can make a strong argument for slang in this context you should go along with the copyeditor's suggestion for a substitute.

Polish and Beyond

By seeing how the copyeditor goes over the manuscript, applying the final polish of correction and styling, you can begin to understand the reasons for the copyeditor's changes. In most cases, the style changes were made to render your style consistent with clear, contemporary usage and with the style of the publication you're writing for. You will also see that the copyeditor called your attention to possible inaccuracies and ambiguities that would confuse readers and distract them from a full understanding of the text. Just as an audience is distracted by a lecturer who gestures excessively or whose notes threaten to fall off the lectern, so readers are distracted from work sloppily presented. Style is the final polish that indicates that the publishing team—writer, editor, copyeditor—has taken care in presenting its work.

Copyediting is not all polish, however. Punctuation, capitalization, usage and appropriate wording are among the working parts of the language, and the copyeditor's close focus on your work pulls him into the text, where he frequently finds himself struggling with what you mean. Every time readers must puzzle over a sentence or phrase, the written work has momentarily failed, and the copyeditor's job is to scout and head off such failures.

Sometimes even the presence or absence of commas can entirely change the meaning of a sentence:

The officers who are based in London are inadequately trained for modern warfare.

Taken at face value, without any commas, the sentence states that all the officers based in London are inadequately trained. By instinct and training, the copyeditor knows that the statement is too sweeping to let pass without a query, for the entire meaning of the sentence rests on those commas. With commas around the clause, the sentence means that some officers, who happen to be based in London, are inadequately trained. In the same vein, writers frequently ask whether there's any difference between "my son Abner" and my son, Abner." To Abner there surely is. "My son Abner" means that Abner is one of two or more sons; "My son, Abner"—a condensed form of "my son, who is Abner"—means Abner is an only son. The copyeditor must attend to this distinction.

The copyeditor can also prevent you from making a careless error and ending up at the foot of a *New Yorker* column with an arch comment. He will keep track of your characters' lives, so that the aspiring singer who shows up in a striking green dress in the morning does not take off a black skirt later in the day unless, of course, you have indicated that she has changed her clothes. If you have written a gritty mystery set in Detroit, he will keep a street map by your manuscript to check all the geographic details. Can the cops really make it from the Fisher Building to River Rouge in just fifteen minutes?

The careful copyeditor, trained for close textual reading, will repeatedly call on you to clarify your work and make its meaning clear to the reader, as these examples demonstrate. Together you and the copyeditor nail down exactly what you mean to say. This last effort to locate and eliminate all the soft spots in the manuscript may be difficult for you, but the success of your work rests in good part on it. Working patiently with the copyeditor on word-for-word clarity, you will ensure that your work, when published, is attractive and meaningful in the true designations of these words.

Shaking Ideas

This look at copyediting outlines the classic restrained approach to the craft. At no time did the copyeditor here rewrite or make a change "because it sounds better that way" or impose a style too rigid for the readers' ease, sins that writers frequently charge copyeditors with and that copyeditors may occasionally commit. The fact is that copyeditors must pick at manuscripts. Dealing as they do with prose that is often raw and careless, some copyeditors become too consistent and conventional and lose their sensitivity to the author's language. If you encounter such an editor, politely suggest that your wording be restored; for passages with no actual errors or style violations, the author usually has the final say on proposed changes. This sentence, by an idiosyncratic but hearty writer in an introduction to a book of reprinted articles, might serve as the test of a sensitive copyeditor:

To go through these articles, for me, is like walking around a room shaking ideas and exchanging hands with forty-odd old friends.

The professional copyeditor will keep his pencil away from *shaking ideas and exchanging hands*. The phrasing may be unconventional, but the voice and idea are clearly the writer's own, and the writer should expect the copyeditor to let her voice come through and express her ideas in fresh and personal language.

Proper expression is, after all, the ultimate goal of everyone concerned with writing and publishing. For all his probings and questions, the effective copyeditor is always sensitive to your intention and intonation. Guided by his respect for, and knowledge of, how words and language work, the copyeditor can help your writing speak to your readers clearly and directly.

How to Write a
Bestselling Novel

by Tom Clancy

L esson #1, as illustrated by the title of this article, is GET PEOPLE'S ATTEN-
TION EARLY.

Obviously I had no intention of making *The Hunt for Red October* into
a commercial success, since it has no sex in it. In fact, my first novel was
never intended as anything more than accomplishing a dream that I'd held
since high school—to see my name on the cover of a book.

I am convinced that everyone has a dream very much like this one—well,
certainly all those who can read, which, unfortunately, isn't quite everyone.
The trick is accomplishing it. I know. I tried for years until the proper set of
circumstances came together for me. Set aside thoughts of Pulitzer prizes and
the *New York Times* list. A novelist is in the entertainment business. Your
job is to tell a story others will find interesting. It will not be interesting unless
it is also entertaining (this explains the relative ratings of NBC and PBS).
Within this philosophical limitation, you can pass on some hard information,
and maybe even a Moral—but before thinking too hard on that one, recall the
words of D.W. Griffith: "If you want to send a message, use Western Union."

Two questions form the foundation of all novels: "What if?" and "What
next?" (A third question, "What now?" is one the author asks himself every
ten minutes or so; but it's more a cry than a question.) Every novel begins
with the speculative question, What if X happened? That's how you start. Your
novel could be based on a real incident; *Red October* was suggested by a 1975
attempted defection of a Russian frigate. You start off with a basic idea ("What
if a Russian sub attempted to defect?") and try to pursue it to its logical (well,
not always) conclusion. "What next?" is the question posed by the fact that—
as in life—a number of different things are happening at once, all of which
affect the central premise of the book.

Fundamentally, all writing is about characters. All great literature (*def*:
"Literature" is written material that, one hundred years after the death of the
author, is forced upon high school students) is about people. People, in case
you never noticed, are the animate objects that do things. Shakespeare's world
of the divine right of kings (not to mention swords, witches and magicians) is
long past, but the people who lived in that world are as real today as they were
in the seventeenth century. My own method of dealing with this fact is to
formulate characters in my own mind. From date of birth until the time the
story begins, I know everything about my characters—which isn't all that
hard when you think about it. Look at your friends and ask yourself why they

are interesting enough to be your friends. What are their good and bad points? What are their foibles and eccentricities—and how did they get them? List these traits, and select a few for your fictional characters.

With that mental image of the characters, you can pluck these living people from the mind, set them down on the "What if?" stage, give them a slight nudge to make them walk around, and then write down what you see. If you do it correctly, the characters will do all your thinking for you, so long as you ask them the right questions. Your characters must become as real to you as your neighbors—if they are not real to you, it's for damned sure that they will not be real to your readers. If they are real to you, you will be able to see the world through their eyes in addition to your own.

Their reality explains why I refer to writing as a self-induced form of schizophrenia. If you find yourself asking yourself, "What would Mr. Jones do in a situation like this?" you're there. But if you stay there too long, you might have to talk to a doctor. One other thing that is difficult to explain to those who do not write is that one's characters can do some surprising things. In *Red Storm* I introduced a character I had every intention of killing off a few chapters later, but he did something so useful that he managed to survive the entire book. (This made me feel a lot better, since I find it very hard indeed to kill off a character.)

Every person you meet— and everything you do in life—offers an opportunity to learn something. That's important to all of us, but most of all to a writer, because as a writer you can use *anything*. There is not a person in the world who does not love to talk about himself and his job; who does not deem himself fascinating; who cannot tell you hours' worth of stories about the exciting life of an insurance agent, real-estate broker, garbage collector or pre-school teacher. And they are all correct. All people *are* interesting, and this is particularly true if *you* are writing a story about insurance, real estate, trash or a day-care center. From those people you will get information, and from their information you get verisimilitude, and verisimilitude is what makes fiction work.

Information and verisimilitude are within easy reach. For some obscure reason, people laud me for my technical research, when the fact is that I spent a total of less than ten working days researching my first two novels—in the field, that is.

Fact: if you can read and dial a telephone, you can find out nearly anything in less than sixty minutes. Name any subject you can imagine, from Ethiopian cuisine to Stealth aircraft, and I guarantee you that somebody has written a book on it. In that book you will find enough detail to convince your reader that you are the world's foremost expert on your subject. Does anybody out there really think I know how to drive submarines? (*Common Cause* magazine did say that I was a naval intelligence officer—they printed a retraction after I asked the reporter why she hadn't called me to inquire.) I never even got aboard a nuclear sub until *Red October* was in final editing. On the other hand, I *have* talked with a lot of people who are or were in this line of work.

Collect stories from people and bank them against the time when you might be able to use them, because sooner or later you will find such an opportunity. There is no such thing as a useless fact.

Writing . . . and Success

Now that we've covered the easy part, we come to the hard part: THE ONLY WAY TO WRITE IS TO WRITE. You can dream about writing, make notes, make outlines, or sketch out your characters all you want, but the book will not get written until you write it. If this were not true, this magazine would not exist, would it?

Like golf, or skeet-shooting, or any other human endeavor, the only way to do it is to *do* it. Any reputable English teacher can give you some hints and tricks, and good criticism, but you have to write some words on paper first.

If you're a writer, you are also *a prioria* reader. You have your favorites; we all do. Copy their style. Why not? It worked for them, didn't it? Examine the way your favorite writer uses language—because this is the key to communicating your characters and your scenes to your reader. I call this plugging words together. Experiment. When all else fails, say everything out loud (or at least think it loudly), and if it sounds like the way you talk—write it that way. With dialogue, always say it out loud. I do it a lot while driving. It gets me some funny looks from passing motorists, but they don't know who I am anyway, so what the hell?

But you have to write. Writing is both the hardest and the most enjoyable work there is. It is hard because you are all alone—just you and the keyboard. There are times when you struggle over every word; and there are times when the paragraphs explode from your fingertips.

But what it really comes down to is your willingness to set everything else in your life aside for several hours per day—every day. Your wife, your kids, your friends, the grass, the car—everything. Writing that book must become the most important thing in your life. If it doesn't, you will fail. If it does, you just might succeed.

And what is success? Success is a finished book, a stack of pages each of which is filled with words. If you reach that point, you have won a victory over yourself no less impressive than sailing single-handed around the world. Maybe you'll get it published. Maybe you won't. I got *Red October* published by the first house I went to, breaking all the rules: No agent, no outline, no proposal, no advance, and a publisher who'd never done fiction.

My greatest good fortune was that I didn't know that I was doing everything wrong; if I'd done a single thing right, I probably would have failed. If I'd known how hard—statistically speaking—it is to get a first novel published, I might have given up and done what my wife told me to do—sold some more insurance. What success really means, I think, is looking failure in the face and tossing the dice anyway. You may be the only person who ever knows how the dice come up, but in that knowledge you have something that millions of people will never have—because they were afraid to try.

A Few Keys to the Kingdom

by Jack Dann

What I'm about to tell you is not particularly earth-shattering, nor even very original, but if you wish to become a writer, perhaps these rules might be of some use.

• You must begin. Every day you must write, no matter what. And writing is usually not fun. It's just hard work. *Finishing* a page or a story or a novel is fun . . . but by then you're already thinking about the next one.

• Being a professional simply means you write and publish. The average writer makes somewhere around $5,000 a year. So even though *you* know you're the next Hemingway or Faulkner, you'll probably need a job. That's good—it puts you in the midst of things, into the middle of life, so to speak. You know, the stuff you want to write about.

• Give the best part of every day to yourself. Get up early and write if you can. Once you've put words to paper, you've conquered the day. Then you can put bread on the table and beer in the icebox. But you must try to write every day. If you can't, read or put your desk in order or do research. It's important to establish the habit of working every day. Inspiration isn't what it's all about. We're all inspired. Writing is about putting words on paper, especially during those times when you're not in the mood. The only way you can learn the craft is by constant practice. If you're persistent enough, and good enough, to sell your first story, you'll have a week of feeling elated, and then you'll worry about whether you can write and sell another. It's the same with finishing a novel. You'll keep upping the ante, trying to do better and more complex work. You'll probably feel that last year's (or last week's) work wasn't very good. Certainly not as good as what you're doing *now*. There's no rest for a writer. It's almost as bad as doing housework, and many writers have even been known to do the dishes rather than face that blank page in the typewriter. (I'm one of the lucky ones who doesn't have that problem.)

• Make appointments with yourself to write. Make yourself feel as guilty as possible. Do whatever you must to get to your typewriter or computer.

• Copy. By that I don't mean plagiarize, but find writers you admire, and read and reread their best work. Dissect their prose sentence by sentence and paragraph by paragraph. Memorize passages if you have to, but get into the weave of the writer's work. It will give an unconscious form and balance to your own work. Don't worry, no one else will know. You will put these unconscious "forms" through your own sensorium.

• When you sit down to write, forget about your favorite authors.

• Read constantly and widely. If you're going to write suspense or fantasy or science fiction, you must be a sophisticated reader before you can do original work in the genre. (There are, of course, exceptions to this.) Genres are quite complex, and they assume a foundation of shared ideas and devices. It's all right to read *anything* and everything that interests you; it's all grist for the mill. Even though you might not be aware of it, you'll be weaving the particular patterns your own work will take.

• Be prepared to be surprised and upset by what you write . . . by what you think. Writing, serious writing, forces you to explore private demons and come to terms with yourself.

• When you put that rough-draft page into the typewriter, don't try to be a critic. The first stages of writing are often intuitive, right-brained work. But once you have a draft, or you become blocked on a story, you must rethink and rework—then you must be as hard on yourself as if you were writing for the *New York Times Book Review*.

• Don't worry that all your writer friends have computers. Just keep putting pages into the typewriter. Keep reworking your prose. This mechanical stopping and starting is good for you. When you've made a few sales (presuming you have a good job and can afford it), *then* buy a computer. If you can't afford it, don't worry. Every time you have to put a page back into the typewriter to correct a bad sentence, you'll smooth out other sentences; you'll get into the habit of polishing your prose.

• If you're having trouble with a sentence or a passage or a plot twist, ask yourself if something doesn't need to be cut. If you have an especially elegant sentence that just isn't working with the rest of your humdrum prose, cut out the sentence. It's probably purple, anyway.

• If you find yourself blocked, take a break and read and take notes and read and take more notes. If you can't stay at your desk, stay in your study (and fight that urge to do housework!) Ask the Little Man for some help.

• Ah, you don't know who the Little Man is? He lives inside your head, and he knows more about some things than you do. The late Richard McKenna, author of *The Sand Pebbles* and many brilliant short stories such as "Casey Agonistes," wrote about him in a marvelous little essay entitled "Journey With a Little Man." The Little Man (or Woman, as the case may be) is your intuitive self. He's the smart writer inside you. When you get an urge to buy a book on the flora of Afghanistan, listen to the Little Man and shell out the money, for, inevitably, you'll find it's just the book you'll need for a project you haven't even thought of yet. (But the Little Man's way ahead of you.)

• Rewrite everything until you feel that what you have on paper corresponds as closely as possible to that wonderful image you originally had in your mind.

• Keep working toward making clear sentences and building solid story structures. Style is really only transparency of thought and idea. Writing well is a result of clear thinking. Cut out everything that sounds nice but doesn't convey the specific meaning you want. Find the exact word to express your thought: that's what Roget made his thesaurus for. The particular way you think, the way you experience and perceive the world, will become your "style." But the very act of writing—the development of your craft—changes the way you see. By working within the confines of your craft (or art), you expand your sight.

• Lest you become too mystically minded, read Strunk and White's *The Elements of Style*, often referred to as "The Little Book."

• And of course you must send your work out to editors. Don't write long cover letters telling your prospective editors that you collect scorpions and juggle apples and saucers. When your manuscript is returned, send it out again the next day.

• The more pleasant alternative to all of the above is to remain a reader. But be warned, you might find yourself waking up sweaty and bewildered in the middle of the night with that restless urge to write.

Index